Housing for the Elderly: Privacy and Independence in Environments for the Aging

J. David Hoglund

University of Charleston Library
Charleston, WV 25304

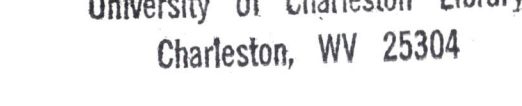
VAN NOSTRAND REINHOLD COMPANY
New York

Copyright © 1985 by J. David Hoglund

Library of Congress Catalog Card Number 85-11213

ISBN 0-442-22784-1

This project has been supported by a grant from the National Endowment for the Arts.

All rights reserved. No part of this work covered by the copyright hereon may be reproduced or used in any form or by any means—graphic, electronic, or mechanical, including photocopying, recording, taping, or information storage and retrieval systems—without written permission of the publisher.

Printed in the United States of America

Designed by Paul Chevannes

Van Nostrand Reinhold Company Inc.
115 Fifth Avenue
New York, New York 10003

Van Nostrand Reinhold Company Limited
Molly Millars Lane
Wokingham, Berkshire RG11 2PY, England

Van Nostrand Reinhold
480 La Trobe Street
Melbourne, Victoria 3000, Australia

Macmillan of Canada
Division of Canada Publishing Corporation
164 Commander Boulevard
Agincourt, Ontario M1S 3C7, Canada

16 15 14 13 12 11 10 9 8 7 6 5 4 3 2

Library of Congress Cataloging-in-Publication Data
Hoglund, J. David, 1955-
   Housing for the elderly.

   Bibliography: p.146
   Includes index.
   1. Aged—Europe—Dwellings. 2. Housing policy—Europe. 3. Architecture and the aged—Europe. 4. Architecture—Human factors. I. Title.
HD7287.92.E8H64 1985   363.5'9   85-11213
ISBN 0-442-22784-1

*For our grandparents, Glen and Mary Stookey,
Marion Exford, and Sophie Schultheis, who have shown us that
growing older can be
a time of wisdom and fulfillment.*

CONTENTS

Preface	v
Acknowledgments	vii

CHAPTER 1 The Intangible Qualities of Housing

Privacy and Independence	1
Social and Behavioral Goals in Housing	2
Environmental Design Research	2
Focusing on the Individual	3

CHAPTER 2 The Elderly and the Aging Process

The Elderly	4
The Aging Process	5
Biological Aging	6
Social Passage	11

CHAPTER 3 Housing, Privacy, and Independence

Housing	15
Privacy	16
Independence	22
Privacy and Independence in Europe	28

CHAPTER 4 Sweden

Sweden	29
The Government	29
Care of the Elderly	31
Financial Security	31
Housing	33
Supportive Special-care Services	35
Supportive Medical Care	35
S-1 Ålderdomshem Papegojelyckan	36
S-2 Teckomatorp Servicecentrum	42

S-3 Västra Fäladen Servicecentrum 48
S-4 Gränna Servicehus för Äldre 54
S-5 Knivsta Servicehus och Sjukhem 59
S-6 Örnen Servicehus 63
S-7 Bostadshotell Kv. Enskededalen 69

CHAPTER 5 Denmark

Denmark 76
The Government 76
Care of the Elderly 77
    Financial Security 77
    Housing 79
    Supportive Special-care Services 80
    Supportive Medical Care 81
D-1 Ordrup Vaenge 82
D-2 København og Omegns Sygehjem 88
D-3 København og Omegns Dagcenter 93
D-4 Omsorgscentret Møllegården 98
D-5 Rygårdcentret 106

CHAPTER 6 Great Britain

Great Britain 115
The Government 115
Care of the Elderly 116
    Financial Security 116
    Housing 117
    Supportive Special-care Services 120
    Supportive Medical Care 120
E-1 Springfield Court 121
E-2 Carpenter Hall 126
E-3 18-24 Banim Street 131
E-4 40-70 Munden Street 136

CHAPTER 7 Future Directions

Bibliography

146

Index

149

PREFACE

My travels in Europe enabled me to visit a variety of housing settings for the elderly in Great Britain, Sweden, and Denmark. The socially progressive attitudes of the Europeans have led them into the most direct confrontation of the issues dealing with housing for the elderly. The Europeans, particularly the English and Scandinavians, are far ahead of the United States in their concerns for such social issues as independence and privacy; and such design issues as spatial manipulation, the use of color and light, and the therapeutic relationships of interior and exterior spaces. More important, they have focused on life's rhythms and patterns, using buildings as therapeutic tools that subtly offer aid and security without removing the individual's dignity.

This book is based upon several important observations and concerns.

Facts:

- The elderly are becoming a larger and more vocal portion of the world's population.

- World economies are facing the difficult issue of how to support, house, and provide health care to a generation that is more numerous, older, and more physically debilitated.

American Approaches:

- Housing policy does not identify with the needs of the individual aged person.

- The outdated forms of health care and types of housing in existence will not meet the demands of the future elderly population.

- New solutions to house our aging population are rarely being attempted.

European Endeavors:

- A higher level of concern for the sustained dignity of the aged members of society exists in Europe than in the United States.

- Europeans give closer scrutiny to the *total needs* of the individual, which extend beyond a mere place to sleep and one hot meal per day.
- European countries with socialized medicine or health care programs that have grown out of socialist doctrine have spawned a variety of residential care alternatives for the elderly.

Cross-cultural Concerns:

- Privacy and independence have become an important part of the vocabulary conceptualizing new forms of housing.
- Unresolved difficulties stemming from bureaucracies split the responsibilities of housing from health care. These needs are not mutually exclusive to the aged individual.
- The current world economy has slowed overall production of housing for that portion of the population in the most substandard housing—the elderly.

Future Directions:

- Privacy and independence will gain in importance for future generations of elderly Americans who were raised in the suburbs.
- New forms of housing must recognize that the provision of a 'bed' does not resolve the elderly individual's total housing need.
- Innovations in residential care will not happen overnight; they begin with carefully calculated steps that probe new concepts and approaches.

This book is organized around three important themes: First, privacy and independence are important social concepts in the design of housing for the elderly. One must understand the total needs of the aged individual and be sensitive to those features of the environment that improve the quality of life. Second, it is necessary to examine such terms as *nursing homes, intermediate care facilities, geriatric hospitals,* or *congregate care facilities*. This terminology stigmatizes forms of housing for the elderly and perpetuates a division between housing care and health care. Finally, examples of European approaches to housing for the elderly are representative of how current concerns, such as privacy and independence, can be facilitated through design.

Chapter 1 focuses on the difficulty that design professionals have in translating social and behavioral goals into a design vocabulary. Standards and design rules of thumb are unresponsive to the daily needs of the elderly. Changes during the aging process, rather than arbitrarily applied accessibility standards, should be the basis for housing design. *Chapter 2* presents an overview of the physiological and psychological aspects of aging. In order to design for concepts such as privacy and independence one must understand what components of the environment have the greatest influence on the individual. *Chapter 3* establishes a conceptual framework of what privacy and independence mean to the individual and how these criteria influence personal identity, self-esteem, and individuality. It is important to recognize that these concepts are vague and open to personal interpretation. The intent, however, is to explore these issues and to spur discussions of these terms among design professionals, sociologists, behaviorists, housing administrators, and users.

Chapters 4 to 6 analyze the governments, social structures, and provision of housing care in Sweden, Denmark, and Great Britain. Sixteen buildings have been used as examples offering particular insights into how social criteria such as privacy and independence have been actualized into government goals, program criteria, and design responses. Photographs and drawings accompany a verbal description and commentary on each building.

Chapter 7 identifies current themes and future directions in housing for the elderly.

ACKNOWLEDGMENTS

My interests in gerontology have been generously supported by the University of Illinois at Urbana-Champaign and the National Endowment for the Arts. The Edward L. Ryerson Fellowship in Architecture enabled me to spend four months visiting housing environments throughout Europe. I wish to thank the Ryerson Committee at the University of Illinois for nurturing my interests and funding my research endeavors. This book would not have been completed without the support of a grant from the National Endowment for the Arts (NEA). Aging research and design quality are critical areas of concern recognized by the NEA.

The interest and support generated by the 1984 *Progressive Architecture* Award for Research accelerated the project beyond its manuscript status. It is important for the profession that research be recognized as an integral part of the design process.

It is impossible to identify all those individuals who provided support, inspiration, references, translations, and time during my travels in Europe. Owe Åhlund in the Department of Building Functional Analysis at the University of Lund, Sweden; Eleonara Sharif at the Swedish Institute; and Gesche Alberts of the Danish Ministry of Social Affairs deserve special credit for their assistance in planning and arranging my visits. I would also like to express my appreciation to the following:

Sweden:
Barbara Åhl, Bengt Lantto, Ivon Magnusson, Lars Källqvist, Arne Åberg, Anna Halla, Karl Grunewald, Arne Clevestam, Elisabeth Edsjö, Christian Gauffin, Hans Smedshammar, Jörgen Larsen, Torbjörn Björkman, Torbjörn Svensson, Mona Åhlund, Birgitta Lindstrom, Jörgen Ralsmark, Jan Helander, Lennarth Andersson, Sven Dahlman, Jan Paulsson, Juri Sonn, Margareta Bowallius, Ulf Melander, and Sture Börjesson.

Denmark:
Erik and Inge Ejlers, Kirsten Laup, Walter Weiss, Elith Berg, and Svend Age Maasen.

Norway:
Harald Engelstad, Aase-Marit Nygård, and Grete Bull.

Great Britain:
Mike Rainey, Kenneth Bayes, Pam Paterson, Joan Butterworth, Jill Jackson, and Evelyn McEwen.

United States:
Jim Anderson, John Replinger, Bruce Hutchings, Ashot Mnatzakanian, Marc Lichtman, Barbara Geddis, Alan Freed, and Maura Wright-Wellington.

And in each country, my sincere appreciation to all of the older individuals who let me into their homes to visit, to talk, and to understand.

Two gentlemen have had a profound effect on the quality of my training and the development of my character. Vic Regnier of the University of Illinois (now at the University of Southern California) and Wally Kroner of Rensselaer Polytechnic Institute have consistently challenged my views, opening my mind to new ways of looking at ideas and concepts. I owe a great deal to them for their academic challenges, as well as for their humanitarian qualities.

My wife, Loretta, accompanied me throughout Europe and provided invaluable support, love, and friendship. The writing of this book has absorbed many weekends, nights, and vacations to complete. She has been beside me all the way, working through new ideas, new chapters, and new frustrations. I could not have done it without her.

> *Good intentions and kind impulses do not necessarily lead to wise and truly humane measure ... meaning well is only half our duty; thinking right is the other equally important half.*
>
> Samuel Howe, 1866
> **Dedication address for a new Institution for the Blind.**

Vigeland Sculpture Garden. Oslo, Norway

1 THE INTANGIBLE QUALITIES OF HOUSING

PRIVACY AND INDEPENDENCE

Design professionals have difficulty translating social and behavioral goals (privacy and independence) into housing design and management—operational criteria—for the elderly. Architects, housing administrators, and social service personnel use words such as *personalization, privacy, independence,* and *environmental stimulation* to conceptualize purpose-built housing for the elderly. These words often become empty phrases because they are the intangible components of housing.

All too often, independence has come to mean grab bars and curb cuts; privacy is equated with a cubicle curtain; and environmental stimulation is identified with bright, garish colors in geometric shapes. Unfortunately, much of the design criteria for the elderly are prescriptive, often found in the form of square footage requirements, fixture arrangements, and standards. Manuals stress dimensions based on the wheelchair and perpetuate the fallacy that all disabled people sit in wheelchairs, and that all wheelchair-bound people have full muscular control of their upper torso. Equally unfortunate is the lack of consideration to what activities are performed in the space and how they are accomplished. Individuals may be able to negotiate a 32-inch door frame on a nonslip floor surface where a 60-inch turning clearance has been provided, but how do they negotiate right-hand transfer from wheelchair to toilet with limited muscular control?

Technical developments in housing have not been balanced with less tangible concerns such as territoriality and personalization. Housing research over the past decade has only begun to focus on issues of privacy and independence. The failures of Pruitt-Igoe in Saint Louis and other large housing developments have led to a closer look at the way environment influences behavior. Psychological studies of sensory deprivation clearly have shown that the built environment speaks, that it affects our behavior, and that it can change our mental outlook.

Privacy and independence must be conceptualized on many levels and communicated in a variety of forms. The environment must reinforce individuality, self-esteem, and dignity. Social criteria, such as privacy and independence, are often conceptualized as issues of detail, rather than as substantive form-giving issues. They are not, however, qualities that can be applied through paint color, material pattern, or graphic symbols. Privacy and independence are criteria that establish a framework for design and decision making throughout the process. They are demanding criteria, because they force us to look beyond traditional responses and forms.

SOCIAL AND BEHAVIORAL GOALS IN HOUSING

Many elderly people will encounter physical barriers and limitations. We need to minimize physical restrictions and encourage access and opportunity. Equally important is the removal of social and psychological barriers that dehumanize the individual. Stereotypes that focus on what the individual cannot do perpetuate negative characteristics. Youthful and fit, we are allowed to be forgetful; the elderly are senile. We make mistakes; the elderly are confused. We use drugs to forget, to calm down, and to escape; the elderly often derive the same results from medications they cannot avoid. We lose sight of the individual amongst a plethora of labels, stereotypes, and behavioral theories.

In the design of housing for the elderly, we must look beyond conventional approaches and address those issues that are important to the individual. Architects are rarely challenged to do something different with housing for the elderly. They are not criticized for doing what has been done before; nor are they praised. We must challenge tradition and accepted practice. Guidelines and standards must be questioned for their appropriateness to a diversified aging population.

The group of European buildings in chapters 4, 5, and 6 illustrate these concerns. Government programs and directives coupled with strong social goals have created a diversity of residential settings for the elderly. National goals have led to more responsive solutions that provide a true sense of privacy and operational independence. Shared rooms in nursing homes and efficiency apartments have become obsolete and outdated throughout much of Scandinavia.

Buildings in these countries respond to their urban or rural context rather than to idealized economic standards. Facilities are conceptualized as housing, using familiar forms, materials, and details.

Housing for the elderly must be conceptualized primarily as residential care. Medical care is only one of many services that the elderly may require as they become older and more physically debilitated. Facilities that stress a medical orientation perpetuate the fallacy that old age is a disease and that it has a cure. This is an unfortunate and inappropriate criterion with which to design housing. Aging is a process that has associated disabilities and difficulties. Housing should be supportive of disabilities and medical needs, rather than allowing the environment to become mechanical and sterile.

ENVIRONMENTAL DESIGN RESEARCH

The writings of Robert Sommer, Edward Hall, Christopher Alexander, Oscar Newman, and Sandra Howell develop a historical perspective of environmental design research. Early laboratory experimentation drew theoretical conclusions between space, its use, and human behavior. "Black-box," or sensory deprivation, experiments emerged from the laboratory to become more observational—a type of candid-camera approach to watching people's use of space and their reactions to certain stimuli. Sommer's *Personal Space* began to delineate between experimental results and development of design criteria. Oscar Newman's *Defensible Space* examined one area of how the environment affects behavior in the urban setting. His connections between housing density, height and size, and rate of victimization are important cornerstones to urban design. *Designing for Aging: Patterns of Use* is Howell's treatise on habitability, which bridges behavior with design by analyzing case studies and developing guidelines for design. It is important that information developed by behavioral scientists be translated so that architects and design professionals can use it in problem solving. Graphic case studies prove to be more valuable than undelineated statistical data. The ideologies represented by behavioral and social scientists must be meshed with those of the individuals responsible for form-giving decisions that influence lives and the way people use space.

Designers must focus their energies on the individual—her needs, her desires, her memories, and her dreams.

To that end, this book will build on existing environmental design research and fill the issues of privacy and independence with new purpose, providing enhanced sensitivity to what they truly mean. Housing must be responsive to its industrialized components, but it must also be responsive to the lives of its inhabitants. Buildings speak a powerful language, and we must heighten our sensitivity to concepts we take for granted and the large role they can play in design as a therapeutic tool in the lives of the elderly.

FOCUSING ON THE INDIVIDUAL

Housing technology has changed very little in the past thirty years, especially when compared with changes in the automotive industry. Codes, standards, and minimum guidelines (which in practice become maximum) allow us to respond to very prescriptive design information. The designer may have no particular user to consider and no empathy for the individual who spends a great deal of time inside the built environment. A vast social distance exists between the architect and the elderly people who will ultimately use the building. As designers, we tend to focus on the tangible features of the building—the bricks and mortar—with very little concern for what actually happens inside the space.

The criteria for the configuration and detailing of any space must come from a sensitivity to the user. In the case of housing for the elderly, it must include an understanding of individual needs, desires, and aspirations, as well as the physical and emotional changes that occur with aging. If housing environments are to provide more independence and privacy, then we must understand what factors will achieve those goals. A house must be the physical setting for life's events, as well as the container for an individual's hopes, dreams, loves, and sorrows.

> A good house is a created thing made of many parts economically and meaningfully assembled. It speaks not just of the materials from which it is made, but of the intangible rhythms, spirits, and dreams of people's lives. Its site is only a tiny piece of the real world, yet this place is made to seem like an entire world. In its parts it accommodates important human activities, yet in sum it expresses an attitude toward life.
>
> CHARLES MOORE, 1975

2 THE ELDERLY AND THE AGING PROCESS

THE ELDERLY

Changing social structures and increased longevity have affected the term *elderly*. The retirement age of 65 has provided the imaginary demarcation when individuals become elderly and able to draw on government subsidy programs. Increasing debate over a mandatory retirement age and concern for flexibility in the "rites of passage" are signals of changing concepts about the aged population. The expanding group of people over 75 has led to the creation of the expressions *old-elderly* and *old-old*.

Because of their numbers and increased political activity, the elderly have become a distinctive social group. Nearly 11 percent of the world's urbanized population is over age 65. Presently, life expectancy at birth is roughly 70 years for males and 75 for women. Men can expect to be outnumbered 3 to 2 by women at age 60 and 2 to 1 at age 75. Although statistical and anthropometric data collectivize the elderly into a distinctive group, it is a fallacy to think that there is any average elderly person. As with all minority groups, however, they have been stereotyped and categorized. Individuals over age 65 are socially, politically, and economically diverse. They have different desires and expectations; divergent ethnic and racial backgrounds determine role models, life-styles, and familial settings.

The personal identity of an elderly individual is often subjugated to a collective identity of what society feels the elderly ought to be. As people age, society begins to attach stereotyped images rooted in devalued characteristics. Old people are classified as incompetent, senile, physically weak, sexually inactive, and at times socially deviant ("dirty old men," "old drunken bum," "mean old witch"). The elderly are commonly grouped into statistical calculations as disabled—as if to be old were a handicap in itself.

Grouping all elderly people into stereotyped images denies the basic characteristics that formulate a person's identity. The historical image of the elderly as frail individuals who require protection subscribes to the "caretaker" philosophy. This attitude is left over from a time when the medical world was unable to help people

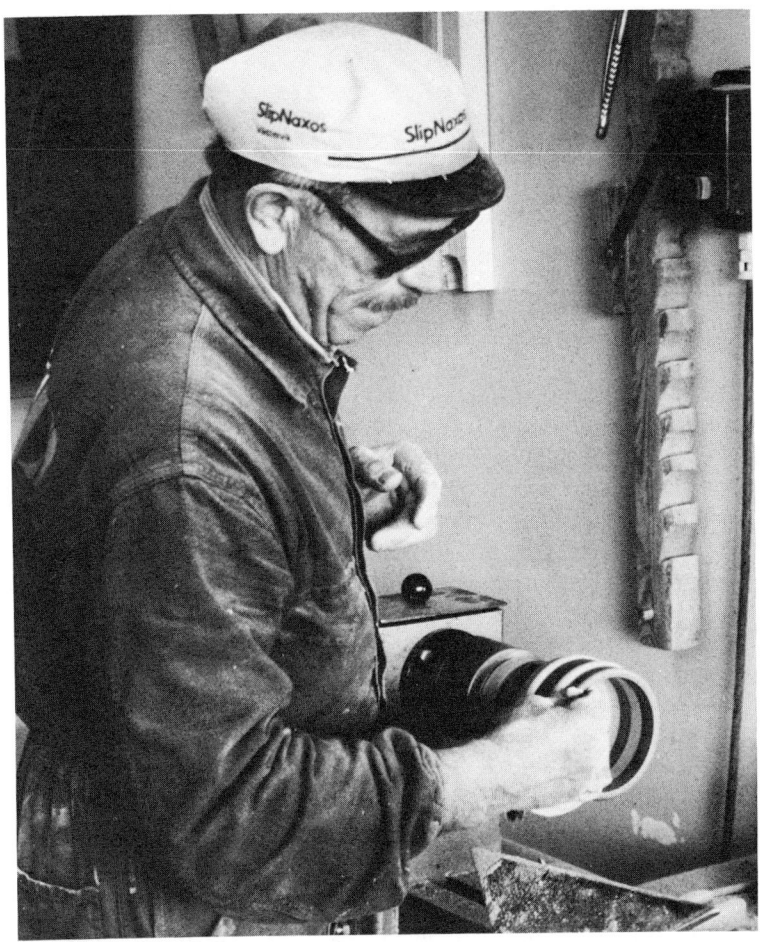

Social changes that occur with aging require constant adaptation. Retired individuals must channel energy into new pursuits.

overcome or mitigate the effects of disabilities. Society has been unable to see the elderly as self-sufficient contributing members. As with the mentally impaired, we have removed them from the mainstream of society and substituted imitation societal structures that reinforce stigmas and deviant images. Our society has lost sight of the individual and has focused on the group. Identities carefully cultured throughout a lifetime are devalued by the stereotyped images held by society. The elderly experience a declining control over their lives and may begin to see themselves as less than what they are. They may even begin to assume characteristics associated with the stereotype. They admit defeat in the midst of a society that refuses to recognize their individuality.

To effect change in society's view, we must focus on the qualities of the individual and his or her personal needs. The first step is to understand fully the aging process that is occurring in all of us. Aging is a result of biological and social changes. Aging is not a disease that can be cured or a handicap that we can design for. Aging is a process that witnesses the rise of any number of concurrent diseases, disabilities, and physical restrictions.

THE AGING PROCESS

Aging is often viewed from two related perspectives: the study of the biological process (geriatrics) and the study of the social passage that occurs over time (gerontology). Advanced age is often seen only as a period of loss: loss of physical ability, loss of peers, loss of worthwhile employment, and loss of security. Obviously, the process of aging is not all losses. An individual is continually developing and expanding with new information and knowledge, new family roles, and new opportunities to pursue personal interests.

Biological aging (senescence) is measured by a decline in the body's ability to maintain a balanced interaction (homeostasis) of the organs, muscles, bones, and endocrine systems. A reduction in the body's homeostasis increases the individual's vulnerability to outside forces. It is important to realize the gradualness of the aging process, which requires constant adaptation. Unlike individuals disabled through a traumatic event who adapt fairly quickly, aging individuals are filled with self-doubts about their capability and the measure of their physical resources. The person may feel exposed and afraid of stressful situations.

The social passages that occur with aging also require constant adaptation. Traditional family roles are often altered. The retired husband is no longer a breadwinner, and the wife must channel displaced child-rearing energies into new pursuits. The quality and quantity of interpersonal relationships may change when the peer group no longer includes fellow workers, and discussions are not centered on "shop talk," raises, and promotions. Elderly men may also find that their male world no longer exists and that social activities are focused on traditionally female interests. Wives of recent retirees may find drastic changes in their routines, which must now include having a man around the house.

Biological Aging

Individuals age at different rates. Biological functions within an individual also age at varying rates and are influenced by heredity and a lifetime of habits. Failing vision and hearing are the most stereotyped images of old age, but failures of circulatory, respiratory, and muscular systems can be as common and more pervasive in their effect. Sensory losses are often cited as the most critical environmental design criteria after wheelchair access; however, loss of function in the endocrine, nervous, muscular, and skeletal systems can be as environmentally determinant. The physical characteristics of advanced age—gray hair, loss of teeth, increased weight, sagging muscles, and wrinkles—are often only a small measure of the biological changes that occur in the body. Stiffened joints, shortness of breath, decreased blood flow, diminished muscle strength, and an inability to sustain physical stress are the invisible characteristics that determine physical competence.

Biological aging leads to an overall loss of strength and endurance of the body's systems. Losses in biological function can lead to perceived changes in competence and affect self-image, ego, and personal strength. Designers must understand the interaction of a constantly changing physical competence with an environment that could provide prosthetic support and enhance greater functioning.

The body is composed of a variety of systems that interact and maintain the body's operation. Communicating systems, such as the endocrine and nervous systems, correlate the various functions in the body, while the mechanical systems (muscular and skeletal) are the machinery responsible for movement. Control systems (digestive, respiratory, and cardiovascular) maintain homeostatic balance. Sensations of taste, smell, sight, hearing, and equilibrium are detection senses, which gather information about environmental changes.

Communicating Systems

Endocrine System: The endocrine system is one of the two communicating systems of the body. Hormones produced by the body's glands control a variety of functions, such as growth, body temperature, metabolic rate, secretion of digestive enzymes, and changes in the reproductive cycle. For example, the release of the hormone adrenaline prepares the body to cope with stress by increasing respiration and circulation of blood to the brain and muscles. Reduced adrenal activity decreases the body's ability to react quickly, purposefully, and with sustained physical activity, thereby increasing the individual's vulnerability.

A major change in the glandular system is the alteration of the hormone cycle in the female and reduced production of sperm in the male. Studies have shown that although there are changes in function, sexual activity can continue well into the eighties. A decline in sexual activity among the elderly is dictated more by societal mores than biological function. Sexual inactivity among elderly females is also due to a lack of partners in the later years—females outnumber males by more than 2 to 1 at age 80.

Nervous System: The nervous system processes information, stimulates movement, and has the capabilities for emotion, reason, and memory. Stereotyped images of neurological change with age have focused on senility, memory loss, and an inability to develop new skills ("you can't teach an old dog new tricks"). Changes in the nervous system, however, also affect movement, reflexes, and reaction time.

The aging nervous system becomes less efficient in the coordination of the muscular, glandular, and circulatory systems. Diminished neuron activity affects the vascular system, reducing blood flow to the brain and limiting the responsiveness of organs and other control systems. Organic changes and diseases of the nervous system affect motor abilities by reducing coordination, which can

Skeletal and muscular changes can alter the body's posture. (ROSENBLAD-WALLIN, 1977; REPRINTED WITH PERMISSION FROM STUS KONSUMENTTEKNISKA, FORSKNING SGRUPP, GOTEBERG, SWEDEN)

Retrieval of memory files requires accurate placement of information and the ability to trace individual memory files. (REPRINTED BY PERMISSION OF EDWARD KOREN)

alter the concept of movement. For example, an individual may become stiff and frozen, mid-stride, while crossing the street, as if the body had forgotten how to walk.

Research in the area of brain functioning, intelligence, and aging is limited. Published studies have shown that elderly test takers do not perform as well as their younger counterparts on the same standardized exam. Studies of this type, however, are unreasonable comparisons of generations that have had different educational opportunities and exposure. Successive generations are more knowledgeable than their predecessors because of higher educational intensity and increased access to information. Longitudinal studies by K. Warner Schaie (1975) conclude that there is little change in intellectual functioning during adulthood, but that there are vast differences among generations. Schaie points out that the large "intellectual" gap occurs because of obsolete skills attained during early adulthood. Although theories of human development point to continued growth throughout an individual's lifetime, it would seem that it is in areas not valued by contemporary society. Measured intelligence concentrates on number and word manipulation, rather than on the range and quality of life's experiences.

Studies of memory loss indicate that the storage capacity does not decline with age, but that the rate of retrieval does. Long-term memory is directly affected by a decline in the organizational processes that enter information. This reduced efficiency in information storage indicates the need for repetitive cuing of information to maintain a constant level of recall. If memory is conceptualized as a large filing system, the storage of information requires efficient and correct placement of files. Aging of the nervous system affects the placement of files—the mind's "secretary" is less able to respond quickly to the coding system and use efficient tracing methods.

Environmental Implications: The built environment requires quick reactions, strength, and agility. Mechanical devices that are time-operated, such as street crossings and elevator doors, may not give the elderly enough time to complete the activity. Negotiation of environmental obstacles, coupled with a reduced agility and speed, may also place the individual in jeopardy. Limited endurance may require the individual to take frequent rests and to travel at times when buses and sidewalks are less congested and easier to negotiate. Other demanding situations may not be so easy to avoid.

Memory loss may require repetition of information through various channels. Buildings with confusing circulation routes and poor graphic symbols make it difficult to find specific places and to retrace paths. Confusion and disorientation can occur in buildings that are symmetrical and repetitive or that appear to be similar. Apartment buildings are notoriously bad for orientation—floor elevator lobbies all look alike and the corridors are unbroken rhythms of anonymous doorways. Orientation can be improved by providing landmarks and increasing the saliency of important directional information. Color coding and patterns have been popular interior orienting tools. Sophisticated coding systems, however, may not always be perceptible or understood, and visual difficulties may limit reception of important information.

Memory loss causes aggravation and stress. The elderly are particularly susceptible to unnecessary stress. The fear of being labeled "senile" can turn everyday forgetfulness into a major trauma. For example, an elderly relative went out to pick up the milk off the stoop and a blustery December wind slammed the door shut behind her. Dressed only in her housecoat, she stood locked outside until she finally was so cold that she broke a window to get in. Her fear of being labeled old and senile kept her from obtaining help from the neighbors. We all need reminders to prod our memory. Self-locking door mechanisms should be avoided; and lights on stoves that remind us they are on are details that make day-to-day functioning easier and less aggravating.

Mechanical Systems

Muscular System: The contraction and relaxation of muscles enables the body to move by using the skeleton as leverage. Reduction of muscle strength and bulk begins at about age 30, and declines until age 70 when it is about half of what it was at 30. Exercise, which provides oxygen to the body, strengthens muscles and improves overall physiological capabilities.

Illness, congenital defects, and disease can weaken limbs or cause paralysis. Diminished physical activity can result in the shortening of muscles and tendons. In its advanced stages, this can cause continually bent joints, affecting posture and the position of elbows and wrists. Muscular atrophy reduces the body's ability to support itself and requires prosthetic support such as walkers or canes. Complete muscle atrophy or paralysis may restrict individuals to wheelchairs.

Abnormal muscle contractions prevent accurate motor ability and limit eye-hand coordination, making everyday functioning difficult. "Tremors" can be the result of tiredness or diseases such as Parkinsons. Tremors make it difficult to operate small buttons, such as on elevators, or to perform precise activities such as inserting a key into a lock. Improper muscular control also makes balance difficult, whether it be standing or seated.

Contraction of skeletal muscles produces heat, which is important for the maintenance of a constant body temperature. Hypothermia is a common problem among the elderly, and reduced heat production by the muscles can add to a homeostatic imbalance. Decreased mobility also affects the kidneys and urinary tract, which operate optimally in a standing or walking position.

Skeletal System: With advanced age, reduced calcium levels make the skeletal system brittle and vulnerable to accidents. Deficient calcium levels are more common in older women than in older men. This deficiency, coupled with changes in gait, leads to a high incidence of hip fractures among elderly women. Healing can be a prolonged and difficult process.

Compaction of vertebral discs and curvature of the spine change the body's stature and posture. A loss of elasticity in the joints reduces flexibility and the range of movement. Bending, kneeling, turning, and rising can become difficult without the support of grab bars or chair arms. Arthritic conditions further affect movement by limiting grasping, pinching, and twisting motions. Arthritis (osteoarthritis and rheumatoid arthritis) is recognized as a major difficulty of old age from which very few people escape. Arthritis affects the joints and may be characterized by swelling or inflammation, which limits strength and dexterity. Manipulation of objects such as hardware on doors and windows becomes difficult and painful.

Environmental Implications: The ability to move about unrestricted is often taken for granted. Temporary conditions such as sprained ankles or broken limbs remind us of how difficult the environment can be when impeded by a disabling situation. We adapt to our environment for the duration of the healing and then return to a "normal" level of functioning. For the elderly, each day requires adaptation to a changing level of strength, agility, and range of motion.

Walking may become a difficult activity, accomplished only when moving slowly and deliberately by shuffling one's feet and using a prosthetic support (cane or walker). Speed and balance are reduced such that the walking surface becomes very important. Slippery surfaces, loose rugs, and raised thresholds become hazardous obstacles. Walking aids, in turn, become a burden when climbing stairs or opening doors.

Severely restricted mobility may require confinement to a wheelchair. Wheelchairs are awkward, space-consuming carts that require the user to function from a seated height. "Barrier-free" standards are based on the wheelchair, its space requirements, and its need to roll. These standards assume that the user has full muscular control above the waist, which is rarely the case for the old-old. Paralysis from strokes or arthritis may affect the entire body's muscular control. The elderly individual may sit in a wheelchair but may not be able to make it move. Anthropometric data must be used with the insight that many of the wheelchair-confined elderly cannot reach, grasp easily, or maneuver precisely.

Bending, kneeling, twisting, and rising can become difficult and painful movements. Low shelves and electrical outlets become impossible to reach, and rising out of a chair is difficult without arms for support. Personal care activities such as hair washing, wiping oneself on the toilet, and getting into and out of bathtubs may be impossible. If these grooming activities become curtailed they may affect socialization because the person is too embarrassed to go out in public.

The environment constantly requires us to manipulate devices that involve grasping, twisting, or pinching. Doorknobs, window latches, lamp switches, stove dials, and water faucets all become obstacles to performing specific tasks. Other activities, such as dialing the phone, may require precise finger manipulation, which is difficult with trembling fingers. "Touch-type" controls such as push-button phones and elevator buttons may be located too close together to properly activate. Hardware devices that do not require precise activation or those that can be operated simply by being pushed or pulled ease everyday tasks and eliminate the need to ask for help.

Control Systems

Digestive System: The digestive tract also changes with age. Lower levels of gastric juices may make certain foods difficult to digest, and constipation may become a problem. The kidneys have less waste to process, but may become overworked by a change in diet, disease, or drugs. Malfunctioning of the excretory system can become a major personal embarrassment and an obstacle to socialization. Reduced bladder control may necessitate frequent trips to the bathroom, limiting long journeys where public facilities may not be available or accessible. Incontinence (an inability to control one's excretory functions) is an extremely distressing situation for the individual, as well as for the family, who may become confused and overwhelmed. Toilet training, diapers, and rubber mattress covers become part of a vocabulary typically reserved for young children. The cleaning process, as well, is undignified and assails our society's view that excretion is an unfortunate necessity, which should be hidden from view.

Malnutrition and improper diets constitute major health problems among the elderly. Deficiencies in vitamin, mineral, and protein intake may be responsible for physiological and psychological changes. An inadequate diet may be the result of insufficient funds, loneliness, changing taste and smell senses, a lack of kitchen facilities, or a diminished desire to expend the energy to cook. Proper eating habits are developed and reinforced by situations that usually focus on family or socialization. For the single elderly person, eating alone may compound the loneliness and the loss of friends and family.

Respiratory System: The body's breathing efficiency declines with age and reduces the ability to oxygenate blood. Oxygen is needed for digestion and cell respiration. Reduced oxygen levels lower the metabolic rate and the body's energy reserve. Pathological changes from pollution and smoking may also lead to pulmonary diseases that restrict respiration. Movement can be severely curtailed by respiration that is sufficient only at rest and entirely inadequate under physical stress.

Cardiovascular System: As with other systems, age brings a decline in efficiency of the circulatory system. The heart must pump harder to achieve the same output. Circulation time increases and there is less of a reserve oxygen capacity for the body to use in times of stress. Reduced blood supply to the brain, especially in cases of arteriosclerosis, may cause short periods of dizziness, blackouts, or blurred vision. Prolonged physical stress, such as climbing stairs, may also cause short periods of reduced blood flow through constricted arteries.

Environmental Implications: Individuals with "invisible" handicaps often suffer from an environment that makes demands beyond their capabilities. Respiratory and circulatory difficulties may restrict physical activity such as climbing stairs. Elevators, which are thought of primarily for the wheelchair bound, also benefit these individuals.

Design criteria for invisible handicaps are rarely found in barrier-free standards. An empathetic approach that responds to the very sensitive needs of an incontinent individual or to the loneliness of unshared meals is required. People who have limited bladder control find that the sound of running water creates a sympathetic release of their own bladder. Decorative fountains of cascading water may provide visual beauty, but they lead to "accidents" and embarrassing situations. Bathrooms should be easily available to people who may need them frequently and are unable to travel very far.

Most eating environments of the elderly usually are not conducive to proper habits. Meals should be an opportunity for socialization and a cornerstone of the day's activities. Programs such as "Meals-on-Wheels" may provide a well-balanced hot meal each day, but they fail to respond to the social opportunity associated with eating and the loneliness of eating by oneself. Purpose-built apartments for the elderly rarely have dining rooms or sun-filled, pleasant eat-in kitchens. Nursing home routines usually revolve around trays and hot and cold carts. *Food service* and *dining* become synonymous terms for an activity that could and should be psychologically supportive and physiologically beneficial.

Detection Senses

Sight: Age causes a variety of changes in the structure of the eye. These changes affect visual acuity, depth perception, and color intensity. Disorders such as glaucoma and cataracts reduce vision and can lead to total blindness. Some visual problems are corrected with surgery or glasses; others require support from the environment. The inability of the eye to focus properly, either from pathological or aging changes, limits the individual's ability to read fine print, discern detail, and interpret environmental changes received only through visual channels.

As the eyes age, it takes longer for them to adjust their focus between objects that are close and those that are farther away. The eye also requires more time to accommodate to various light levels. Glare and sudden changes in light level can cause momentary blindness until the pupil can adjust. Illumination levels must be higher to compensate for a reduced amount of light reaching the retina.

The lens of the eye is normally transparent, but it yellows and thickens with age, causing changes in perception of color. Blues, greens, and purples become difficult to distinguish, and slight changes in hue can go undetected. Colors that are closely related may blend together and alter depth perception; edges of stairs and changes in floor level may go undetected. Peripheral changes to the eye can cause "tunnel vision," where images are focused only at the center and blur toward the edges.

Hearing and Equilibrium: The ear is a receptor for sound waves and maintains equilibrium. The ability to hear allows us to communicate directly with one another and to monitor the environment. A limited loss of hearing can make it difficult to distinguish different sounds, especially speech from background noise. Many forms of hearing loss occur at different frequencies—if the high frequencies are lost, then only vowels, and not consonants, are heard. Frequency losses make speech seem unintelligible and confusing. For these types of hearing loss, increased volume does not make the message understandable. Those who have difficulty understanding what is said may be considered senile.

Damage to the inner ear causes imbalance and reduces the brain's feedback about the position of the body. Coordination of visual information with the equilibrium senses allows us to negotiate and interpret our environment. A lack of equilibrium can result in unsteady maneuvering.

Taste, Smell, and Touch: Taste and smell are the most subtle detecting senses. The number of olfactory and taste bud receptors declines with age and makes fine discrimination difficult. Sweet and salty tastes may be difficult to distinguish, and food may not seem as enjoyable. Smell provides gentle cues about the environment and the people who are around us. A reduced ability to smell is not a major handicap, but it is a form of sensory deprivation that limits the quantity of information one receives about the environment.

The skin also experiences a diminished sense of pain and pressure with age. Sensitivity to temperature changes may be reduced, causing an individual to inadvertently burn or scald himself or herself. Subtle changes in the texture of walls and materials may not be discernible.

Environmental Implications: Visual acuity allows us to interpret our environment and communicate with one another. Buildings clearly are geared to our sense of sight: light, color, and proportion are qualities evaluated only by our visual perception. Sight and hearing are important monitoring devices that constantly interpret the environment and warn us of danger. The other detecting senses add more subtle information about the qualities we perceive—softness, hardness, roughness, the direction of breezes, and the smell of flowers.

The loss of any or several senses requires that the others focus more sharply on providing information. For this reason information must be provided through a variety of forms. Redundant "channels" (for example, visual and audible alarms) assure that the information is available to everyone. For the elderly, increased deprivation of all the senses requires that information not only come through several channels, but that the message has clarity and intensity.

Visual changes require a greater design sensitivity to scale, dimension, and distance. The visual range of many elderly people closes slowly, so that objects at the ends of the fingertips take on primary importance. Landmarks 20 to 30 feet away may not be distinguishable from the background clutter, and details may not be perceptible. Reflected light patterns on highly polished floors become blinding spots. Windows at the ends of corridors and luminous light fixtures are sources of light for which the eye cannot properly compensate. Objects and people appear to be large dark featureless shadows against a blinding background of light.

Blurred vision may make it difficult to perceive edges or to read signage that is too small. Light patterns and shadows falling across the floor may appear to be edges or steps or may actually obscure a change in level. Gradual changes in light level and tactile cues at edges can prevent misinterpretation of visual information. The use of nonreflective materials by designers can improve visual acuity by eliminating peripherally refracted light that leads to blurred vision.

Audible information should be clear, concise, and slow so that it does not become garbled. (Public address systems are notoriously bad.) Unnecessary background noise, such as the hum of equipment, should be eliminated because it interferes with understanding conversation. Some background noises are valuable for orientation, as well as to signal when and from what direction people are approaching. It is also important to remember that increasing volume does not always increase reception of information.

Tactile messages offer opportunities for exploration by architects. It is important that the vocabulary be consistent and that the messages offer information. Tactile cues on walking surfaces can provide "paths," warn of edges, and locate amenities. For the elderly person dependent on handrails to ease mobility, wall surfaces and the handrail itself offer information about paths of travel and the individual's location in the building. Changes in air movement can signal open doors, edges, or the juncture of different rooms or corridors. The warmth of the sun, the chill of ceramic tile, and the heat of a radiator can all offer familiar orienting qualities.

Social Passage

The Swiss psychologist Carl Gustav Jung spent much of his life developing a philosophy that focused on old age as the true pinnacle of the individual's lifetime. Jung felt that only those individuals who lived to an advanced age could experience the full range of joys, sorrows, and other life experiences that lead to a fully enriched life. He saw old age as a period of personal fulfillment and growth—a time of true insight and privilege.

The role of the wise elder has lost its place in our society, as well as in our families. Our culture stresses the early years as important periods of growth and development; middle age has become the pinnacle, and old age the downward slide to death. Society has been unable to see the elderly as self-sufficient contributing members. We force them to retire at age 65 and we remove control of the most meaningful events in their lives. We create sterile, nonstimulating environments that stress staff convenience rather than the individual's preference or comfort. We remove the elderly from informal social opportunities by providing all services in one building, so that they never have to leave.

Prominent psychologists and sociologists have established theories about the changes that occur with advanced age in our culture. Some changes are linked with the biological aging process, while others are a result of the interrelationships of the environment, the individual, and behavior. Theories such as those of disengagement, continuity, activity, and environmental press offer insights into the psychological changes that occur with aging. The environmental designer must be sensitive to the subtle, often invisible, changes within the aged individual.

Disengagement Theory

Disengagement, which is a prominent and controversial theory, claims that as people age they withdraw from social roles and interpersonal relationships. At the individual level it may be selective;

Individuals may disengage themselves from some roles and not from others. Retirement may remove valued social roles and leave the individual searching for new ways to feel needed and valuable. Men may find retirement a difficult period of adjustment to a world that revolves around conventionally female activities and roles.

that is, the withdrawal may be from some roles and not from others. As Robert Atchley points out (1972), with each withdrawal the individual becomes more self-centered and inward-turning.

Much of the disengagement theory is based on a concept of societal equilibrium. Equilibrium is achieved when the youngest and fittest are in positions of authority and control. This leads to the concept of retirement, which weeds out older participants and transplants them into lesser valued roles. Advocates of the disengagement theory believe that as individuals age they inevitably become less efficient, hence, less productive. Reduced expectations and forced retirement can then be viewed as a beneficial complement to a biological decline. Compulsory retirement, however, may not be viewed as beneficial by a 65-year-old individual who has not reduced his or her expectations, social roles, or the quality of interpersonal relationships associated with middle age (see activity theory). A forced change in social roles may lead to confusion, alienation, and fear. Mutual satisfaction can occur only when there is a simultaneous disengagement by the individual (who recognizes a declining physical reserve) and society (which recognizes the same decline).

Society has developed rules by which disengagement can occur. The rites of passage establish retirement at a particular age (65), require ceremonial events (retirement parties), stipulate gift-giving (watches), and provide images for future social roles (fishing, traveling, and grandparenting). Disengagement, however, is a much more gradual process that involves a constantly changing withdrawal from certain roles. Total disengagement may occur when the individual has no physical reserve beyond a mere day-to-day existence.

Activity Theory

The activity theory is disengagement's complement and its antithesis. Activity offers the perspective that individuals maintain the norms of middle age into old age. The foundation of this theory is that older people deny aging and continually struggle to maintain the roles, appearance, and activity levels associated with middle age. If culturally valued roles are removed by society through forced disengagement, then the individual will replace it with a different valued role in which to channel his or her energies. Volunteer groups, church societies, and clubs reinforce an individual's self-worth by providing an outlet for skills and roles developed at work or at home.

Continuity Theory

The greatest social changes that occur with aging relate to personal value and self-worth. A primary interest of human psychology and the elderly is focused on maintenance of culturally valued roles and patterns. Major gerontological theories, such as continuity, recognize that as the individual develops she or he acquires habits, preferences, and commitments, which need to be reinforced and supported as that person's image of who she or he is. People spend most of their lives developing qualities and surrounding themselves with objects that create a personal self-image. Continuity theory states that with advanced age we develop a stronger need to maintain our habits and routines, but that we still adapt to changing phys-

Ecological Model: Environmental Press and Competence. (FROM *ENVIRONMENT AND AGING*, BY M. P. LAWTON. COPYRIGHT © 1980 BY WADSWORTH, INC.; REPRINTED BY PERMISSION OF BROOKS/COLE PUBLISHING COMPANY, MONTEREY, CA)

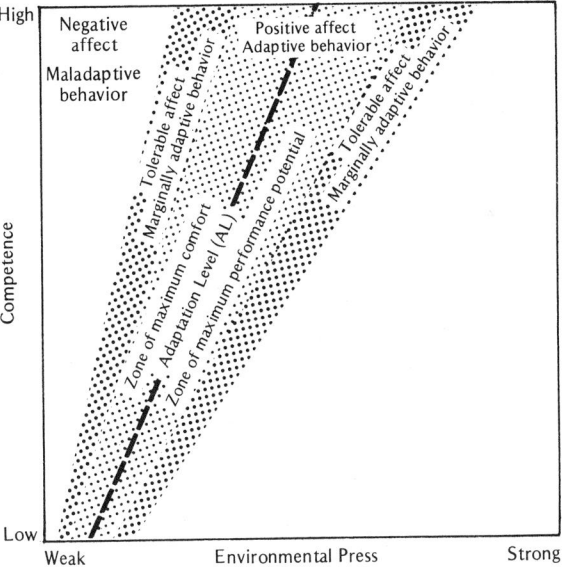

iological capabilities, new situations, and life's experiences. Old age is not static but evolutionary.

The activity and disengagement theories each have a narrow view of adaptation to old age—denial that it exists or detachment from associations. Continuity theory recognizes diversity in the elderly population.

Environmental Press and Competence

Lawton and Nahemow (Lawton, 1980) have conceptualized the person/environment interdependence in their ecological model of environmental press and competence. The shaded zone of the diagram represents a balance of competence and environmental demands. If the environment becomes too demanding and surpasses the individual's competence, the outcome is negative. The same is true if the environment is not demanding enough; the encounter is negatively valued because it is unstimulating.

The ecological model allows for a qualitative measure of several variables. All elderly people are not alike; they have different amounts of physical reserve, endurance, stamina, and strength. Different environments place different demands on the individual in different ways. Negotiating a busy urban sidewalk is generally considered more stressful than preparing dinner; however, either activity may provide a balanced adaptation for individuals with different competence.

The person/environment relationship has strong design implications—the environment can be too challenging or not stimulating enough to each individual. The elderly are not a homogeneous group that reacts predictably to stimuli. The level of adaptation varies with the individual and the environmental setting. It is also important to recognize that the level of adaptation will change with the individual over time. Also, personal prostheses (hearing aids, walkers, etc.) can raise competence and alter the level and quality of adaptation.

Environmental Implications

The environment in which we place elderly individuals may not alter society's stereotyped view of the aging process, but it may begin to focus attention on specific issues. Age-segregated buildings isolate the elderly from the mainstream of society, minimizing their value and role in society. Age-integrated facilities, or age-segregated facilities in an age-integrated area, can offer an expanded social role for the elderly. Access to shopping areas and public conveniences can reinforce normative social patterns and lead to informal social opportunities. Residents of age-segregated housing may have nothing more in common than their age category (over 65) and their address.

A simple interpretation of such social theories as disengagement and activity can lead to erroneous design responses. While disengagement may require structure, clarity, and definition in the environment, activity requires greater choice, independence, and flexibility. One must understand the variety of social changes that occur within the individual throughout the aging process. An environment that forces socialization will not limit people from disengaging but may actually increase its chance. On the other hand, an environment that does not foster shared social opportunities can lead to withdrawal by those unable to actively pursue them.

Opportunities for socialization should follow life's rhythms and patterns. Certain daily activities are considered social and others private. Although shared bathrooms and bedrooms make roommates more familiar with one another, it may not create a friendship or social bond. It is inappropriate for an environment to force socialization as the solution for a natural disengagment. It is equally inappropriate to disguise economic considerations as social and behavioral goals. Semiprivate rooms are just that, *semi*private; they are the result of economic efficiency, not profound, socially therapeutic goals.

The environment must provide a measure of flexibility and adaptability. A "high-press" environment may provide positive outcomes for the individual who can cope and feel a sense of pride in that accomplishment. As physical competence declines, however, the press level may need to change for that individual to maintain the same sense of accomplishment. Environments that accommodate only a static level of competence will reinforce failure for those unable to adapt and passivity for those who are not tested to their fullest potential. Environments must have choice and variety, providing opportunities to be fully tested, as well as opportunities to merely survive.

3 Housing, Privacy, and Independence

HOUSING

The house is an object of unusual fascination for contemporary society. Economists use housing starts and interest rates to project future economic growth. Census studies measure housing quality to develop economic profiles of the population. Trade magazines, such as *Housing*, and vanity magazines, which include *Better Homes and Gardens, Metropolitan Home,* and *Good Housekeeping,* expound the virtues of the house as an object of art. With all of its many facets, what relevance does the house have in the life of an elderly individual?

Housing fulfills a temporal need for shelter, but it also becomes infused with emotional qualities. The home is a place for retreat, a place of security and comfort that provides a sense of continuity and familiarity. For the elderly, these qualities of home become more important when the outside environment seems threatening and unfriendly. The environmental range may close in as physical competence declines. The single-family home may become an apartment, a few small rooms, or finally, only a bed. For many institutionalized elderly, the memory of home is only a photograph or a favorite bed quilt.

The home provides a private turf that has definable edges; an important territorial distinction that reinforces our control over objects and events. Control over our environment symbolizes a self-determined life-style and preserves the qualities of independence and privacy. With changing physical competence, the environment will exert more and more control over the individual. For elderly people, a place of their own can become the only constant, reliable ingredient in their lives.

Although housing forms and quality vary by country, the elderly portion of the population consistently can be found living in older, substandard housing. Studies of the elderly and their satisfaction with housing point to high levels of contentment and overall satisfaction, although individual measures, such as security, may rate low. Many theories have been established about this curious satisfaction with substandard housing. One explanation is the individual's overall expectations. The current generation of "older" elderly were born in the first decade of this century. They have lived their mature lives through two world wars, the depression, and periods of great unemployment. Having a place for themselves and their family has been a precious commodity. The possession of housing, not necessarily its quality, is important.

Future generations of elderly people undoubtedly will have higher expectations for housing quality and life-style. Those individuals who have lived the American dream of a large house in the suburbs will come to expect certain qualities in their future housing. The suburban home has provided unparalleled independence for an individual's activities and life-style. Retirement communities, "congregate" housing, and nursing homes must respond to upcoming generations that are enjoying unquestioned privacy. Accompanying the social opportunities for increased privacy and independence has been a rise in economic standards; our society has become more affluent with larger houses, more expensive cars, and fancier vacations.

Privacy and independence are concepts that we identify with the home. Housing quality is measured by the privacy it affords the individual. Privacy is often quantified by the number of rooms and whether or not there is a private toilet. Purpose-built housing is conceptualized by the measure of independence and privacy provided to the residents. Intermediate care facilities, independent apartments, and sheltered dwellings offer distinctive levels of care and become stigmatized labels for housing forms.

Privacy and independence are important social qualities that designers interpret into design criteria for housing. Conventional rules will not provide privacy and independence for the elderly unless we understand *their* needs in terms of *their* physiological capabilities. Classifying some housing forms as independent is a misunderstanding of that quality, which has a profound role in every individual's daily life. Some individuals may require more assistance to complete specific tasks, but they should not be robbed of independence in other areas of daily living.

This chapter will examine the characteristics of independence and privacy, and how they are conceptualized in our society. Privacy and independence are important qualities for the elderly individual. These terms play a major role in the design of purpose-built housing for the elderly, as well as in the way in which we conceptualize housing forms. Whenever we group together a number of individuals for the purpose of support and care, we create an institution. It is unlikely that we will completely remove institutional settings from our society. It is possible, however, to reexamine our institutions and make them more homelike and more residential, infused with the qualities of privacy and independence.

PRIVACY

The word *privacy* has become an important part of our twentieth-century vocabulary. We use it to conceptualize the quality of a place or the spirit of an idea. We use it to describe physical separation from others, as well as the internalization of our thoughts and visions. It is possible to have privacy on a crowded street, and at the same time, it may prove to be impossible to attain privacy alone in a room. Privacy exists at many levels, with both physical and spiritual requirements. The activities of our daily lives require periods of spatial separation, as well as a sense of space that transcends physical barriers.

Certain aspects of privacy are easily recognized and have become an accepted part of our culture. We have unquestioned aloneness in the bathroom for grooming, bathing, and defecation. We may share these functions only with spouses or small children. We expect a measure of spatial separation and visual privacy for these functions whether we are in our own home or visiting a public building. If our expectations are not upheld, or if we are accidentally intruded upon, we may feel uncomfortable and vulnerable.

Research studies, Supreme Court cases, and national debates argue the protection of privacy as an individual's basic right. Most aspects of privacy, however, are guaranteed only by learned cultural responses. To assure privacy one must have the capacity to protect it. Institutions, by their nature and method of operation, disregard the basic spatial and spiritual qualities of privacy. Economics dictates shared nursing home rooms and small apartments with sleeping alcoves. Institutional routines focus on ease of operation and staff convenience to maximize efficiency. Hospitallike patterns place visual observation above privacy; modesty and aloneness are not respected. In the rush to provide economical, efficient, and safe housing care, we have ignored the less tangible qualities that make life worth living.

The Many Forms of Privacy

Privacy, by its nature, is interactional; there must be an *other*, as well as a perceived boundary. The *other* may be a person, a sound, or merely the sensation that we are not alone. The boundary may be as real as a wall or as vague as a social courtesy. The maintenance of a boundary requires the consciousness to control it, the strength to enforce it, and the respect of others to preserve it. If any of these three qualities of the boundary is lost, then our privacy is subject to invasion.

It is important to understand that privacy exists at many different levels and in many different forms. When we speak of privacy we must focus on whether it is the privacy of an event, of a life-style, or of a thought. The environmental response may depend on our sensitivity to privacy's many implications. Responding with a wall and door may provide a spatial segregation, but it may not fulfill an individual's need for privacy.

Privacy of Event

It is important to realize that we conceptualize privacy in many different forms—usually related to our daily activities. The most common form is the privacy of an event. We expect privacy for bathing, dressing, sex, sleeping, and defecation. We conceptualize the boundary as a physical separation by the use of walls and doors. We may control the boundary by locking the door, but we usually rely on common courtesy and the respect of others to maintain the boundary of our privacy. Walls with doors are used because they physically define a territory and provide a visual and auditory separation for our private events. Special activities such as taking medication, oxygen treatments, or cleaning dentures may require unique forms of privacy so that we may conceal certain aspects of ourselves. We often fear the discovery that we are not all that we seem.

Privacy of Life-style

The way in which we live daily is a result of a lifetime of habits and preferences. The time at which we eat, the way in which we dress, and the length of time we like to sleep are as much a part of us as are the color of our hair and the shape of our nose. We do not like to change our patterns, because they provide a sense of order and familiarity.

As we age, the environment places more control over our daily patterns. Certain activities take longer and require more energy, but we adapt to the changes we recognize in ourselves. Changes that are dictated by external forces are not easy to adapt to and remove the qualities of a self-determined life-style.

Privacy of life-style may require territorial boundaries as physical as walls to conceal aspects of our daily routine that we do not care to share. The amount of money in our checkbook, the neatness of our home, and the clothes we wear around the house are all aspects of our private life-styles. The rhythms and patterns of our daily life may not require physical barriers, but rather the intangible quality of freedom to do as we please.

Privacy of Thought

At a spiritual level, privacy is required for contemplation, reflection, planning, and goal-setting. Privacy leads to the development of our personality, the concept of who we are, and the perception of our role in society. Our dreams, goals, and aspirations are all tied into a very personal, private way we plan our lives. Our most private thoughts are all our own, unless we voluntarily share them. Many components of our personality and emotions have external features, but our thoughts, our pains, and our sorrows can be completely internalized.

Our thoughts cannot be physically invaded. They can, however, be affected by noise, activity, and interruptions, which bombard the mind with conflicting information. A lack of continuity between our thought patterns and the eventual outcome of our actions can lead to confusion and disorientation. We "learn" that our response to certain stimuli will have no effect, so we withdraw. The privacy of our thoughts may not be physically invaded, but they are manipulated in such a way that they have little meaning.

The Concepts of Privacy

Privacy and Economics

The words *public* and *private* are usually thought of in terms of economics—ownership and possession. In our democratic society, governmental intervention into the affairs of the individual is an ongoing area of debate. Privacy, or the right to be left alone, has never been constitutionally guaranteed. Property and possessions are legally secure, but our need for aloneness is protected only by mutual respect through learned social behavior. Privacy is only as secure as our ability to protect it and reinforce the boundaries of our personal space.

Historically, privacy has been guaranteed only to the wealthy through land ownership. This concept is still very much alive and can be witnessed in the social stratifications of the lower and middle classes. With increased family income comes the ability to purchase more space and more sleeping rooms. As a society, we are not fully egalitarian—certain "basic qualities" of life are seen as privileges rather than as rights. Nowhere is this more apparent than in the housing settings we provide through our welfare system. We congregate large groups of people into small living quarters and place them in unfamiliar high-rise buildings. Institutional settings for the elderly and mentally handicapped are well known for their wards where four to twelve people sleep in a common room. Institutions disregard privacy because the individual has no way to purchase it (except perhaps by a reward system) and no way to protect it. Private nursing home rooms, apartments with a private bedroom (rather than a sleeping alcove in the living room), and a private bathroom are reserved for the economically privileged. Our society does not offer a rich blend of opportunities to all citizens.

Privacy and Individual Identity

Privacy is fundamental to the development of our individuality. Individual identity is reflected in our habits, preferences, and activities, as well as in the physical attributes of our space and property. As social animals we are predisposed to a dichotomy. We want to identify with a group—to be part of the clique—but at the same time we foster an individuality that represents an image of uniqueness. We engage in territorial marking by decorating and modifying our surroundings. We personalize our home with objects such as photographs, which represent a historical continuity to our identity. We extend our territory into spaces we do not own by claiming a "turf" that acts as a buffer to our own private areas. Individuals and groups claim spaces in the community by establishing familiarity and tenure. People begin to associate public spaces or objects such as park benches or chairs at the pool as part of their private territory. We extend a spiritual quality of privacy into the public realm. If the public environment is unsupportive of private needs, then the individual may feel vulnerable or uneasy. The individual may retreat into a fully secure territory where privateness is assured and his or her individual identity is stable.

The home has become synonymous with a person's identity, because it embodies both the spiritual and the physical needs for privacy. The home truly becomes "castle," because in it we are free from the demands of others, free to establish our own identities, and free to live with unquestioned privacy. The territory that we call home differs among individuals; it may be a house surrounded by land, an apartment, or even a single room. The true expression of a person's identity is most often witnessed in his or her most secure territory. That territory represents all that is stable and familiar; it may be as close as the clothes we wear or as large as the neighborhood we live in.

Privacy and the Institution

Stereotyped images of the elderly are part of the institutionalizing process in which the older individual begins to accept and emulate the characteristics of the group. Institutions are based on a strong group identity where privacy, self-expression, and individuality are manipulated. These highly structured and authoritarian organizations (i.e., the military, prisons, and religious groups) often undermine those aspects of individuality that contribute to a strong individual

Privacy and the Elderly

Privacy and Shrinking Life Space

With advancing age, the elderly experience a narrowing life space caused by physiological, psychological, and economic changes. Initially, retirement may mean relocation to a smaller dwelling and a smaller circle of friends. The death of a spouse or decreased physical competency may again cause relocation into a smaller dwelling in a new area. Physiological changes may reduce the frequency and range of travel, as well as the ease with which it is performed. Further biological changes may require an increased dependence on others to assist in performing routine daily activities. The intervention of an attendant or helper may also mean that the private turf, as small as it may be, must be shared and available to someone else. With each change there is a reciprocal loss of territory and possessions—a casting off of those things that are considered burdensome. A decrease in physical territory and the number of possessions may intensify the value of those items that have been retained and protected.

Institutions and other communal supportive housing environments often require an individual to compromise his or her perceptions of privacy, territory, and boundaries. Changing physical competence also requires compromise between the need for assistance and the need to retain a sense of dignity and privacy. Biological changes will alter the individual's physical mastery of the environment and the ability to protect the boundaries of privacy. An individual may require more assistance in performing activities that are considered private, such as bathing and toileting. The individual may have to relinquish certain lifelong-held views of privacy in order to complete certain tasks without expending all of his or her personal energy. The environment should respond to maximize other aspects of privacy in the performance of that activity. If physical intimacy must be shared with an attendant during bathing, then the boundaries of privacy should expand. The need to share with another person does not necessarily mean the total abandonment of the need for privacy from others.

We surround ourselves with the objects and events of our lives.

identity. The prohibition of personal possessions, forced common sleeping arrangements, and group hygiene facilities subjugate the importance of the individual. The only safe, secure, uninvaded territory into which to withdraw is the mind and the imagination. No turf exists, no private place away from others; there are no barriers, no walls, no shared courtesies. Even the body is subject to the probing and touching of indifferent strangers—a form of human contact we extend to others only in times of shared intimacy.

The repetitious, sterile qualities of most institutional buildings are derived from the modular component, the room, which reinforces anonymity and the sameness of the individual. Rights become "privileges," the family becomes "visitors," and given names become pet names such as "Sweetie," "Cutie," and "Lovie." A lifetime of habits and preferences are lost to the patterns of institutional routines and staff availability. Individuality is lost to an overpowering need for efficiency, cost effectiveness, and quality control.

Privacy, Aloneness, and Loneliness

Privacy's inherent antithesis is publicness or socialization. We all need periods of aloneness and periods of fellowship. The rhythms of our lives are built around appropriate periods and events for socialization and withdrawal. Both qualities are positive, but they become painful and undesirable when they are forced upon a person in unwanted forms and at inappropriate times. Loneliness is a difficult problem for the elderly. Many become housebound by infirmity or fear. It is important, however, to distinguish between aloneness and loneliness. There is a carefully balanced duality between loneliness and fellowship.

The theory of disengagement (see chapter 2) speaks of a natural reduction in interpersonal relationships that accompanies a withdrawal from certain social roles. The continuity theory, however, recognizes a need for the elderly to maintain culturally valued roles and images. Loneliness results when there is a forced disengagement from society or when the individual is no longer able to physically maintain the quality of social interaction she or he requires. Forced interaction will not resolve periods of loneliness if the individual does not perceive himself or herself as lonely or if the fellowship is under someone else's control and manipulation. The encouragement of spontaneous fellowship does not necessarily mean that we should remove the barriers between the public and private realms, but rather that we should reinforce those activities that are social and those that are private.

Privacy and Design

For architects privacy has always represented an organizational framework for design. Single-family homes are planned on a hierarchy of public and private zones, with walls to define edges and doors to create barriers. Large open office areas are arranged on a reward system of increased privacy for increased responsibility and status within the company. Privacy becomes a very measurable quality that can be quantified by the size, height, and character of the wall.

Privacy is recognized as positive. We use the word *private* to describe the characteristic of an area, of a particular space, or of an available life-style. Privacy is popular. It sells housing communities, houses, health clubs, apartment buildings, and parking spaces. We recognize the physical attributes of privacy, even though we may have different requirements for it.

Privacy in the design of housing for the elderly becomes difficult to measure or describe. Housing administrators and architects suddenly find vast differences in their conceptualizations of privacy. The physical attributes of privacy are compromised by economic, operational, and efficiency goals. We begin to replace actual privacy with symbolic gestures that we rationalize as being adequate. Instead of a bedroom with walls, we provide a sleeping alcove in the living room of an apartment so that the individual has "less to take care of." We provide multibedded nursing home rooms so that residents can "socialize more easily," and when they want to be alone, they can pull their cubicle curtain closed around their bed. Such physical features that we label *private* for the elderly we would find unacceptable or substandard for ourselves.

As designers, we use standards and invoke concepts that have no basis in fact. The problem is heightened because traditional concepts of privacy may not fulfill all the requirements for an aged individual. A wall with a door may provide physical separation, but it may not provide any measure of privacy if it is opened at will by strangers, or if the individual is physically or mentally unable to control its use and operation. We must go beyond traditional images and concepts of privacy and sensitize ourselves to those factors that place the control of privacy back in the hands of the aged individual.

Privacy and Personal Care

Personal care activities are those functions of daily living associated with hygiene: using the toilet, washing one's face, combing one's hair, bathing, dressing, and undressing. It may also include medication or medically related treatments that become important aspects of the elderly individual's life. Personal hygiene activities are time-consuming, arduous, and at times hazardous. For the physically impaired elderly, personal care activities can be the most difficult activities of the day since they require the greatest degree of physical dexterity, balance, and energy. These activities may also be the

to perform these basic events may restrict his or her desire and opportunities for socialization. In turn, a lack of privacy in the performance of these activities may also limit an individual's desire to expend the necessary energy. It may seem simply easier not to get dressed than to expose oneself to embarrassment and indignity.

For the elderly, the largest compromise comes when they must admit that they need assistance to perform the basic rudiments of personal hygiene. The elderly individual must share the most intimate events with another person and expose his or her imperfections. It has been noted by many psychologists that the inability to take care of one's personal hygiene becomes a pivotal influence on a person's self-image and sense of worth.

> When it was no longer possible for a patient to continue what for him or her had been standard practice in bathing, the patient who had managed to cope effectively with many other tough problems of chronic illness and aging seemed to give up altogether. . . . The need to make radical changes in his bathing patterns seemingly was perceived by the patient as a major landmark of failure.
>
> ALEXANDER KIRA, 1976

To ease the psychological strains, it is important that the elderly individual have environmental support to maintain an independent pursuit of these activities. Privacy must also be maintained for the individual performing the activity, as well as any attendant who may be there to assist. It is important that the privacy be "operational" rather than merely conceptual. Providing the spatial requirements for an accessible bathroom based on a particular handicap does not guarantee privacy. A bathroom that is too small for the individual, a wheelchair, and an attendant means that the door will most likely be left open.

Bathing should be rejuvenating as well as soothing and representative of care and concern between a staff member and the individual. Unfortunately, most bathing practices in nursing homes resemble car washes. The bathing process is usually complete with a line of residents sitting in their vehicles, with each staff member in charge of a specific task such as soaping, scrubbing, rinsing, or drying. It may seem like a humorous analogy, but it is a common approach because of its efficiency and effectiveness for the staff.

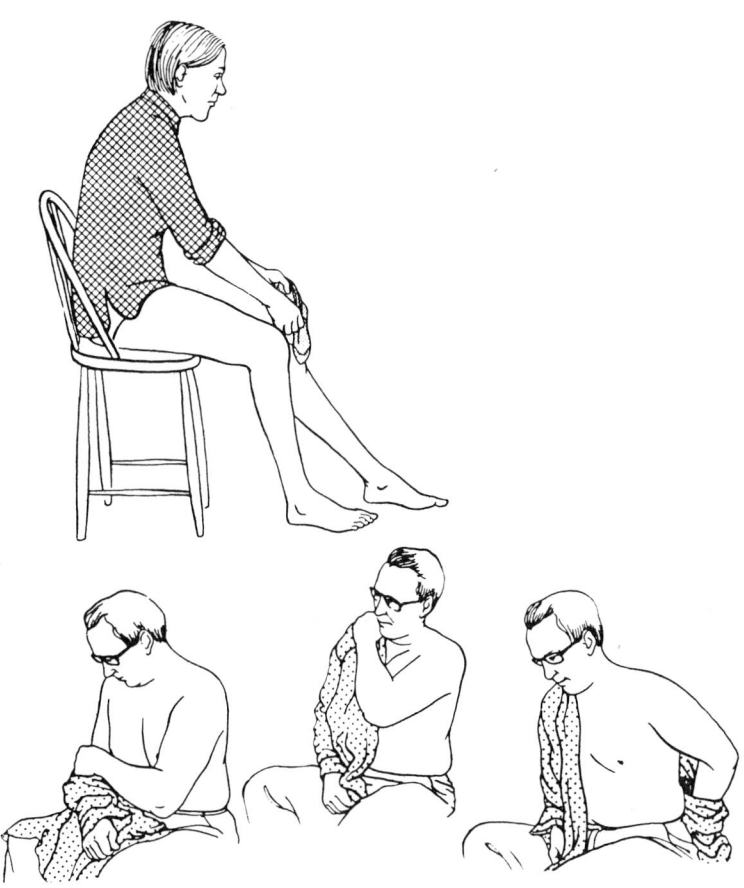

Daily changes in physical competence can make the most simple personal care activities difficult. (ROSENBLAD-WALLIN, 1977; REPRINTED WITH PERMISSION FROM STUS KONSUMENTTEKNISKA, FORSKNINGSGRUPP, GOTEBERG, SWEDEN)

most frustrating to perform because of daily changes in competence. Buttons and zippers become impossible to manipulate, dizziness makes leaning over the sink dangerous, and a flare-up of arthritis may make perineal cleaning impossible. Because cleanliness is such an important part of an individual's self-image, the inability

Privacy and Sleeping

Although sleeping and sexual patterns may change for the aged individual, the requirements for privacy—aloneness and solitude—remain much the same. Physiological changes may require more time for rest and rejuvenation of the body. The bedroom may be used for much more than traditional nighttime activity. The elderly may also find that they must spend more waking time in bed, and that the bedroom becomes a necessary focus of other functions, such as socializing, eating, and bathing. Considerations for space, light, view, and access become much more important.

The bedroom represents a private area away from the demands of others and allows the individual to pursue his or her independence. In our youth the private bedroom indicates a level of maturity and growth that allows us to be alone within the security and unity of the family. As we grow older, the bedroom becomes a private zone in which individuals share intimacies. The bed takes on a sexual connotation and is usually screened from the views of others. In her 1980 study of housing for the elderly Sandra Howell discovers that many recently widowed elderly people refuse to give up their double bed because it provides a continuity of life-style and is a sentimental reminder of their spouses.

The bedroom is traditionally placed at the back of the house as the ultimate and most private zone for escape and sharing. In the attempt to economize and miniaturize housing for the elderly, the bedroom becomes an alcove off a living area or a small room that is accessed from the kitchen. There is no attempt to provide a sense of spatial separation or zoning that protects the private character of the bedroom. Nursing-home settings further miniaturize the living zone by creating a space that will only accommodate a bed and a chair. There is no privacy in shared rooms and no opportunity for spatial separation or aloneness; all aspects of the individual's life are public. Operational criteria require that doors be left open to the corridor so that the staff can see into the rooms as they go by.

The criteria for maintaining privacy of the bedroom are more straightforward than those for personal care. Privacy of sleeping requires spatial separation as well as visual and auditory isolation. The door must be under the control of the individual and must be closed to fully provide a sense of aloneness. Shared rooms will never provide the privacy that we would require and expect for ourselves. No amount of personalization, zoning of floor space, or provision of curtains will fulfill the requirements for privacy of the bedroom. Nursing-home-type settings involve not only the issue of privacy of event (as in sleeping) but privacy of life-style as well. Nursing home rooms become the focus of socialization, sleeping, leisure, and eating activities.

Privacy and Responsive Design

Institutional buildings can lose many of their "institutional" characteristics by a careful combination of design quality and operational support. Programs and standards that deny privacy must be changed, and the criteria that establish privacy must be reexamined. Real privacy must be available to the individual, and the staff must respect that privacy in its daily operations. Design alone will not provide privacy if there is no support from the staff. The environment can have a major role in reinforcing the behavior of both the staff and residents. The creation of spaces with edges and of progressive levels of privacy and publicness provides gentle reminders of ownership and allow individuals to claim turf outside their private space.

Naive assumptions about privacy will not provide the quality of housing care the elderly require. Rules of thumb and guidelines do not respond to the subtle qualities of housing that strengthen our self-esteem and support our individuality. Designers and housing administrators must focus on the criteria that make an event, a life-style, or a thought private. We must explore beyond cubicle curtains and closed doors to identify those design responses that make privacy an operational fact in the life of the elderly.

INDEPENDENCE

By nature, we are a society based on cooperative activity. Our societal structure is organized in such a way that everyone puts something in and gets something in return. Because of our lack of self-sufficiency we depend on support from one another and look to the community as a whole for resources.

In contemporary society, independence is a prized possession, an ideal worth striving for. Independence is associated with strength, self-reliance, and leadership. The reverse is true of dependence; it is a quality we fight to avoid because it signals helplessness and weakness. We are all born completely dependent, but the signs of our maturity and growth are measured by the development of our independent qualities. The terms *dependent* and *independent* gain negative or positive connotations when the behavior is appropriate or inappropriate. (Newborns are dependent, which is appropriate.)

The literature on independence and the disabled stresses two important themes. The first theme is that the balance between independence and dependence changes throughout the life span. The need for dependence or independence varies in quantity in different aspects of the person's life. The balance is highly individualized. For instance, physical dependence on other persons for food preparation or house cleaning is not inappropriate if domestic tasks were never part of that individual's self-determined life-style. The second theme relates to this careful balancing. That is, excessive independence may deplete the individual of energies that could have been better spent in other endeavors. The image of the superhuman disabled person conquering all odds is fine for television movies, but has very little to do with the day-to-day life of the disabled or elderly person. Once the individual has ascertained what tasks can be tackled by creative techniques, she or he can accept assistance when it is needed. It is important that independence not be asserted as preferable to dependence, but rather, that as little as possible be done to undermine those aspects of independence that are valuable to the individual.

The Many Forms of Independence

The "barrier-free movement" has focused attention on the need for accessibility. Unfortunately, this emphasis has incorrectly equated barrier-free standards with independence. Independence is often conceived of as a freedom from enclosures or barriers. Barriers may be physical, as in objects that restrict passage, or figurative, as in social restrictions that prevent certain activities and opportunities. Another type of barrier is a psychological restraint, which is an internalized form of the physical barriers and restrictions.

As with privacy, independence exists in many different forms. Restrictions to independence dictate the need for greater access and opportunity, as well as a greater understanding of the restriction itself. Providing curb cuts and kneeling buses will not provide independence if the individual is socially crippled by stigmas and stereotypes.

Physical Barriers

Physical barriers have their greatest influence on the physically disabled. Steps, curbs, narrow doorways, and small toilet stalls all represent physical features that can restrict the independence of a disabled individual. Unintelligible signage and confusing paths of travel also place the individual at the dependence of others for help and assistance. Current public awareness and government standards now support the removal of physical barriers. Ramps, grab bars, and parking spaces for the disabled represent a step toward eliminating physical barriers. Standards and anthropometric data now expound the virtues and dimensions of the average disabled person. Contrary to popular belief, not all disabled people are wheelchair-bound, and they may not have full use of their arms, vision, or hearing. Although the removal of physical barriers is important for the elderly, one must remember that most accessibility standards do not respond to the particular needs of the aged individual.

Social Barriers

Social barriers are more subtle than their physical counterparts. Many social barriers are difficult to recognize because they are an accepted part of our culture. To maintain a sense of our own "purity" we isolate those members of society whom we view as different. The mentally retarded, the very frail elderly, and the severely deformed are often prevented from participating in the mainstream of society. As a society, we remove their rights of choice, privacy, and free will. We institutionalize them and reinforce negative characteristics and role models. A common reaction toward

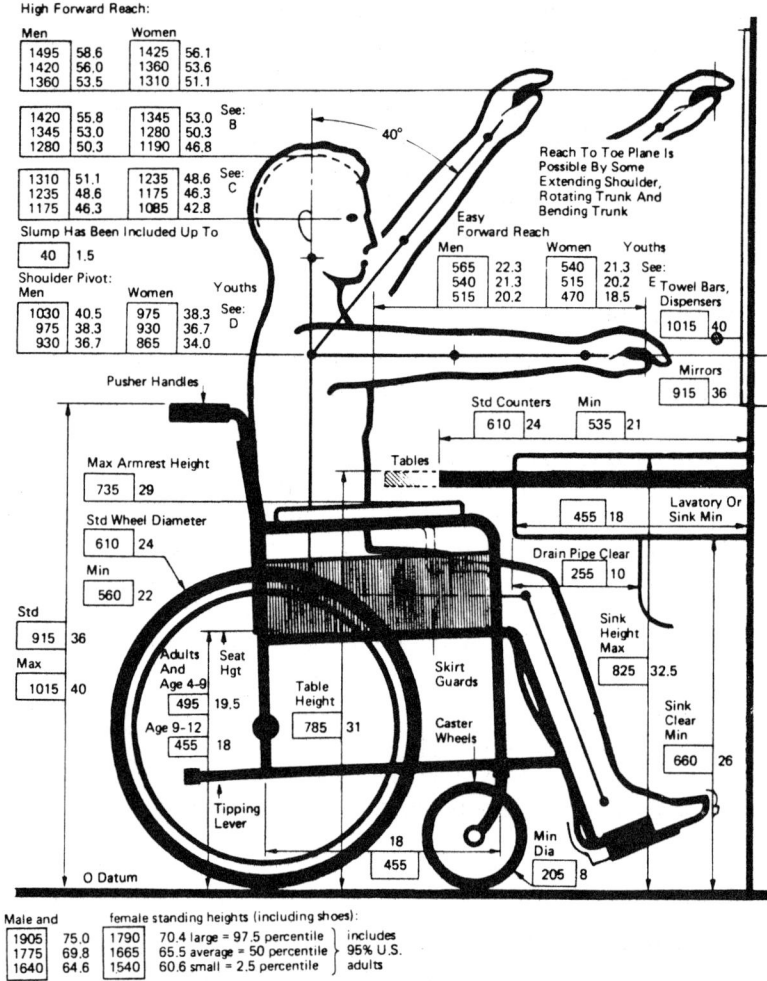

Anthropometric data offer the dimensional characteristics of the disabled individual. The average height, reach, and grasping ability that assumes full muscular control above the waist is rarely applicable to the wheelchair-bound elderly. (FROM *ARCHITECTURAL GRAPHIC STANDARDS*, RAMSEY-SLEEPER, 7TH ED., 1981; REPRINTED BY PERMISSION OF JOHN WILEY & SONS, INC.)

24 HOUSING FOR THE ELDERLY

the disabled is that they deserve compassion and pity. The difficulty is that this reaction is devoid of respect and is a response that builds up our own personal sense of security.

Humanism and good will are perverted to the debasement of the very individuals whom they would help. Handicapped individuals are ordinarily labeled, frequently segregated from their able-bodied peers, and compensated for their "pitiful" station in life.

L. W. HEAL, 1980

Psychological Barriers

Psychological barriers are even more difficult to identify. They have no physical quality, such as a step. Psychological barriers are often the result of a person being told (not necessarily verbally) that she or he is unable to do something or achieve a particular goal, often before she or he has attempted it. In contrast to the children's story, "The Little Engine That Could," instead of believing "I think I can, I think I can!" the environment reinforces failure and strips the individual of the opportunity to try. The environment can become so controlled by others that the outcome has no relationship to the activity. This is usually referred to as "learned helplessness."

Freedom from Barriers

It is important to understand the variety of barriers that restrict independence. There has been an inordinate focus on accessibility standards, which relate to a very small part of the overall issue of independence. For the elderly such standards do not account for the full range of physiological changes that restrict accessibility. Dizziness, a lack of endurance, and unsteady balance are requirements for which there are no standards. In fact, most accessibility standards are inappropriate for the majority of the old-elderly population because they require upper body strength and precise maneuvering. Grab bars, handrails, and gently sloped ramps are actually useless to a large percentage of the elderly population.

Independence does not come from freedom of physical barriers alone. In fact, for many of the elderly there will always be physical barriers that cannot be removed. Independence comes from a quiet acceptance of one's limitations, an adjustment of expectations, and the channeling of energies into those pursuits that are rewarding and fulfilling. Independence should not be diminished by a physical dependence on another individual or a prosthetic device. Independence comes from a self-determined life-style.

The Concepts of Independence

Independence and Goals

Society has viewed a barrier-free existence as an important goal for the disabled and the elderly. Independence, in this sense, has been established as a social, clinical, and economic goal. As a social goal, independence is associated with the freedoms we expect as citizens of a democratic country. Independence is not only the freedom to come and go at will, but also the freedom to participate in all activities and opportunities afforded the mainstream of society. Clinically, independence is often conceptualized by social workers and therapists as the ability to perform certain activities by oneself. The provision of prosthetic devices and the training of "independent living skills" are ways to reintegrate the disabled individual into society to assume his or her "normal" life pattern. Recently, independence has gained primary importance as an economic goal by governments that can no longer afford to maintain individuals on social welfare. Independence has gained the support of our society because it has a built-in financial reward. The more individuals are able to do for themselves, the less society will be required to assist them financially. Social programs (homemaking, meals, transportation, and so on) that support the elderly in their own homes clearly are less costly to operate than purpose-built housing. Independence is a financially feasible social goal. Because of the pressure of granting independence to the elderly as an economic goal, the social and clinical opportunities have followed as well.

In the past, independence for the elderly focused on housing forms that provided a low level of support at a centralized location. Currently, "independent housing" means the opportunity to live at home with support services brought to the individual. Meals-on-Wheels, district nurses, and home helpers provide unobtrusive services that allow the individual to live "independently" at home. Independence has not gained widespread support in other housing settings such as nursing homes. Nursing homes provide all of the individual's daily needs whether they are required or not. Activities are performed for the individual because it is faster and easier. Independence is not viewed as financially rewarding in "heavy care" settings. Independence is a goal often used in conceptualizing housing, but is rarely found as an operational and design goal in supportive housing for the elderly.

Independence and Individual Identity

Dignity is an external measure of worthiness or importance attached to an individual, as exemplified by the term *dignitary*. Dignity can also become a personal measure of self-worth, which is often linked to self-determination, pride, and a careful balance of independence and dependence. It is important to focus on those factors that the individual uses to measure his or her own worth. As with privacy, independence becomes a strong measure of who we are and what our role is in society.

An individual's identity is a meshing of past accomplishments, areas of expertise, preferences, and habits. A consistency in life's rhythms reinforces those behavioral patterns that provide a historical continuity. Changes in rhythms require adaptation and reevaluation. If changes occur in areas that are the cornerstones of the individual's identity, then adaptation will be difficult and painful. Physical strength and mental prowess may decline, leaving the individual full of self-doubt and feeling less valued. The elderly man with impaired hearing perceives the wearing of a hearing aid as a symbol of old age and thus as a devaluation of his worth in society. At some point the individual must accept the fact that these aids can actually increase the ability to function more independently in society.

Independence and Risk

Independence is derived from a process of growth and risk taking.

Throughout our youth, boundaries are set to limit our exposure to hazardous situations. Crossing the street, using a power lawn mower, and driving a car are activities that signal a level of maturity and independence. Parents allow their children to take risks so that they will grow and develop within constantly changing parameters. Chronological age and peer group standards are often used to signal an increased opportunity to accept risk as well as an increased opportunity for independence from the family unit. Independence is often developed concurrently with a strong self-image. The development of a strong self-image begins for many of us the first time our mothers send us on an "important" errand as a young child. Crossing the street and arriving at the small corner grocery store assumes a level of normalized risk that our parents somewhat reluctantly let us take. The entrusted responsibility creates a strong image of ourselves as reliable and genuinely helpful members of the family unit. We complete the task and are acknowledged for our productive, well-done effort. We feel encouraged, grown-up, and ready for the next challenge.

To facilitate an individual's evolving self-image, the environment must reinforce his or her uniqueness and offer freedom and meaningful choice as well as a level of risk. Risk taking is an aspect of ordinary life that is necessary for normative human adaptation. The elderly are often removed from all potential hazardous situations and not accorded the dignity of risk.

Forgetfulness, hearing loss, and physical weakness are often viewed as conditions that make everyday life more dangerous. Although this may be true, not all activities become a risk to the individual. The environment and daily activities can be adapted to provide a level of normative risk. The difficulty is that adaptation requires a highly individualized approach, which must respond to a constantly changing ability to master the environment. Chronological age and peer group standards do not provide a comparable set of parameters for normative risk taking among the elderly. Instead of a highly individualized approach, we substitute a system that bars any risks and requires staff to perform the most basic activities. Supervised performance of activities is usually ruled out because it requires longer and more intensive staff contact than is economically feasible.

Independence and the Elderly

Independence and Dependence

The aging process leads to a gradual increase in dependence. Dependence may be on physical devices that provide prosthetic support or on individuals who assist with daily living tasks. An increase in dependence does not necessarily constitute a loss of independence. Independence and dependence can coexist as a balanced way of life for the elderly. The individual must recognize when that balance is achieved and how best to preserve those qualities of independence that are most important.

Creating an environment that achieves some balance between independence and dependence is the designer's goal for creating effective barrier-free design. "Excessive independence . . . may wear a person out. Being goaded by independence, he may insist on doing for himself only to be depleted of energy and emotional resources that might well have been spent more usefully. Glorification of independence must give way to an appreciation that independence and interdependence go hand in hand" (Goldsmith, 1976). The individual must be allowed to choose when and where dependence is most beneficial. The aging process requires constant adaptation by the individual and may require a shifting balance from day to day.

Rhythms and Patterns

Gerontological theories have identified the importance of maintaining behavioral patterns into old age. Rhythms and patterns are important parts of our life-style, which we do not commonly associate with independence. Independence is usually conceptualized in terms of the performance of specific activities rather than the order of life's events. Rhythms of work and play, weekday and weekend, night and day are important measures of our life. The independence of our life-style is guaranteed by our ability to control the events in our lives. The time at which we eat, go to sleep, and bathe are cornerstones of our individuality and our self-determined life-style.

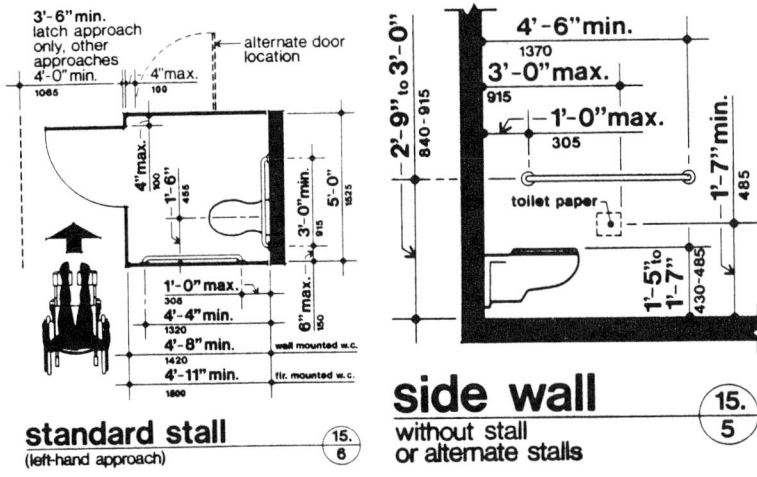

The functional requirements of independence. (REPRINTED FROM FEDERAL REGISTER. "ARCHITECTURAL AND TRANSPORTATION BARRIERS COMPLIANCE BOARD; MINIMUM GUIDELINES AND REQUIREMENTS FOR ACCESSIBLE DESIGN," AUG. 4, 1982)

The rhythms and patterns of life are often removed from the control of the elderly. Meals, sleeping, and bathing schedules respond to the working patterns of the staff and administration. Other rhythms, such as joy and sadness or giving and receiving, are often lost in an environment where there is little reason for euphoria or where there is only the opportunity to receive. The elderly have become the forced receivers of society's goodwill and generosity.

Independence and Responsive Design

Designing for independence has been equated with the use of accessibility standards. Building codes, health department regulations, and anthropometric data offer conflicting information about the designing of spaces for the disabled. Designers translate this information into practice without understanding how the space is used or the purpose of the required dimension. Economic constraints compound the issue by translating minimum standards into maximum standards. A portion of the disabled population benefits by these standards, but only when they are universally used and properly executed. An "accessible" toilet stall may be inaccessible if it is too far away or if it strips the individual of his or her dignity. "Accessible housing" requirements (for example, 10 percent of housing units in new apartment complexes must be accessible for the handicapped) may fulfill a housing need, but they may also socially handicap the disabled individual who is unable to visit friends in 90 percent of the housing units, which are not accessible to the disabled.

Functional requirements for independence should not be considered to the exclusion of other social and psychological needs. This is especially important for the elderly. The elderly will always be confronted with physical barriers that cannot be removed; functional independence may be impossible for those too frail or weak. Wheelchairs provide movement only to those able to make them move, and certain activities may be possible only with the assistance of another individual. In this case, accessibility requirements for the bathroom should not be based on right-hand transfer to the toilet and a five-foot turning radius for the wheelchair, but rather on spatial requirements for a wheelchair and another individual who provides transfer assistance.

The majority of accessibility standards do not respond to the needs and requirements of the aged population. Ramps are difficult for wheelchairs to maneuver on and difficult to negotiate with a walker. Handrails are too high, grab bars are too far away to be useful, and any door is simply too heavy to open. Accessibility standards are valuable, but they must be responsive to the user or else they perpetuate an image of inadequacy for those unable to function in a presumably accessible environment.

Many design criteria that can facilitate functional independence do not appear in barrier-free standards. Accessibility is only one of many requirements for physical functioning in the environment. The redesign of fixtures and devices in the home can aid independent living by easing the physical demands on the individual. New computer systems open doors and windows and control light switches. Toilets that automatically wash and dry the perineal area are already on the market in Europe. Bathroom sinks that tip forward for hair washing from a seated position provide arm support and easier access. Hand-held shower nozzles, adjustable-height kitchen counters, and blade-handled faucets maintain the individual's control over the everyday activities of his or her life. Passive and active alarm systems that summon help in an emergency retain a level of normative risk for the individual.

Social and psychological barriers to independence are difficult to respond to. There are no design guidelines that remove stigmas and pity from our society. The challenge to the designer is to create an environment in which stereotypes and myths are less likely to flourish. Housing environments that appear forbidding, cold, and institutional will reinforce negative qualities about the individuals living within. Perhaps congregate housing needs to be conceptualized and detailed as individual dwellings and nursing homes should be planned as grand old residential hotels. There are numerous analogies that can offer interesting concepts for new forms of housing for the elderly.

PRIVACY AND INDEPENDENCE IN EUROPE

The following three chapters offer examples in which government programs, social goals, and design responses have combined to provide housing for the elderly that offers privacy and independence. The sixteen buildings from Sweden, Denmark, and England were selected for their variety and quality. In many ways they do not represent the true picture of the level of housing care that exists in these three countries: the buildings illustrated represent some of the best state-of-the-art facilities in existence. They are important to examine because of the future directions they signal for the United States. These facilities address three specific and important points.

First, these facilities exhibit a high level of concern for the individual and his or her sustained dignity. Pension systems that exist in Sweden and Denmark provide for the financial security of the individual. Support services maintain the individual in his or her own home as long as possible or as long as desired. The variety of purpose-built housing settings all offer privacy by eliminating shared rooms and in many cases eliminating efficiency-type apartments. Independence is facilitated by offering an accessible environment, as well as the freedom of choice, the ability to come and go freely, and the dignity to take risks provided by living alone.

Second, the variety of needs that the aged individual may have are addressed. "Housing needs" also encompass economic security, social opportunity, and health care. The facilities that are illustrated offer a variety of approaches from segregation of these housing components to "campus care" to respite care. The variety of solutions presented in the following chapters reflect the tendency of governments to address separately health care and housing care.

Third, the variety of housing settings speaks of a concern for experimenting with new concepts, ideas, and approaches. These buildings respond to their local context, their role in the community, and the opportunities they can offer rather than idealized economic standards that lead to "rubber-stamped" housing. Small facilities and large facilities, rural solutions and urban solutions, hotellike facilities and houselike facilities coexist under the same government goals and design directives.

4 SWEDEN

Sweden has the fourth-largest land area in Europe, approximately the size of California with a population comparable to that of New York City. The vast majority (90 percent) of Swedes live in the southern half of the country. Sweden has a large elderly population; 17 percent of the inhabitants are over the age of 65 and have an expected life span of 73.1 years for men and 79.5 years for women. Population projections expect the oldest group of elderly people to increase the most. It is anticipated that the over-90 age group will double by the year 2000. Currently 20 percent of the elderly population is over 80 years old.

Sweden's care of the elderly has long been admired and praised for its comprehensiveness and the quantity of economic support. This has not always been the case. The Old Age Pension Act was not established until 1913, and major housing reforms did not start until the 1930s. A cohesive social welfare program was not established until the 1940s when the Social Democrats assumed power and abolished the "poorhouses" that warehoused the physically and psychologically dependent elderly.

THE GOVERNMENT

Sweden has a parliamentary form of government and a constitutional monarchy. Political power is concentrated in the cabinet and parliament (Riksdag), with ceremonial and symbolic duties performed by the monarch. The central government sets the national policy and directives, levies taxes, and is chief administrator of the country. With a decentralized form of government, Sweden places responsibility for the welfare of the citizens directly on the regional and local governmental units—the county councils and the municipalities.

The county council (*landsting*) governs Sweden at the regional level. Sweden is divided into 24 geographic counties, which vary in size and population. The primary responsibility of each county is to provide and administer a coordinated health service and medical care program consistent with national policy. The county councils have the authority to collect taxes from their citizens to support these programs.

The local level of government is the municipality (*kommun*). In

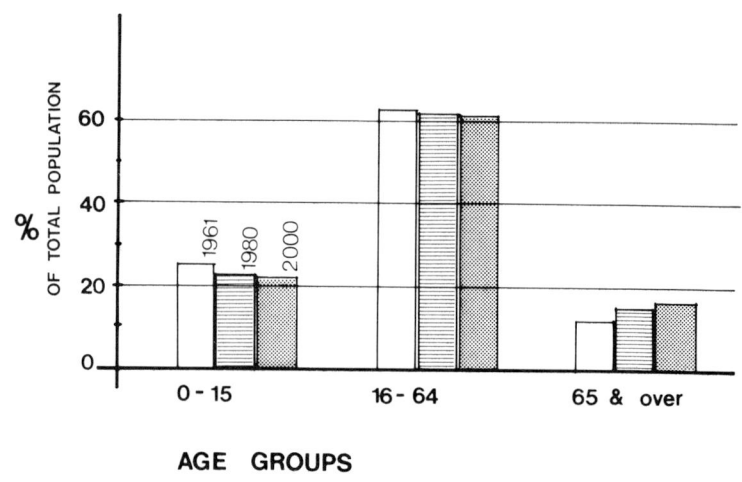

Swedish population structure.

1984 there were 284 municipalities providing social welfare (care of the aged), housing, education, leisure, arts, sanitation, streets and parks for their citizens. The *kommun* is also able to levy taxes to support its programs and activities.

County councils and municipalities are essentially autonomous self-governing units, enacting central government directives as they see fit. Government subsidy of programs, however, usually provides the necessary incentive to maintain a coherent national policy across governmental boundaries. County councils do encroach on municipal authorities since the county government is responsible for overall long-term planning and coordination of services. The relationship between these two governmental bodies appears to depend on the relative power, size, and financial motivation of each group.

Sture Börjesson, the Secretary for the National Commission on Aging, offered the following observation in a recent letter:

> Discussions and stories of care of the elderly can scarcely be pursued without getting into the question of the limits of jurisdiction between county councils and municipalities. It has often been unavoidable for them to adopt different standpoints, both in individual cases and in more general assessments—not so much with regard to the question of whether a certain person needs care or service, or whether a certain form of care or service is needed, but rather with regard to the question of which authority is responsible for providing this care or service.

The key concepts to define clear limits of jurisdiction are coordination and cooperation so that individual care recipients are not caught between the spheres of interest of different authorities. The municipalities and the county councils have come a long way in their joint efforts to clear up these problems through, for example, agreements to share costs in cases where their spheres of responsibility border on and overlap each other.

STURE BÖRJESSON, 1984

CARE OF THE ELDERLY

As a welfare state, Sweden has constructed a safety net of economic and social support to protect all citizens. As an egalitarian society, this net is a right of all citizens, not a privilege of income or class distinction. The creation of this welfare state has also placed the responsibility of care for the "disadvantaged" with the government. Care of the unwell elderly has become the responsibility of the government, not of the family. This approach is inconsistent with traditional family settings but has become compatible with current shifts within the Swedish family structure. In many cases individuals are unable or unwilling to care for their elderly relatives, who require greater and greater levels of care.

The basic goal of old-age care in Sweden is to provide elderly citizens with a financially secure future in good, modern housing, with supportive medical and special care services. Beyond these basic aims, the government has set five guiding principles to direct county councils and municipalities in the planning of services and facilities for the aged.

1. The principle of NORMALIZATION, which means that to the greatest possible extent each individual should be given the opportunity to live and function in as normal a setting and under as normal conditions as feasible.
2. The principle of VIEWING A PERSON AS A WHOLE, which means that the overall psychological, physical, and social welfare needs of a person are assessed and dealt with in a single context.
3. The principle of SELF-DETERMINATION, which means that personal integrity is respected. People should have the right to determine their own lives and make their own decisions. The right to personal security and the right to decide things for oneself must be combined in old-age care.
4. The principle of INFLUENCE AND PARTICIPATION, meaning that individuals should be able to influence not only their own environment but also society as a whole Elderly people, too, want to assume responsibilities and feel they are needed.
5. The principle of PROPERLY MANAGED ACTIVATION, which implies meaningful tasks carried out in close partnership with other people in a normal, stimulating environment.

SWEDISH INSTITUTE, 1981

Financial Security

The Old Age Pension Act was established in 1913 (the U.S. Social Security Act was established in 1935) to provide financial support for the elderly portion of the population. Economic security is now provided through three types of pension plans and several forms of housing assistance. The three types of pensions are the basic pension, supplemental pension (ATP), and partial pension. Pension payments usually begin at age 65, but can begin as early as age 60 or as late as 70. It is well recognized that many pensioners (those registered in the pension program) have a greater material wealth than during their youth.

The Basic Pension

The basic pension is paid regardless of income. The Basic Pension system includes:

1. Old-age pension
2. Pension supplements
3. Additional Benefits: municipal housing allowances, wife's supplements, children's supplements, handicap allowance

Old-age pensions are based on an amount set by the government, which is indexed to rise with inflation. In 1984, single pensioners received SKR 19,488 (US$2,467) (based on US$1 = SKR 7.90) annually and married couples received SKR 15,936 (US$2,017) each.

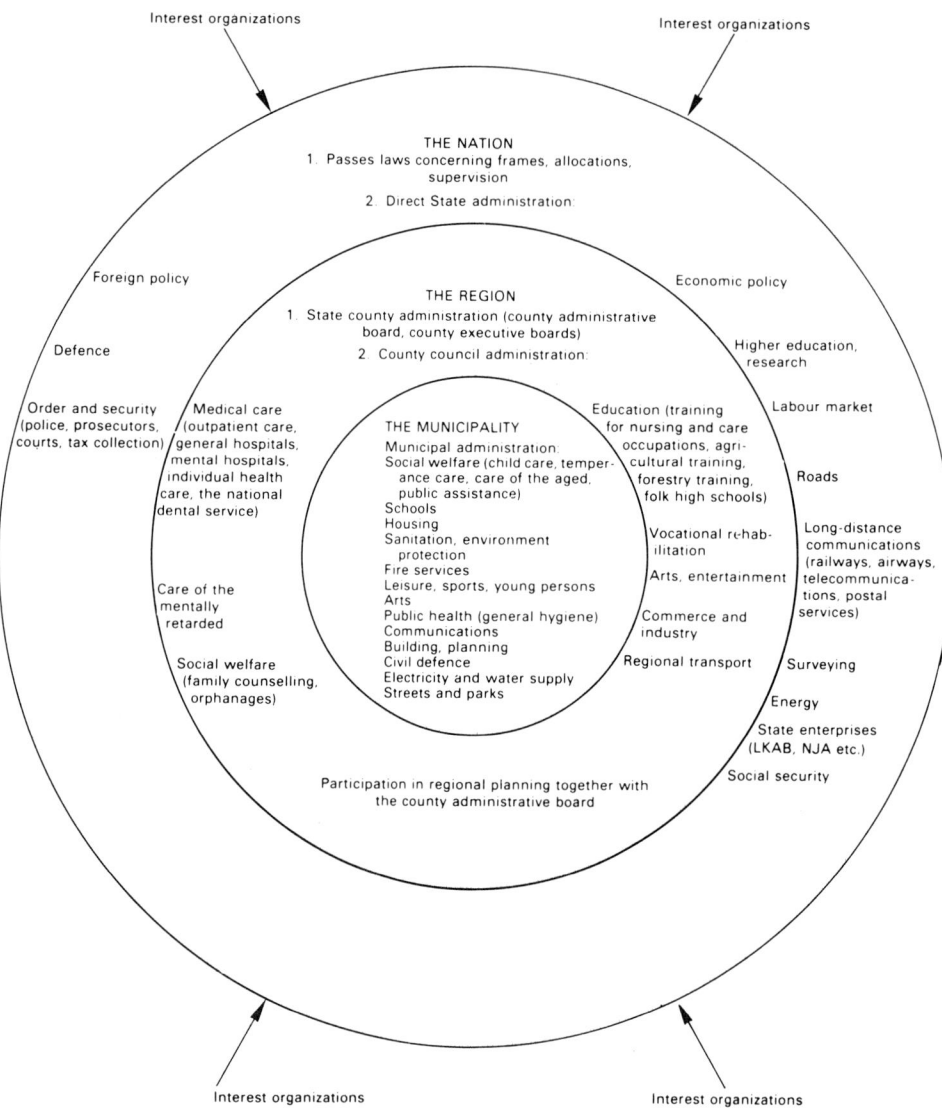

The division of responsibilities. (FROM *LOCAL GOVERNMENT IN SWEDEN*, BY AGNE GUSTAFSSON, THE SWEDISH INSTITUTE, MINISTRY OF LOCAL GOVERNMENT, 1978; REPRINTED BY PERMISSION OF THE SWEDISH INSTITUTE)

Pension supplements (for those with only the basic old-age pension) provide an additional income equal to 45 percent of the basic pension, raising the total benefits to SKR 29,232 (US$3,700) annually for a single person. Additional benefits include the following:

- Municipal housing allowance: income-related payment that varies by municipality. In many communities it actually covers the total cost of housing.
- Wife's supplement: income-related payment to a retired man's wife (over age 60) with no pension of her own.
- Children's supplements: payment to an old-age pensioner with a child under age 16.
- Handicap allowance: a variable payment to an old-age pensioner with reduced physical or mental functioning (for handicaps that began before age 65).

The Supplemental Pensions (ATP)

Supplemental Pensions include:

1. Old-age pension
2. Permanent disability pension
3. Temporary disability pension
4. Widow's pension
5. Children's pension

Old-age supplemental pensions are payable in addition to basic pensions for those who have worked for at least three years. The size of the pension is based on an average of the person's 15 highest income years. A full ATP pension amounts to 60 percent of this average income, which is adjusted for inflation. This Supplemental Pension program is financed by the employers.

The Partial Pensions

Older workers are eligible to receive a partial pension at age 60 and to continue working part-time. The worker must work at least 17 hours per week and is compensated for 50 percent of the difference between the earned income and a full pension income. The subsequent old-age pension is not reduced due to these payments.

Housing

The Swedes have placed a high priority on providing good, modern housing for the elderly. The municipalities are responsible for assuring that all of their citizens have adequate housing. For the elderly, this includes housing that is accessible and barrier free. As of 1977, the Swedish building bylaw requires that all new buildings, including residences, be suitable for the disabled. Since 88 percent of the Swedish elderly live in traditional single-family houses or apartments, accessibility has become a major issue. Sweden's focus is clearly on adapting existing housing stock so that the elderly may remain at home. In addition, there are a variety of purpose-built housing settings where residents can obtain a level of service and support otherwise unavailable in the community housing market.

Type of Housing	Percent of Elderly Population	Comments
Ordinary Dwellings	88%	
Pensioners' Dwellings	3%	30,000 total flats in 1980.
Service House or Residential Hotel		20,000 total flats in 1980.
Old-age Residential Homes	4%	70% of residents are over age 80
Long-term Care Centers, Hospitals, Nursing Homes	5%	

Where the Swedish elderly live. (STATISTICS COMPILED FROM THE SWEDISH INSTITUTE, 1981)

The nomenclature for building types always raises obstacles when translating between languages: words can have distinctly different connotations. Also, terms such as *skilled care* and *protected dwelling* become unfortunate labels that stigmatize the housing environment. The Swedish government is constantly experimenting with new approaches, new types of service, and different rural and urban solutions that do not fall into neat categories. The following synopsis of Swedish housing care is offered merely as a tool to further understanding.

Ordinary Dwellings

Pensioners in a rental apartment or in owner-occupied housing are eligible for a municipal housing allowance or a central and local government subsidy. Pensioners are also eligible for allowances to make adaptations to accommodate disabilities and improve accessibility to their apartments. Pensioners in owner-occupied dwellings are also eligible for such an allowance, as well as for loans for home improvement or modernization.

Pensioners' Dwellings

A pensioner's dwelling may be either a designated apartment in an ordinary apartment house or a "flat" in a purpose-built building. These types of apartments are sometimes referred to as protected dwellings or sheltered dwellings (see British sheltered housing in chapter 6). Pensioners' homes are owned and managed by the municipality. The standards, as well as the number of apartments per building, vary by location. The individual apartment usually contains one or two rooms plus a kitchen (in American real-estate terminology, an efficiency or one-bedroom apartment). Facilities may include a few common social areas, and home help is usually available.

Service Houses and Residential Hotels

Service houses and residential hotels are similar to pensioners' dwellings. There are more common facilities (restaurant, activity room, doctor, and chiropody services), as well as a higher level of support. The apartments are linked to a central, staff-monitored control station. Assistance can be actively summoned by pulling any of the cords located throughout the apartment. Passive systems summon help if the resident has not performed a certain activity within 24 hours, such as flushing the toilet or opening the refrigerator. These alarm systems provide a sense of security for those elderly who are afraid of falling and not being found.

Old-age Homes

Old-age homes are also owned and operated by the municipality. Residents are usually older (the average age is 84) and in need of more assistance with daily living tasks such as meal preparation and bathing. Common meals are provided, as well as around-the-clock care from a specially trained staff. "Apartments" typically consist of one bed–sitting room with a private toilet and a "tea kitchen" (hot plate and small refrigerator). Shared lounges, dining rooms, pubs, hobby rooms, libraries, and physical activity rooms are found in most facilities. Old-age homes provide nonmedical care referred to as personal care in the United States.

Nursing Homes, Long-term Care Hospitals, and Psychiatric Hospitals

Nursing-home care is the responsibility of the county council (*landsting*) as part of required health care. The type and level of care in Swedish nursing homes are consistent with those in the United States. The difference appears to be in the quality of care, which is guaranteed and provided by the Swedish government rather than private, "for profit" health care groups, as it is in the United States.

Long-term care hospitals and psychiatric hospitals are specialized medically oriented settings provided by the *landsting* for the chronically ill and often mentally impaired elderly. It is important to realize that nursing homes and long-term care hospitals are not considered housing for the elderly and in the past have not adhered to the five guiding principles of services and facilities for the aged.

There is a growing concern within the government and special interest groups to "deinstitutionalize" these settings and to consider linking long-term care facilities with municipal social-welfare centers (see S-5: Knivsta Service House and Nursing Home). Groups like the Swedish Planning and Rationalization Institute of Health and Social Services (SPRI) have been looking at the particular issues of institutional settings such as nursing homes. Recent competitions have involved design professionals and behaviorists in the shaping of new residential settings for the chronically ill.

Supportive Special-care Services

Many elderly people need supportive services to maintain them in their own homes or in appropriate residential settings. The municipal governments provide a group of services collectively referred to as home help. The principal component is the homemaker service, which provides pensioners with house cleaning, food preparation, laundry, and personal care assistance. In 1983, 60,000 homemakers provided services to 20 percent of the elderly population. Other home-help services include transportation, snow clearing, and training to compensate for deteriorating physical conditions. These services are provided at a minimal charge (or free) to pensioners who are identified as being in need of such services.

Services are available collectively at locations commonly referred to as day centers. Day centers may be built as part of a housing facility for its residents and pensioners in the local community, or as freestanding structures in a local neighborhood. The services provided vary only slightly from facility to facility and are consistently well equipped and of a high standard. Common services include a restaurant (occasionally also a pub); hobby and activity rooms (for weaving, metalwork, and woodworking); a library; and facilities for chiropody, hairdressing, bathing, physical therapy, and physical exercise (gymnasium, pool).

Day centers are open daily to pensioners of the community on a drop-in basis (in some communities there may be a choice of several centers). Transport services or reduced taxi and bus fares are available to shuttle pensioners between home and the day center. Participants seem to be naturally gregarious and open, actively seeking new challenges. Medical professionals or families may request social workers to contact elderly individuals who have become socially disengaged.

Supportive Medical Care

In general the elderly portion of the world's population places the heaviest burden on medical care systems. The elderly are inappropriately placed in hospitals, usually because there are no facilities that provide care for a prolonged convalescence. In Sweden, nearly 50 percent of the medical care in hospitals is given to the oldest 10 percent of the population. In most cases, it is not medical care that is required, but rather, intensive support with daily personal care.

Home nursing is a growing form of medical care in Sweden—40,000 patients in 1979 had a visiting doctor or nurse. Special monthly allowances defray the cost of this service. Nursing homes and long-term care centers provide places for those who cannot be treated at home. Social health insurance pays all costs up to 365 days, after which the patient must pay an income-related fee per day. Other forms such as respite care and day medical care are being explored and expanded (see S-4: Gränna).

Summary

The difficulty with the Swedish system of care for the aged is the division of responsibilities between municipalities and county councils. The elderly face a plethora of intertwined medical, social, and economic difficulties. Very few municipalities or counties are set up to review individual situations, coordinate services and benefits, and inform the individual. In some cases, pensioners are not aware of what services actually are available to them.

The division of housing and health care has led to difficulties in fulfilling the principles of normalization. A normal home setting has been attained in most municipally supported housing. Swedish nursing homes and long-term care centers, however, are based on a health care model. The quality and level of social service in nursing homes is not consistent with other housing forms.

S-1

ÅLDERDOMSHEM PAPEGOJELYCKAN
(Home for the Aged in Papegojelyckan)

LUND, SWEDEN

TYPE OF HOUSING:	Old-age home
OTHER ELEMENTS:	Day center
NUMBER OF UNITS:	68 single rooms
	2 double rooms
ARCHITECT:	Sten Samuelson
BUILT:	1977–78
OWNER:	Municipality of Lund

Physical Description

The Ålderdomshem Papegojelyckan contains 70 typical residential rooms in a two-story, three-wing brick and wood building. The home is located on the edge of a newly developed multifamily housing area called Papegojelyckan (Luck of the Parrot). The home is linked to other residential buildings and a community park by way of numerous landscaped paths and parking areas.

The rooms are organized into six clusters of twelve rooms. Each cluster shares a dining room, parlor, balcony or terrace, residents' kitchen, laundry facilities, and sitting room. Each cluster is a wing of the building, which is linked on one end to the central activity and program spaces and on the other end to a long circulation space with small sitting areas.

Residential Care

It is difficult to categorize the approach to health care in terms of American terminology. The residential care offered at Papegojelyckan falls closest to what we call personal care, but, with an average resident age of 86 years, it encompasses aspects of skilled care as well. Medical care is "distributed" from a central concierge desk in the building lobby. All rooms are linked to this desk by a call system. Because no extensive medical care is provided, the room is held up to one year if the resident must move to a hospital.

Two meals (lunch and dinner) are served every day in each of the six dining rooms, and the breakfast meal is delivered to the resident's room to be eaten at his or her leisure. Each resident room has a "tea kitchen" (hot plate, refrigerator, and storage) so that residents can prepare their own snacks or coffee or tea. Meals can also be eaten in the restaurant, or residents can prepare their own meals in the specially equipped residents' kitchen located in each wing.

Rooms

The room entrances are designed to be as residential as possible. The doorways are recessed to create a front "stoop" where mail and newspapers are delivered. Each room also has a doorbell. The rooms are spacious (160 square feet—15 sq m, with a 50-square-foot vestibule—4.6 sq m), and each has a private bathroom. The bathrooms are all accessible to wheelchair users, each with a roll-in shower. The rooms have large bay windows, which look out onto the courts between wings of the building or out on the paths adjoining the other multifamily housing. Except for the hospital-type bed, which is provided, the rooms are furnished by the residents and can be completely redecorated with wallpaper and carpeting.

Adult Day Center

A major component of this facility is the adult day center program. Elderly community residents are free to attend any community day program at any facility in town (inexpensive public transportation provided). Attendance is voluntary and unscheduled. The Papegojelyckan facility is fully equipped with a wood shop, craft room, weaving room, sauna, swimming pool, rotating library, cafeteria, billiards, and pub. The large meeting room is used for a variety of programs and games. The community activity area also contains a medical and physical therapy suite.

The interior courts at Papegojelyckan.

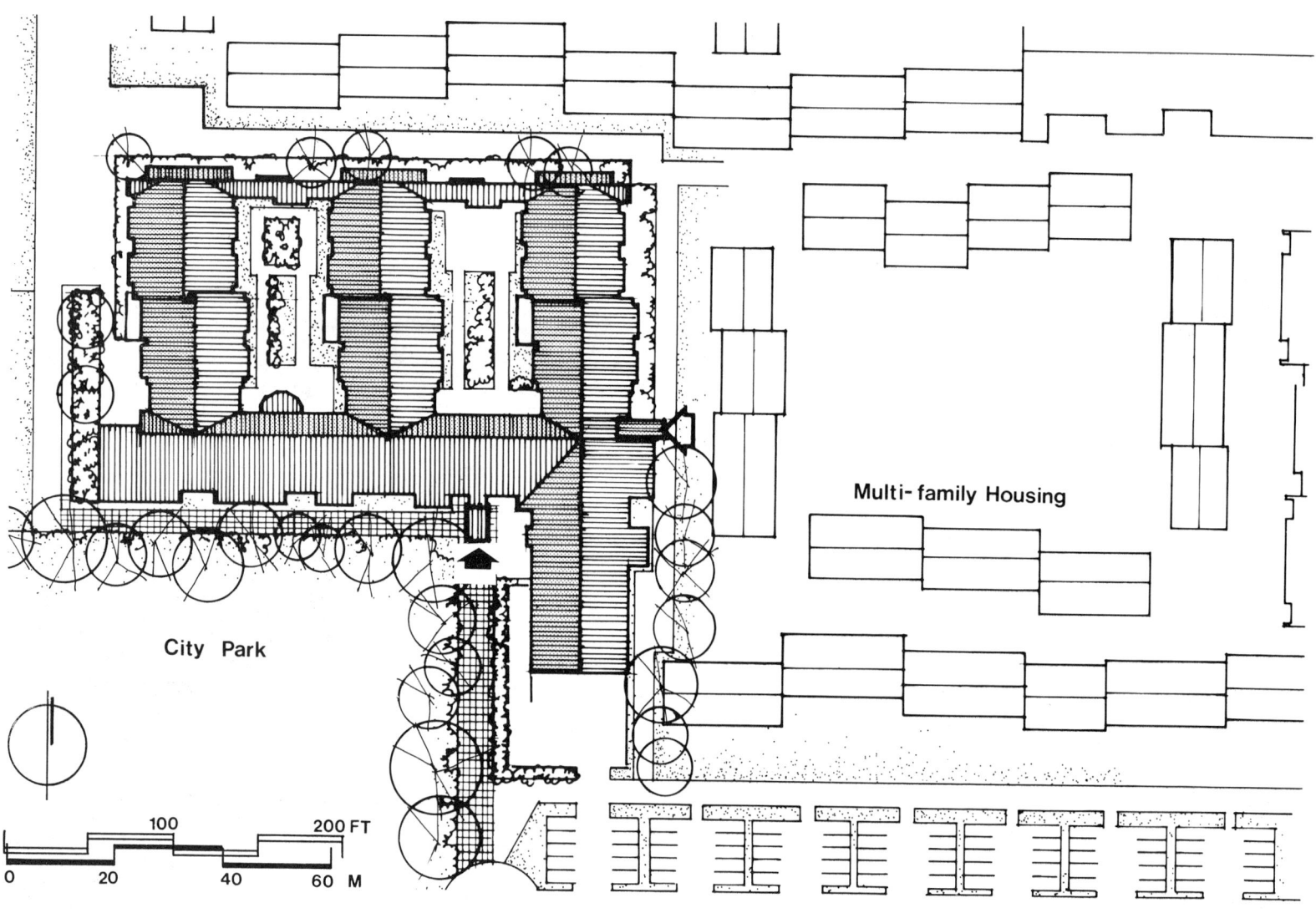

Site plan of Papegojelyckan.

Ground floor plan of Papegojelyckan. The residential wings are located north of the main circulation corridor. The day center activities and public areas are located to the south.

1. Typical resident room
2. Dining room for 12 residents
3. Shared living room
4. Pantry for residents' use
5. Laundry for residents
6. Resident storage room
7. Sitting room
8. Smoking room
9. Sitting area
10. Garden courtyards
11. Swimming pool
12. Gym
13. Medical suite
14. Ceramics workroom
15. Carpentry room
16. Weaving room
17. Activity room with stage
18. Entry
19. Reception/Concierge
20. Billiards
21. Library
22. Restaurant
23. Pub
24. Kitchen
25. Administrative suite

Residents enjoy previewing activity from the second-floor balcony above the lobby and cafeteria.

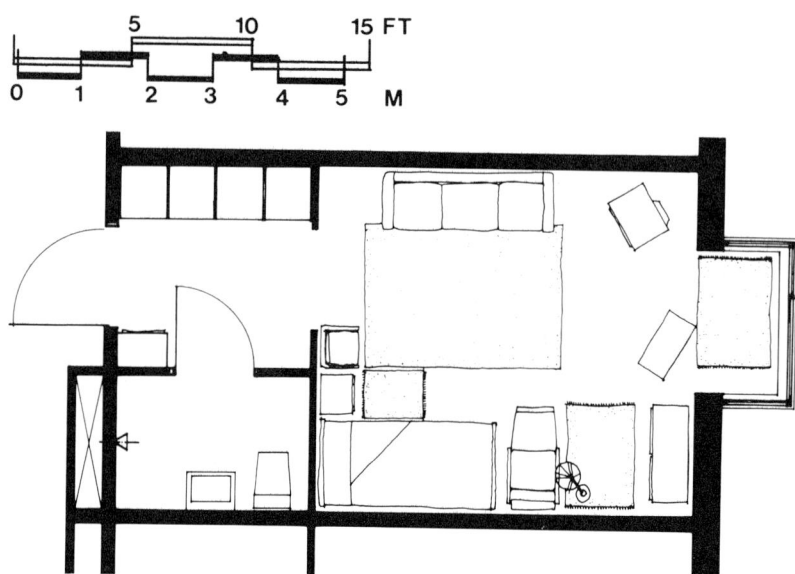

Typical private resident room: Each room has a private bathroom (with shower), several storage closets, and a tea kitchen (refrigerator and hot plate). Residents can bring their own furniture.

Commentary

Assistance is provided to residents in terms of the services that they require. Services (except meals) are not provided for those who can continue to provide for themselves. The goal is to keep the residents as independent and self-sufficient as possible. This approach may change as the residents age and require more assistance. The staff already sees an increasing need for care from residents, who have aged a number of years since the facility opened.

The day center offers necessary services and social activities for older community residents. The result has been that these facilities, which were intended to be shared with Papegojelyckan residents, are usually "taken over" by the more active elderly people from the community. Papegojelyckan residents are generally more frail and less active, and seem to be unable (or unwilling) to compete with their younger counterparts. The residents, as one staff member pointed out, like to sleep in the afternoon and take advantage of the facilities when the community residents have left.

Strengths

Residential scale and detailing.
Operation that promotes independence and personalization of rooms.
Residential setting in multifamily neighborhood—age-segregated housing in an age-integrated neighborhood.
Range and types of activity spaces, lounges, and parlors.
Residents' rooms are large enough to be more than just bedrooms.

Weaknesses

Too many "quiet" lounges and sitting rooms within the residential clusters. Arvid Hultquist (96-year-old resident) proposed that there be fewer lounges, as well as a more compact design to minimize travel distances.

Too many services available within the facility; the residents have no need to go out into the community. Medical care, groceries, activities, and social opportunity are all brought to the resident.

Residential corridors suffer from an institutional, sterile appearance—hard surfaces with little texture, glare from lighting fixtures, and a lack of natural light weaken the otherwise residential appearance.

The materials, roof lines, and landscaping all add to the residential character.

S-2

TECKOMATORP SERVICECENTRUM
(*Teckomatorp Service Center*)

TECKOMATORP, SWEDEN

TYPE OF HOUSING:	Pensioners' dwellings
OTHER ELEMENTS:	Day center for the elderly
	Day care center for children
	Public library
	School cafeteria
NUMBER OF UNITS:	16 apartments (two-room and three-room)
	50 children in day care
ARCHITECT:	Olle Hansson
BUILT:	1979
OWNER:	Municipality of Svalövs

Physical Description

The Teckomatorp Service Center is located on the southern edge of town between an existing residential neighborhood and an existing school. The town is an agricultural community that is not unlike small farm towns in the American Midwest. The houses are simple detached dwellings with large flower gardens and well-manicured yards.

The Service Center is a collection of one-story, brick- and wood-sided buildings with sloping corrugated roofs. The heart of the complex is a building that houses the program spaces—town library, cafeteria, arts and crafts, lounge space, and central kitchen. To the east of this building are seven small buildings that contain the 16 pensioner apartments. The complex is surrounded by both private and community gardens. To the west are three small, residentially scaled buildings that house the day care program for children of different age groups. To the south is the existing school with its ball fields and parking areas.

The use of small building components retains the rural character of the area. The apartment "buildings" appear typical of local single-family housing. The extensive use of gardening areas (private and common) allows the residents to continue previous gardening and farming activities and adds to the rich look of the area.

Residential Care

The main building is the common ground for all users. Young children, school children, the elderly, and townspeople all share in the use of the cafeteria, library, and arts and crafts room. Each user group has a distinct entrance and there is a careful hierarchy of private and public zones to reduce potential territorial conflicts. No attempt is made to force interaction among elderly residents and youthful users. The library was conceptualized as a zone where interaction could be spontaneous and by choice. Overzealous activity by the children is monitored by the librarian. The elderly and the children share in holiday celebrations and exchange "services"—skits are provided by the children, and stories are read by the elderly. The success of this center (and it is a success, according to staff and residents) stems from the lack of forced interaction—some children will wander over to watch television with the pensioners; and elderly residents often help the children with their gardens. It is the director's view that "the success is up to the pensioners, because the children don't consciously think about it . . . to them it [interaction] is natural."

Apartments

Both two-room and three-room apartments exist, all with private patios off the living room and common garden areas near the kitchen. Current Swedish planning has eliminated the efficiency apartment as being inadequate for elderly residents. Two-room (one-bedroom) apartments are provided for single residents, and three-room (two-bedroom) apartments are provided for couples. The large entry vestibules are typical of Swedish housing.

Apartments at Teckomatorp.

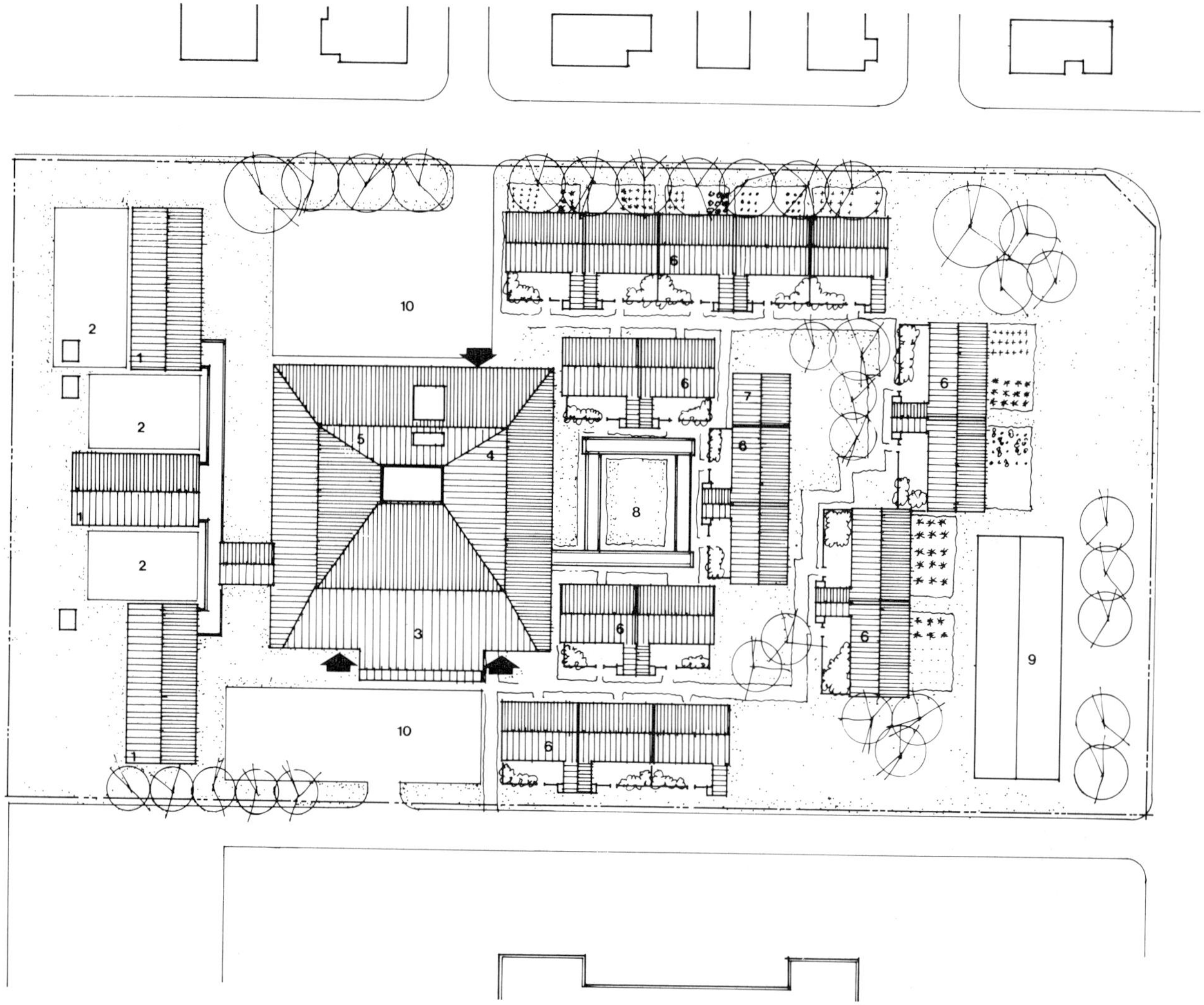

Site plan of the Teckomatorp Service Center.

1. Day care center buildings for children
2. Play areas
3. Public library
4. Day center for the elderly
5. Cafeteria
6. Pensioner's dwellings
7. Laundry facilities
8. Community garden
9. Apartment building
10. Parking areas

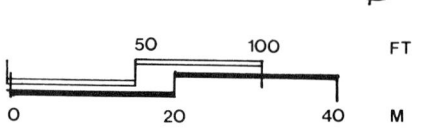

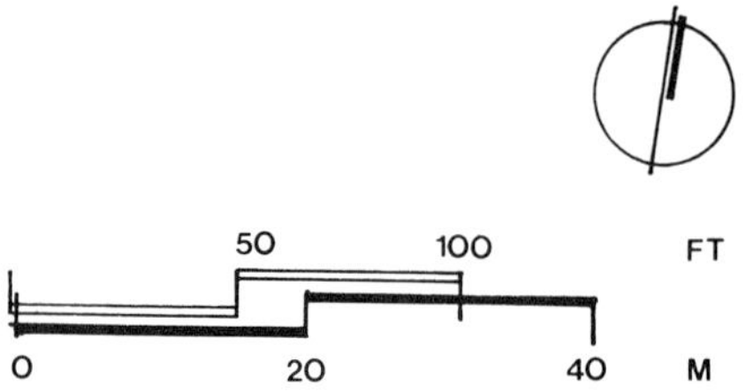

The buildings for the day care center for children repeat the architectural vocabulary of the sheltered dwellings.

All the apartments are equipped with passive and active alarm systems. The active alarm system is activated by the resident in case of emergency. The passive alarm is set off automatically if she or he does not use the toilet or open the refrigerator by 10 A.M. If the passive alarm is set off, the service center director checks with the resident to make sure he or she is all right. Although some residents object to the Big Brother aspect of the passive alarm, most react favorably because of the security that it affords should they fall and not be able to activate an alarm.

Commentary

Teckomatorp is a small (population: 1,500) farm town surrounded by acres of open fields. The town found itself in need of many services and programs that could not be financially supported as independent facilities. Teckomatorp needed a library, a day care center for children, and a cafeteria for the school (which included elementary through high school levels). The growing elderly population found themselves without a network of supportive services

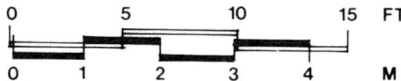

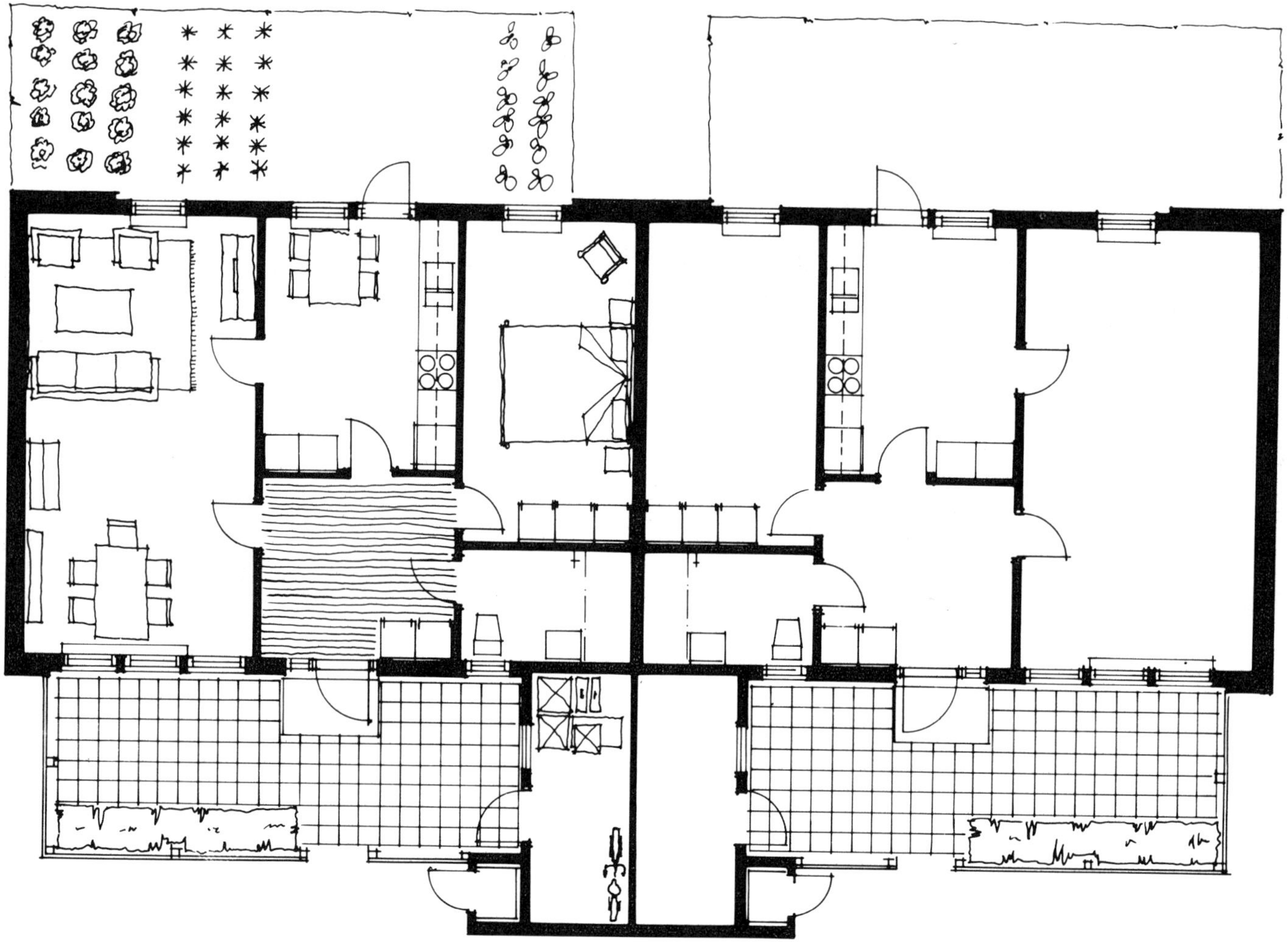

Typical apartment cluster: one-bedroom apartment.

Each apartment has a private garden terrace.

to maintain them in their own community. Sheltered dwellings, a meals program, and day center activities were identified as critical services presently lacking in the elderly community.

The solution to all these needs was a highly creative multifaceted service center for the whole community. By centralizing services near the existing school, construction and operating expenses were reduced, and a high level of age-integration was achieved. Apartments for the elderly, a new library, and the day care center for children share space as well as a common architectural vocabulary.

Teckomatorp Service Center is one of the first Swedish experiments combining activity centers for the elderly with day care for children. This approach is being tested in many American facilities as well. Combination of such facilities can obviously be handled in a number of different ways, from complete amalgamation of services to isolated and disparate services. The Teckomatorp Service Center takes a more neutral stance: some activities succeed by their combination—shared meals, for instance—while others need to be distinct, and appropriate for each age group. In some cases, the combination of pensioners and children is inappropriate—due to either cultural or social distance. In Teckomatorp, this is not a problem. The service center approach retains the cohesive spirit of a small town, where the pensioners are commonly grandparents or great-grandparents of the children at the day care center and the school. Interaction and contact are spontaneous and frequent.

Strengths

Centralization of services provides a feasible array of programs for the small rural community.

Residential scale consistent with the rural community.

Provides continuity of lifestyle by providing areas for gardening.

Provides opportunities for spontaneous interaction between elderly residents and other community users.

Careful attention to private territories and common zones established by different user groups reduces conflicts.

Weaknesses

Except for the library, there is no place where elderly residents can just watch the day care children without being involved with them.

More adult-oriented services should be combined with the library (perhaps a post office, bank, town meeting hall, etc.). The major interaction opportunities currently are with children rather than with other adult groups.

S-3
VÄSTRA FÄLADEN SERVICECENTRUM
(Västra Fäladen Service Center)

LANDSKRONA, SWEDEN

TYPE OF HOUSING:	Pensioners' dwellings
OTHER ELEMENTS:	Day center
NUMBER OF UNITS:	58 apartments (two-room)
ARCHITECT:	Sten Samuelson and Inge Stoltz
BUILT:	1977–1978
OWNER:	Municipality of Landskrona

Physical Description

The service center is located in the town center of a new residential community in Landskrona. When completed, this new multifamily community will consist of five villages with approximately 350 dwellings. The service center for elderly residents consists of a low-rise building with 28 apartments linked by a bridge to a ten-story building with 30 apartments and a one-story day center.

The day center is designed as a storefront operation in the commercial heart of the village center. The activity spaces are arranged along the main street with other shopping spaces. The day center contains an activity zone (weaving, arts and crafts, meeting room), which is farthest removed from the village center and thereby keeps it more private for the residents. The residents' cafeteria, which provides 100 meals per day, is located as an intermediate zone next to the pharmacy and medical clinic for the village.

The low-rise structure is a long three-story building with apartments arranged along the south side of the corridor. Each corridor has small bay windows, which create small sitting areas along the north side and face a day care center for children. The building is a simple composition of repetitive brick bays set off by white painted wood balconies.

The ten-story mid-rise structure was originally intended to be a 20-story landmark for Landskrona and its new community. At ten floors it succeeds as a monument of unusual triangular forms and composition of materials. The plan consists of a pinwheel of four apartments arranged around a central core. Each floor is "different," as the architects selected a variety of elements such as jutting triangular balconies, rectangular recessed balconies, and triangular bay windows off the kitchen. These elements, clad in white aluminum panels, contrast with the heavy brick walls from which they seem to spring. The form is distinctive in a setting of plain stucco town houses.

Residential Care

The Västra Fäladen Service Center complex signals two commitments to integration of the elderly into the larger community.

First, in the development of any new large community there is usually a desire to create a balanced society. A major component of a balanced community is an imitation of the age structure and family structure of the society as a whole. By providing housing for the elderly in its first phase, the development group made a commitment to offer housing for older members of families relocating to Västra Fäladen, as well as to those elderly individuals interested in moving to a new community.

Second, Västra Fäladen made a commitment to increase the independence of its elderly residents by integrating them on the northern edge of its new town center. The hope is that commercial activities and public transportation will be more easily accessible without being created specifically for elderly users. There are opportunities for the elderly residents to socialize with village residents coming to the town center for shopping and medical care. The service center has also arranged for the public to use the cafeteria to get coffee and rolls while waiting at the adjacent medical center.

The north side of the 10-story apartment building. The bridge connects the "tower" to the low-rise apartments for the elderly.

Apartments

The mid-rise building has essentially two floor plans but attains a number of different apartment types by using a variety of balconies and bay windows. Consistent with the Swedish belief in the therapeutic benefit of private outdoor space, each apartment has a balcony. All the apartments in both buildings are equipped with passive and active alarm systems that send signals to the reception desk in the mid-rise building. The system is activated by pulling the cord (active system) or not flushing the toilet in a 24-hour period (passive system).

Commentary

The ten-story mid-rise building would actually be considered a "high-rise" by Swedish standards. Buildings of this size are a controversial building form for the housing of the elderly; it is not a common Swedish approach. Local service providers feel it is too flashy and wasteful. The elderly residents have voiced their preferences for the low-rise building; they are afraid of being isolated on the upper floors. Many of the "tower" residents are afraid to use the balconies on the upper floors—even though there is a wonderful view of the ocean. Several people laughingly pointed to the triangular bay windows—"What do you do—buy a triangular table and chair?"

One rationale for the vertical scheme was that apartment dwellers would have a view of the harbor at Landskrona, where many of them had lived and worked. The distant view did not seem to be as important to the residents. They pointed out that the low-rise apartments all have views onto a pedestrian path where there are *people!*

The main street becomes a focus of activity in which the elderly can participate.

Site plan of the new housing community, Västra Fäladen: The complex consists of small villages around a town center that has small shops, services, and a day care center for children. The housing for the elderly (10 and 11) is located at the north end of the town center.

1. Existing high-rise housing
2. Existing low-rise housing
3. Village M
4. Village K
5. Village L
6. Town center
7. Support services
8. Shopping center
9. Day care center for children
10. Low-rise housing for the elderly
11. Mid-rise buildings to house the elderly

(FROM "BOLIGBEBYGGELSEN VÄSTRA FÄLADEN, LANDSKRONA, 1979)

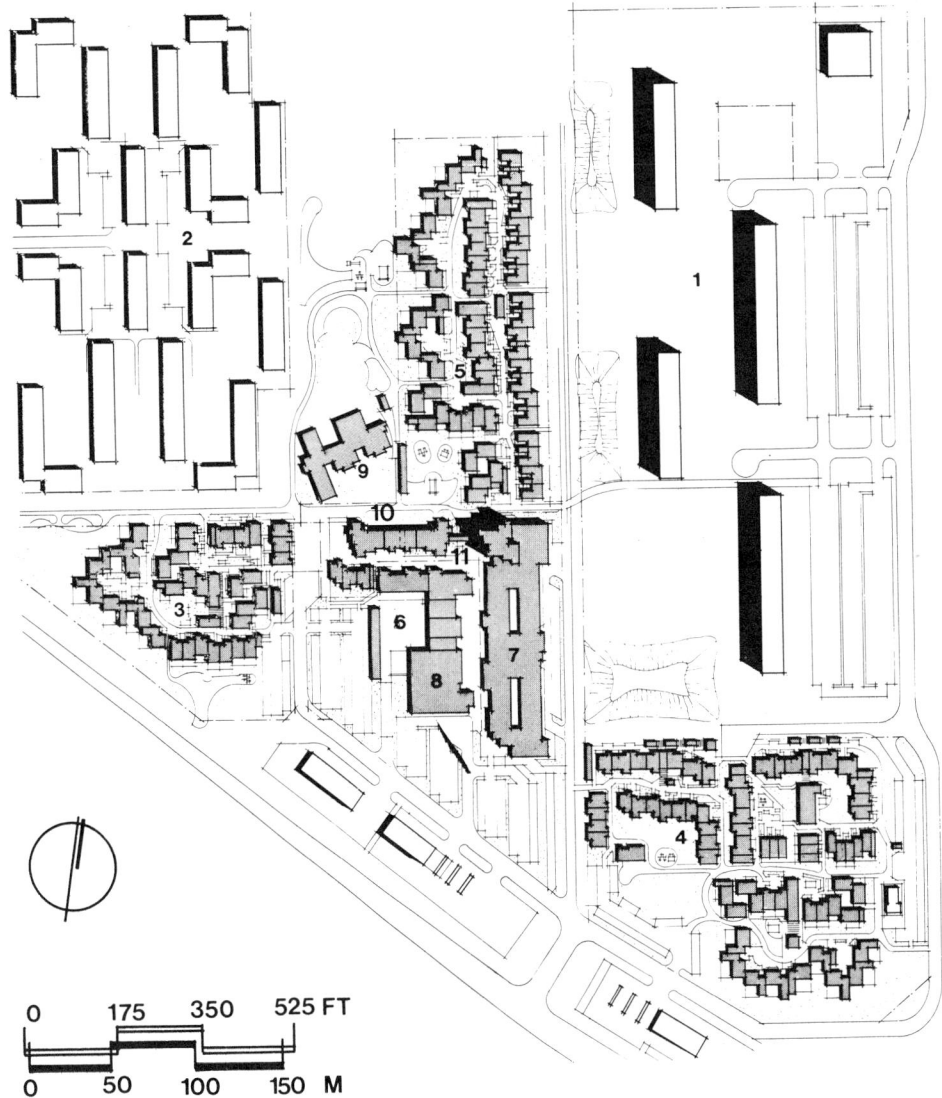

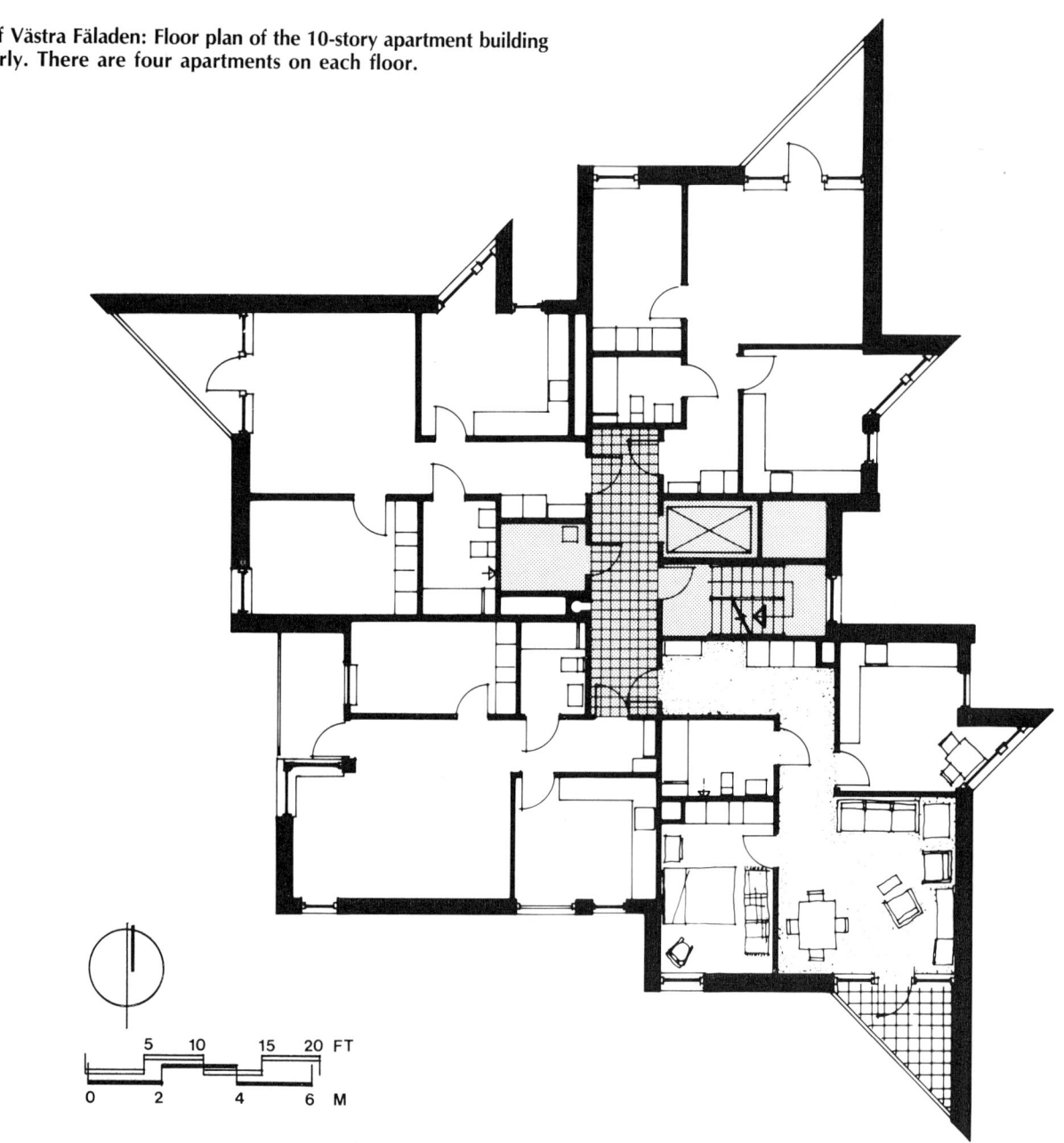

Floor plan of Västra Fäladen: Floor plan of the 10-story apartment building for the elderly. There are four apartments on each floor.

Strengths

Location at the heart of the new community.

Cafeteria for the elderly can be shared with the community and operates as a storefront activity like the other commercial ventures along the main street.

Community-oriented services (medical care, pharmacy) are built as part of the service center, eliminating duplication of services and integrating the elderly into the mainstream of the community.

Visually, the ten-story building is an exciting play of form and material.

There are very few typical apartments, although they are all based on the same two units.

The 20-story version, as originally had been planned, was not built.

Weaknesses

There are only four apartments per floor, which minimizes opportunities for socialization and isolates people on the upper floors.

The ten-story building has only one elevator, which leaves the residents stranded if it is unoperational for any period of time.

The sitting areas in the low-rise building are too small, resembling bumps in the corridor. (A resident pointed out that people rarely use them.)

High-rise living is not typical for these former Landskrona residents.

Västra Fäladen apartments for the elderly, looking east. Apartments on the left are in the low-rise building, the 10-story "landmark" is beyond.

S-4

GRÄNNA SERVICEHUS FÖR ÄLDRE
(*Gränna Service House for the Elderly*)

GRÄNNA, SWEDEN

TYPE OF HOUSING:	Pensioners' dwellings
	Short-term nursing-care unit
NUMBER OF UNITS:	30 efficiency apartments
	16 one-bedroom apartments
	7-bed nursing-care unit
ARCHITECT:	Helmer Flensborns
BUILT:	1979
OWNER:	Private building company and rented to municipality
	Nursing-care unit operated by *landsting*

Physical Description

This facility replaces an older, outdated old-age home in the town of Gränna and is located on the edge of the downtown area, adjacent to new multifamily housing. The building is a two-story, U-shaped plan with apartments in each wing and common services at the center. The sloping roof, vertical yellow siding, and balconies with flower boxes all add to the residential qualities of this form of housing.

Each wing has approximately twelve apartments that have a common lounge ("day room") and a room for personal storage. The center portion of the building contains all of the common activity spaces. There is a large, restaurant-style dining room and meeting room on the ground floor and an arts and crafts center for batik, ceramics, and woodworking on the upper floor. There is also a personal care suite, which includes a hairdresser, foot care facility, and laundry room on the second floor. The seven-bed nursing-care unit is located at the end of the east wing.

Residential Care

Pensioners' Dwellings:

Sweden, like other countries, is faced with an increasing aged population that is living longer and maintaining its independence longer. "Residential hotels" and "old folks' homes" (similar to a personal-care-level nursing home) are forms of housing for the elderly in Sweden that no longer respond to current philosophies of independence, privacy, activity, and a residential quality of life. The Gränna Service House represents these philosophies for a portion of the aged population that needs a small measure of assistance but that by and large can live independently. They do not require intensive medical supervision or a complete array of housekeeping and personal hygiene services.

At Gränna each resident has his or her own "home," complete with a kitchen. The majority of apartments contain one room and a kitchen (a spacious version of the American efficiency apartment). Residents have a rental contract to live at Gränna, so that they are not displaced if they are hospitalized for greater care. Housekeeping and meal services are available for purchase—residents pay only for what they use. This allows the residents to obtain different levels of support and minimizes overprotection by the staff.

Short-term Nursing Unit:

The seven-bed nursing-care unit at Gränna represents the latest in current Swedish thinking. A common gap in services for the elderly occurs between hospitalization or intensive medical care and resumption of an independent life at home. Many elderly patients are forced to stay in a hospital bed because there is no support network to let them convalesce at home. This respite care unit provides that support for elderly residents of the Gränna community. Pensioners can stay for three to four weeks, relying on medical

The Gränna Service House looking north.

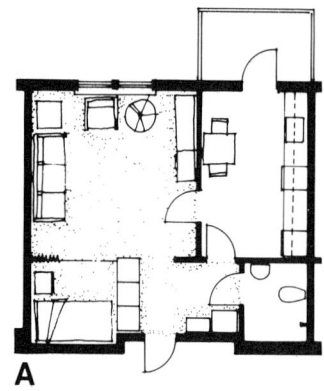

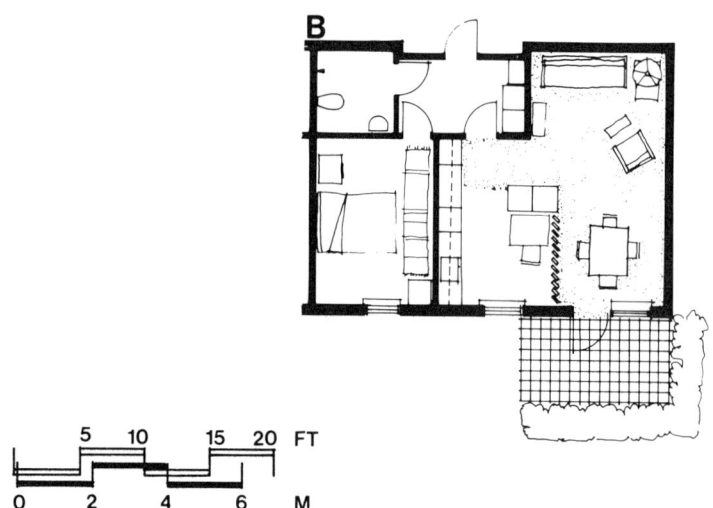

Apartment plans: typical efficiency apartment (A) and one-bedroom apartment (B).

assistance from the nursing staff and using the activities of the service house. The nursing unit has proven to be very successful and has demands beyond its capabilities.

Apartments

There are five different apartment types—two efficiency models and three one-bedrooms. All apartments have a balcony or grade-level terrace accessible either from the kitchen or living room. The apartments are all planned with an entry room as the heart from which all rooms are approached. The entry zone is an extremely attractive device to enhance the privacy of the efficiency apartment. The kitchen of the efficiency unit is not open to the living space, which further reduces the all-purpose feeling of the typical efficiency apartment. The kitchen is a spacious, well-equipped room with the balcony/terrace at one end, which opens it up to the outside. The sleeping niche is deep enough to completely contain the bed, maintaining the living area as a room for activities other than sleeping or food preparation and eating.

Commentary

Gränna is a representative example of current housing thought in Sweden. Services are provided for those who require them rather than as a rule of operation. Residents maintain their dignity and self-esteem by determining those areas in which they need assistance. The service infrastructure is such that residents can maintain a life in Gränna as they age and require more assistance, without having to move to another "level of care" facility. The services and building can potentially provide a prosthetic support for the life of the resident.

Strengths

The choice of services, which allows residents to determine those areas in which they need meal, housekeeping, or personal hygiene assistance.

The efficiency apartments are well planned to maintain privacy

Ground floor plan of the Gränna Service House.

1. Efficiency apartment
2. One-bedroom apartment
3. Common lounge
4. Resident storage
5. Janitor's room
6. Public toilet
7. Meeting room
8. Dining room
9. Kitchen support
10. Office
11. Entry
12. Medical clinic
13. Staff support
14. Private room
15. Semiprivate room
16. Bathroom
17. Nurse's station and treatment room
18. Pantry
19. Storage
20. Terrace

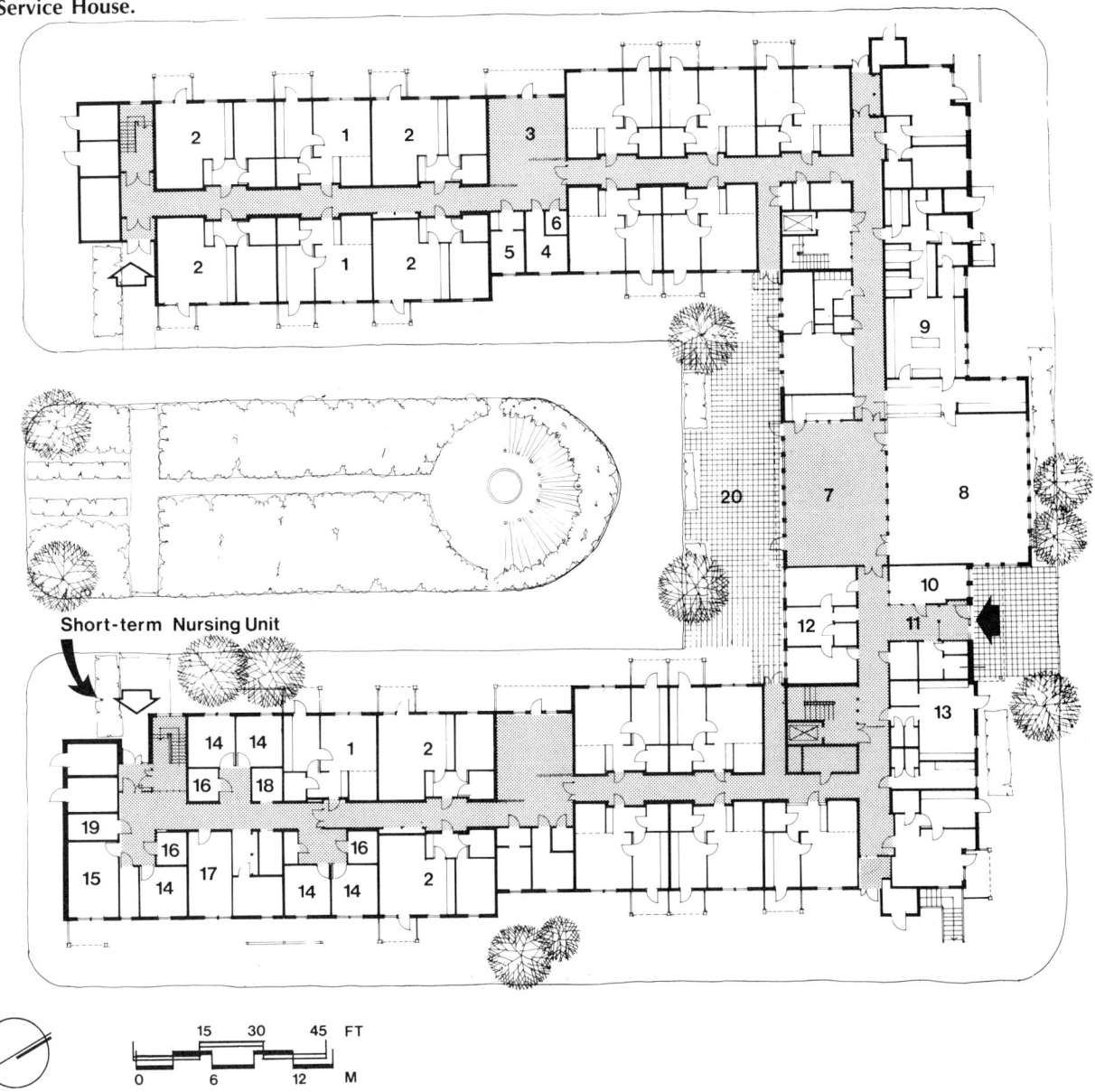

The interior court looking northwest

and a separation of activities of sleeping, living, and food preparation and eating.

The short-term nursing-care unit provides a place for pensioners to convalesce in a noninstitutional setting.

The residential scale of the facility.

The corridors are opened up with natural light in the lounges and small porches at each apartment entrance.

Weaknesses

The short-term nursing-care unit has no lounge space or dining room.

The efficiency apartment is almost large enough to create a separate, private bedroom. It seems to be an unusual compromise of space.

S-5
KNIVSTA SERVICEHUS OCH SJUKHEM
(Knivsta Service House and Nursing Home)

KNIVSTA, SWEDEN

TYPE OF HOUSING:	Pensioners' dwellings
	Nursing home
OTHER ELEMENTS:	District medical services
	Day center
NUMBER OF UNITS:	62 one-bedroom apartments
	30 private nursing-care rooms
ARCHITECT:	Arne Clevestam
BUILT:	Apartments: 1981
	Nursing home: 1982
OWNER:	Municipality of Uppsala
	Medical services: Nursing home owned and operated by the *landsting*

Note: At the time of the author's visit, this project had not yet been fully completed, making it difficult to analyze. It is included, however, because it signals a new form of housing service for the elderly with cooperation between housing providers (*kommun*) and the medical care providers (*landsting*).

Physical Description

Knivsta is a small, almost rural town that has grown up along the railroad between Stockholm and Uppsala. The service house site is located between the railroad station and a residential area of Knivsta. This project acts as districtwide service for the elderly of Knivsta and outlying unincorporated areas. Housing, meals, activities, counseling, therapy, and medical, dental, and nursing care are all available.

The complex is organized around a central core, which contains the kitchen, restaurant, meeting room, offices of the social workers, pharmacy, hobby area, exercise room, and administrative offices. To one side are the *landsting*-operated medical services and nursing home. On the other side of the core are the 62 apartments, located on two levels along three residential wings.

The complex is a series of one- and two-story elements set as wings off a main "spine" linking medical and housing services. The buildings are simply constructed of red brick and sloping corrugated metal roofs.

Residential Care

The Knivsta Service House represents a joint venture between the *landsting* and Uppsala *kommun* to provide a range of housing settings in a continuum of care for the elderly residents of the Knivsta area. This project also represents an economical solution that eliminates duplication of common elements offered by both groups. Elderly pensioners receive assistance that responds to all their needs, which are rarely totally physiological, financial, or psychological. In addition, the limitations imposed by an aging body can impede access to the services that are available and the coordination of those benefits. At Knivsta, pensioners obtain housing, medical, and social assistance through the coordinated efforts of the social workers and insurance office. The continuum-of-care setting also assures the elderly residents of a constant role and stable future in the Knivsta community.

Apartments

All 62 apartments are one-bedroom arrangements, although there are two different size units. Both apartment types share a similar arrangement of rooms off an entry space, and all apartments have a balcony or grade-level terrace. The larger apartment, planned for couples, has an eat-in kitchen and a more spacious bedroom.

Apartments at Knivsta

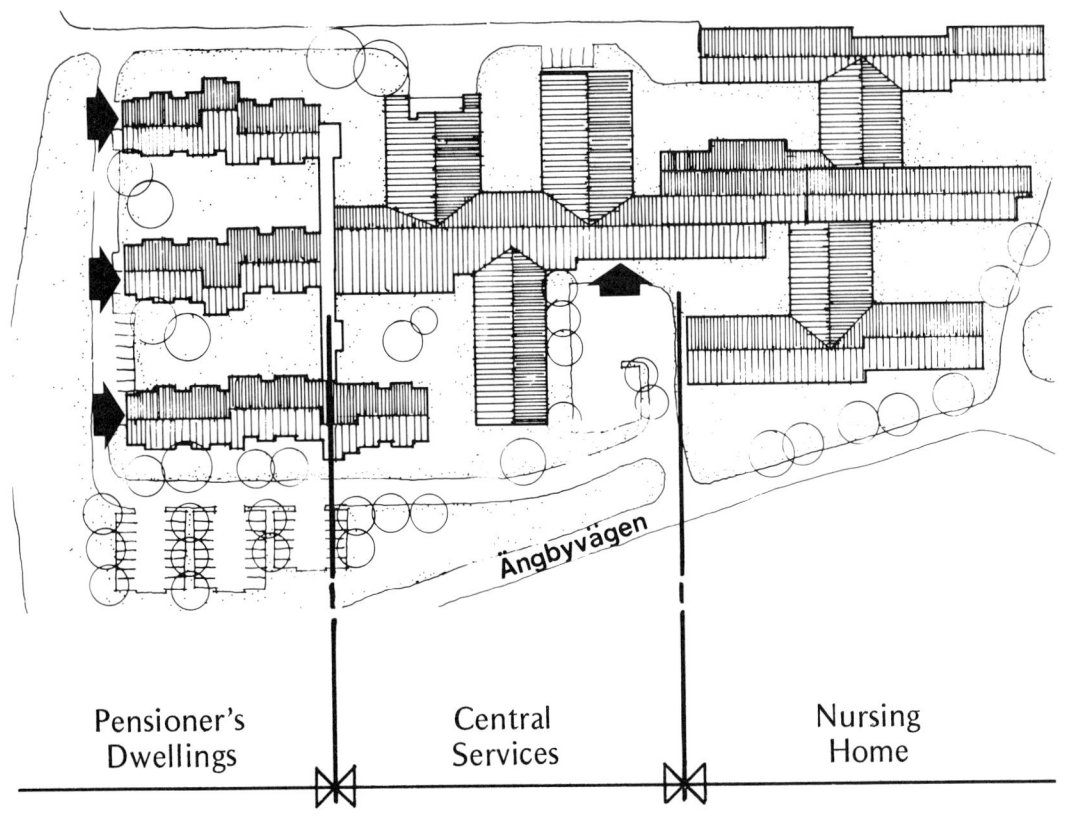

| Pensioner's Dwellings | Central Services | Nursing Home |

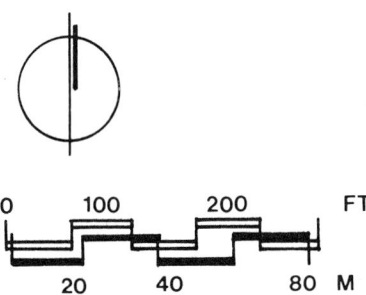

Site plan of the Knivsta Service House.

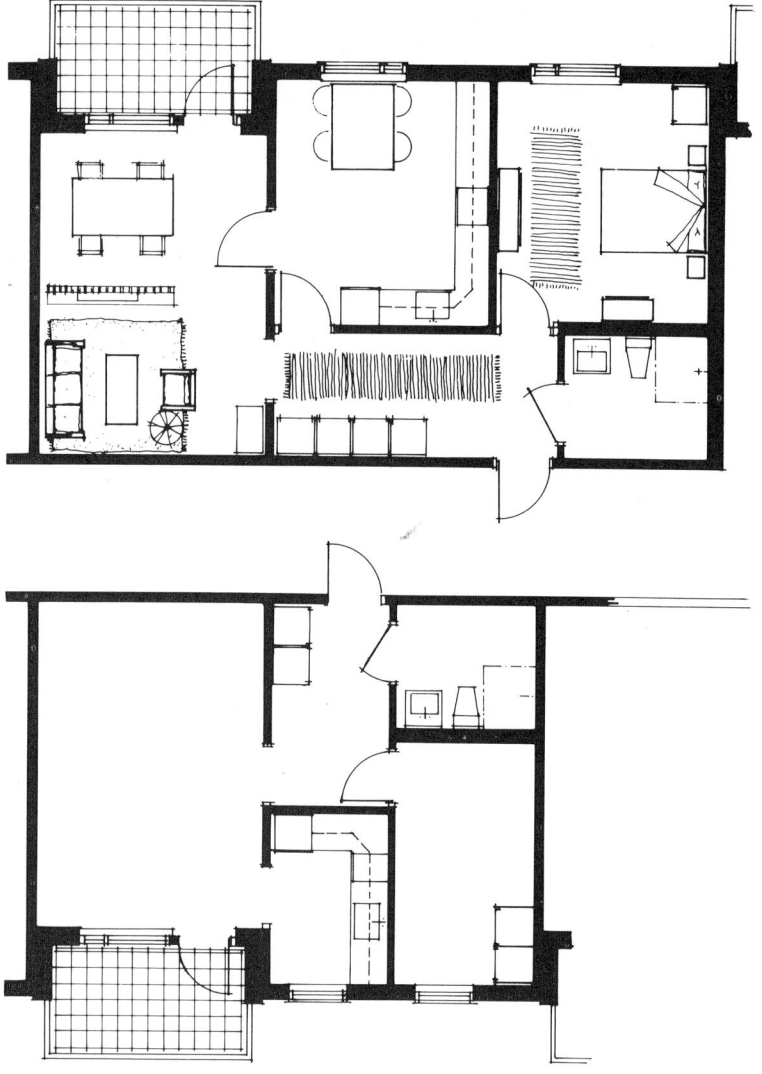

Commentary

Continuum-of-care or "campus" approaches to housing for the elderly are hotly debated in both Europe and the United States. The Knivsta Service House can loosely be considered a continuum, even though it has only two housing forms ("protected" or nursing). This is because the service house supports other elderly members of the community through its "outreach" program—there was no need to create other special forms of housing.

Strengths

Economy from shared facilities.
Coordination of benefits and assistance available to elderly pensioners.
The massing complements the rural housing and small commercial structures of the community.

Weaknesses

The size of the complex—especially the travel distances.
Nursing care and housing are situated as polar opposites on the site.

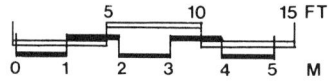

Apartment plans.

S-6
ÖRNEN SERVICEHUS
(Örnen Service House)

UPPSALA, SWEDEN

TYPE OF HOUSING:	Pensioners' dwellings
OTHER ELEMENTS:	Day center
NUMBER OF UNITS:	36 one-bedroom apartments
	11 two-bedroom apartments
	(3 three-room arrangements;
	8 two-and-a-half-room
	arrangements)
BUILT:	1980–81
OWNER:	Municipality of Uppsala

Physical Description

Örnen's outstanding feature is its location. The building is located on the main shopping street at the end of a pedestrian mall in downtown Uppsala. The 47 apartments are distributed between two buildings, which are linked by the day center on the ground floor. The buildings are set at right angles to each other and hug the edges of the corner site. The building that faces the main shopping street is four stories, with the ground floor containing administrative offices and a restaurant. The other building is set back from the street with a green space and is only three stories—maintaining the residential scale of the side street.

The two buildings and several adjacent historical residences (to be converted into housing for the elderly at a later date) enclose a landscaped court. Pipe rails lead residents along different textured walkways to a central recreation/sitting area complete with a gazebo, life-size chessboard, tables and chairs, and gardens.

The ground floor day center provides services to its building residents and to elderly residents of the downtown area. The primary feature is a restaurant-style dining room, which has a storefront appearance along the main shopping street. The day center has a lending library, laundry facilities, and hobby area. The hobby area, which faces the garden court, is complete with a wood and metal shop, as well as a weaving room and game room.

Residential Care

A large percentage of Sweden's elderly population is located in the city centers. Uppsala's Social Welfare Board recognized the pressures felt by their "inner-city" pensioners—the lack of adequate housing and support services to maintain them in their own dwellings. The Örnen Service House addresses these two issues. The service center provides meals and opportunities for socialization unavailable in the community. Services present in the downtown area—food stores, beauty shops, and medical care—were not duplicated in the Örnen Service Center. It is important that the pensioners maintain an active role in the community.

Apartments

Consistent with other Swedish housing projects, all apartments have balconies. Apartments located along the main street also have eat-in kitchens, which extend with bay windows over the sidewalk for views up and down the pedestrian mall. All apartments are tied into a central passive and active alarm system, as well as to a telephone to the reception desk.

Örnen has a variety of apartment arrangements; the majority are one-bedroom apartments for single pensioners. There are also numerous two-bedroom apartments. The two-and-a-half-room arrangement provides a standard bedroom for couples and includes a smaller guest bedroom. The three-room apartments provide two equal-sized bedrooms, so that siblings or friends can live together.

The apartments are spacious and arranged in a typically Swedish fashion based on the entry room from which all rooms can be reached. The apartments are all accessible to the disabled—although none are specifically adapted to them. An early planning decision was made to adapt apartments to the specific needs of the tenant.

View of the courtyard and building B from building A.

All apartments have balconies. The railings and infill panels allow views to the ground from sitting height.

All bathroom walls are reinforced for the installation of grab bars tailored to the specific requirements of the particular disability of the resident. This obviously benefits the disabled resident and also removes the institutional character of adaptations for the disabled from the apartments of those who do not require them. The kitchen is a compromised version of the Swedish *fokus* kitchen, which is totally adapted for the physically disabled. Careful attention was given to the arrangement of appliances, the location of the appliance controls, the depth of the sink, and under-counter rolling storage carts. The balconies all have built-up deck floors, which maintain the floor level across the threshold, and open railings, which allow residents to see the ground from a seated position.

Site plan of Örnen.

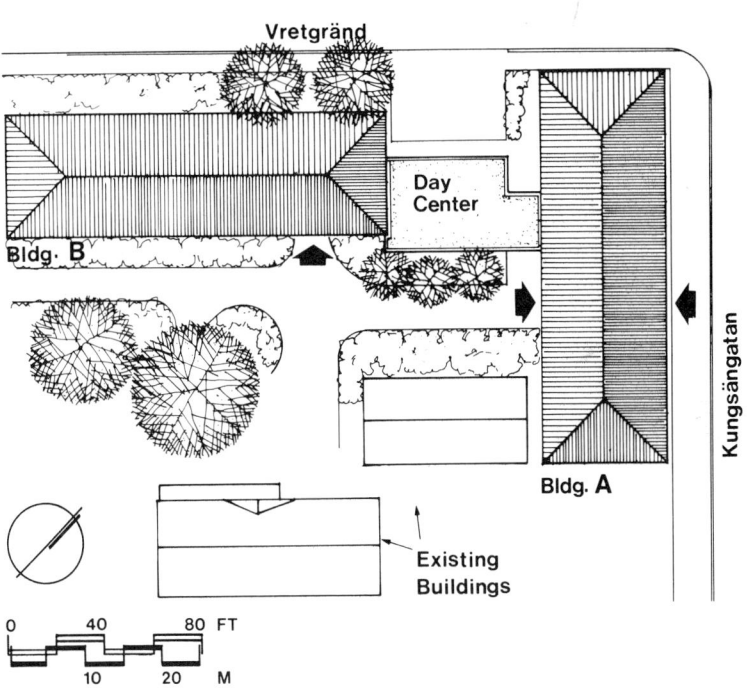

Rendering of Örnen from pedestrian street. (REPRINTED BY PERMISSION OF THE UPPSALA KOMMUN SOCIALFORVALTNINGEN)

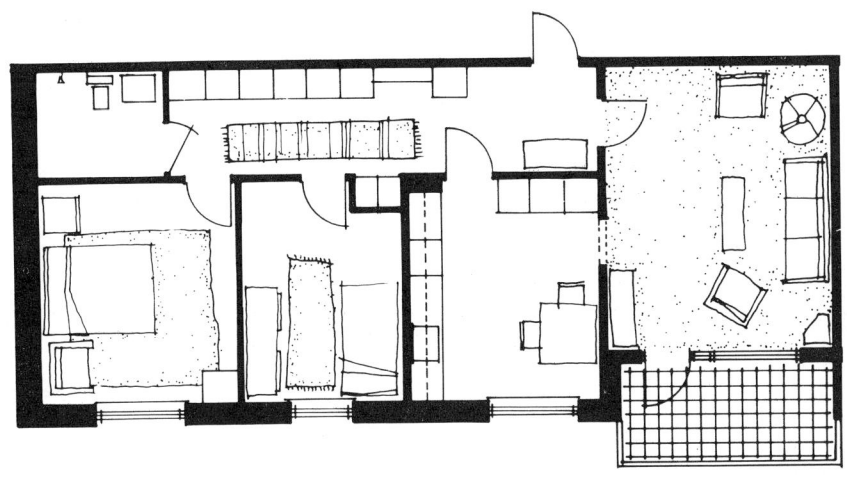 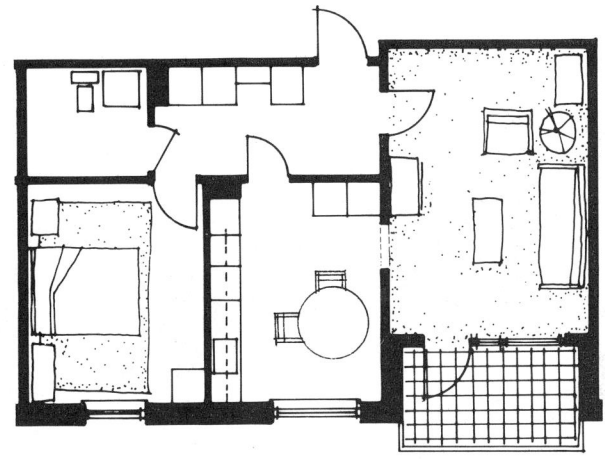

A TYPICAL 3-ROOM APARTMENT   A TYPICAL 2½-ROOM APARTMENT

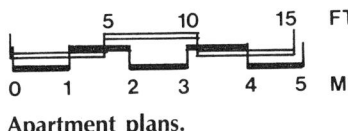

Apartment plans.

Commentary

Normalization was a key concept in the planning of Örnen. The qualities of a normalized life are apparent in the planning concepts through the detailing of the apartments. The downtown location allows residents to maintain an active, integrated role in the community. The service center provides only those support services that are not available in the community. The apartments are planned with variety and flexibility to meet the varied housing needs of the elderly population. The design responds to the requirements of the disabled, without overinstitutionalizing the environment or removing life's challenges.

Strengths

Downtown location.
Variety of apartment plans and arrangements.
The juxtaposition of the urban setting and the garden court (which is accessible to other local residents).
The apartment detailing, which subtly responds to the varied needs of disabled residents.
The tailoring of adaptations for the disabled to the specific user, which avoids compromise locations, sizes, and types.
The scale, detailing, and residential character, which respond to its main street location differently from its residential side street location.

Weaknesses

The garden court seems overly structured and limits the range and types of activities that occur.
There is no provision for parking (except for vehicles for the disabled) by residents.

Building B is set back from the street and is lower in height.

S-7
BOSTADSHOTELL KV. ENSKEDEDALEN
(*Residential Hotel in the Dalen District of Enskede*)

ENSKEDE, STOCKHOLM, SWEDEN

TYPE OF HOUSING:	Pensioners' dwellings Residential hotel
NUMBER OF UNITS:	14 one-bedroom apartments (adapted for the disabled) 86 efficiency apartments 115 one-bedroom apartments 72 single personal-care rooms
ARCHITECT:	Stockholm's Building Division
BUILT:	1978–79
OWNER:	Stockholm Municipality

Physical Description

Kv. Dalen is a new satellite residential community of Stockholm—a Swedish version of the suburbs. When completed there will be 1,700 dwelling units located in neighborhood clusters around common green spaces. The residential hotel for pensioners is located at the southwestern edge of the site, adjacent to the town center and the Tunnelbana (subway) station.

The facility encloses a courtyard on three sides with several five-story building components, which are laterally offset to make the overall size seem smaller. The design uses three different colors of stucco (wine red, rose, and beige) and various roof lines to further reduce the perceived scale of the building. The ground floor contains the common facilities; hobby room, physical therapy facility, medical suite, administrative offices, and a few apartments. The upper floors contain the bulk of the 287 dwelling units distributed between two different levels of care—independent apartments and personal-care suites, which have shared common dining and lounge space. Attached to the facility is a portion of the town center, which provides central services to all the residents of Dalen. The center contains a library, a meeting hall, a 25-meter swimming pool, a restaurant (which also provides meals for the pensioners), and space for several commercial ventures (hairdresser, bank, florist, and so on). Immediately adjacent and across the pedestrian boulevard is a grocery store with several other small shops.

Residential Care

The Swedish health care system works at building a supportive infrastructure capable of maintaining the elderly in the community. Visiting housekeepers, nurses, and social workers, as well as reduced transportation costs and social centers, have delayed the point at which institutionalization must occur—that is, a centralization of dependent pensioners who require more assistance than can be delivered to their homes. As would be expected, the pensioners who have reached this point are frailer, more physically debilitated, and in need of more medical care than their counterparts of ten years ago. This does not mean, however, that they are unable to function independently in different aspects of their daily living; the cross section of institutionalized elderly residents is truly diverse.

Facilities such as the residential hotel at Kv. Dalen offer a variety of living arrangements with varying degrees of intervention. The facility has three dwelling types at two different levels of care. Residents can live here, as members of the community, sharing common facilities, without having to move to a facility with another level of care somewhere in the community. The resident's home is his or her home forever.

Apartments

The one-bedroom apartments are unusual by Swedish standards. The eat-in kitchen is typical in that it is spacious and has a small balcony for access to the outdoors. The rest of the apartment is quite curious, however; the bedroom is accessible from the living

View of the Kv. Enskedalen town center from the Tunnelbana (subway) elevated platform.

View of the Residential Hotel from the town square looking northeast. The ground floor has activity spaces and all apartments have balconies.

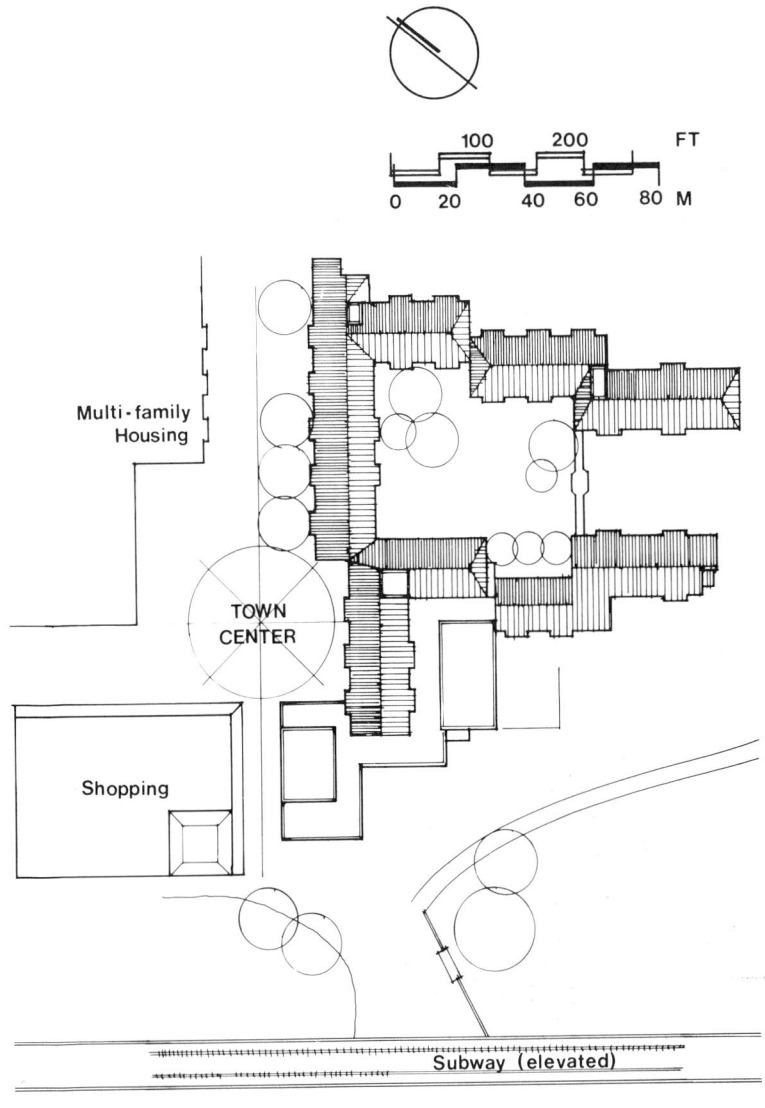

Site plan of Bostadshotell Kv. Enskedalen.

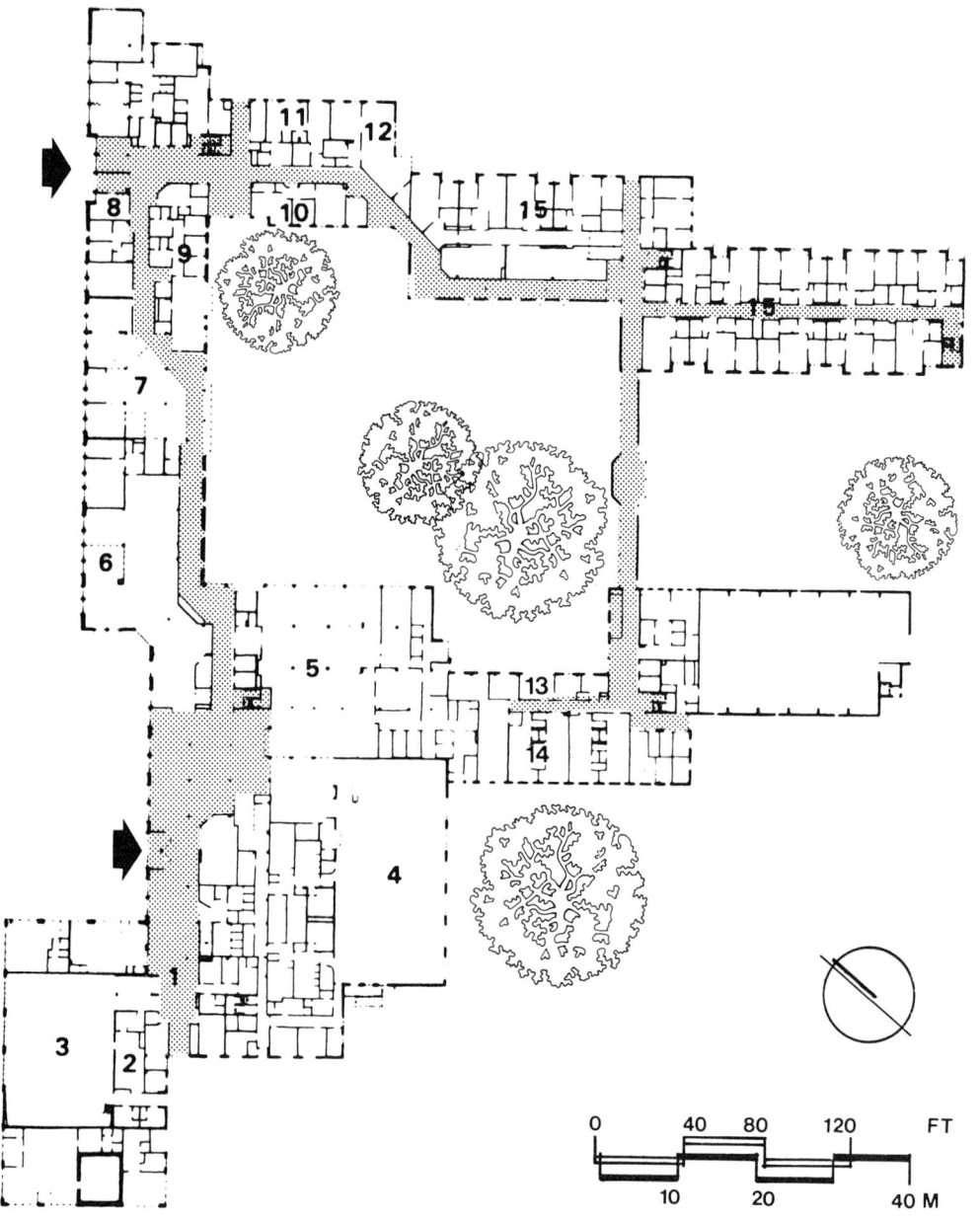

Ground floor.

1. Entrance hall
2. Office
3. Meeting hall
4. Swimming pool
5. Restaurant
6. Library
7. Club room
8. Foot care
9. Physical therapy
10. Administrative suite
11. Medical clinic
12. Staff room
13. Special care staff
14. Special care
15. Apartments

(REPRINTED FROM "STOCKHOLM BYGGER BOSTADSHOTELL," ARKITEKTUR, NO. 2, MARCH 1979)

room and remote from the bathroom, which is off the entry hall. The storage space is huge and located in the most used area, near the living room and bedroom. The efficiency apartments, on the other hand, are well zoned and organized to maintain the privacy of the individual. They are similar to the apartments at Gränna (see S-4).

The personal-care suite consists of 24 rooms, which share a common lounge, dining room, pantry, and central bath for those who need assistance. The rooms are bed-sitting rooms, each with a private bathroom and a small tea kitchen recessed off the entry hall.

Commentary

The residential hotel at Kv. Dalen is representative of age-segregated housing in an age-integrated community. This facility goes one step further by developing a program of services and activities that can be shared with the community at large. Instead of having a

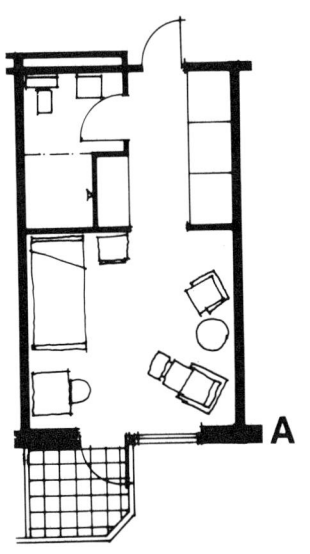
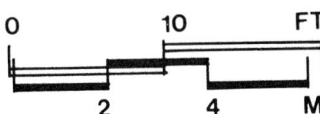
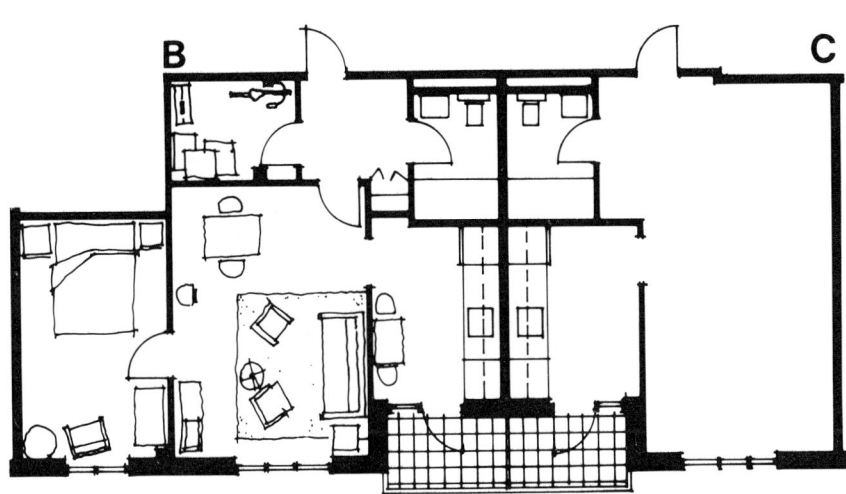

Apartment floor plans: typical personal care room (A), one-bedroom apartment (B), and efficiency apartment (C).

The town center location of the *bostadshotell* keeps the elderly active in the community at large.

separate library, swimming pool, and restaurant, the pensioners are given the opportunity to maintain their roles in the community and remain socially integrated.

Strengths

The provision of housing for the elderly in the new community of Kv. Dalen maintains a balanced community representative of the society as a whole.

Shared use of generic services (library, restaurant, and so on) that do not need to be specialized for pensioners.

Variety and levels of support available to pensioners who require varying degrees of assistance to maintain independent lives.

Location in the town center, at the hub of the activity and movement.

Weaknesses

The one-bedroom apartments are poorly zoned and organized.

Travel distances between apartments and program spaces can be extremely long.

The size of the facility is overwhelming.

Unfortunate location adjacent to the cemetery.

When the community was originally planned and sited why was the housing for the elderly located adjacent to the cemetery?

5 DENMARK

Denmark is one of the five Nordic countries composing Scandinavia (Denmark, Finland, Iceland, Norway, and Sweden). Denmark has a population of 5.1 million people, 70 percent of whom live in the Copenhagen metropolitan area. Studies indicate that 14 percent of the population are over the age of 64 and 20 percent are over the age of 60.

Denmark is recognized as one of the first true welfare states, having set the pattern for social systems in countries such as Sweden. Social policy for the elderly started with the Old-Age Assistance Act in 1891 and has evolved with important reforms beginning in 1933 (national health insurance). Changes in housing policy occurred throughout the 1960s and 70s; the government assumed control of the nursing home industry in 1969, abolished old-age homes in 1974, and created rent and mortgage subsidies in 1979.

THE GOVERNMENT

The powers of Danish government are divided among three branches—legislative, judiciary, and executive. Laws are passed by the parliament (Folketing) and are signed by the reigning monarch. The executive powers formally belong to the monarch, but in practice are exercised by a group of ministers. These ministers, along with the prime minister, constitute the formal government of Denmark. Denmark, like Sweden, has a decentralized form of government with home rule. The counties and municipalities are responsible for providing services and welfare support for their citizens.

Unlike Sweden, Denmark's division of regional responsibilities for welfare is not clear-cut (that is, medical care at the county level and social care at the local level). Responsiblity for medical care and social care is divided among the central government, county councils, and municipalities, based on the degree of specialization of the particular service. For instance, family doctors, physical therapists, and dentists operate on the local level, coordinating services with publicly owned clinics and personnel. Hospital and associated outpatient care is provided by Denmark's 14 regional county councils. Specialized institutions, as well as research, are established by the central government and operate as adjuncts to the National Hospital in Copenhagen.

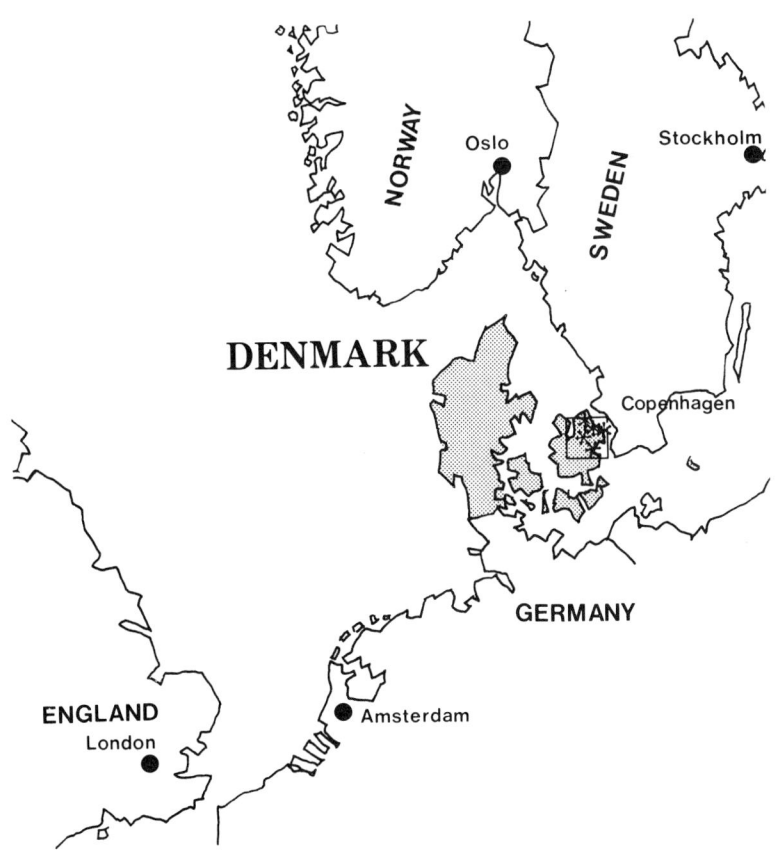

The 14 regional county councils (*amtskommuner*) coordinate services and benefits, and provide expert help to the local authorities. Specialized services (adoption, drug abuse, alcoholism, and so on), which are difficult for the local municipalities to administer, are provided by the county councils.

Denmark has 275 municipalities (*kommuner*), which act as the source for advice, guidance, and social assistance. Since 1933, it has been the responsibility of the local community to provide old-age care to its inhabitants. The municipalities coordinate income maintenance benefits, housing, medical care, and specialized services for the elderly. They supervise the operation of nursing homes, provide home help, and build housing. The central government reimburses the municipality for 50 percent of the operating costs, and the other 50 percent is raised through taxes levied by the local government.

CARE OF THE ELDERLY

Denmark provides a variety of economic and social programs as safety nets for the population. Denmark expends approximately 29 percent of its gross national product for the social security of its citizens. The Old Age Assistance Act of 1891 represents an important point in Danish care of the elderly; it was the first piece of social legislation that targeted income and housing assistance for a specific group of needy persons. Care of the elderly in Denmark focuses on financial security, housing, supportive social services, and health care.

The basic goal of Danish care of the aged has been to maintain the elderly in their own homes; or, at the very minimum, in their own communities. Complementary principles of normalization, privacy, and independence have been used to formulate a system of care that is based on recognition of the individual, rather than the group.

> Normalization, which has been the target of services for handicapped persons in Denmark for decades, means that handicapped persons should be given possibilities of a life as close as possible to the normal, meaning that they should have conditions of life corresponding to what is normal in society, meaning also that services should be given in accordance with the needs of the individual.
>
> N.E. BANK-MIKKELSEN, 1980

Financial Security

Financial security in the form of cash assistance has been reformed many times since its inception in 1891. Formerly, pensions were available only to the old and disabled who were unable to provide for themselves. Changes and reforms led to the Old Age Pension Act of 1956, which entitled all elderly people to some form of state pension; and finally by 1970, uniform entitlement regardless

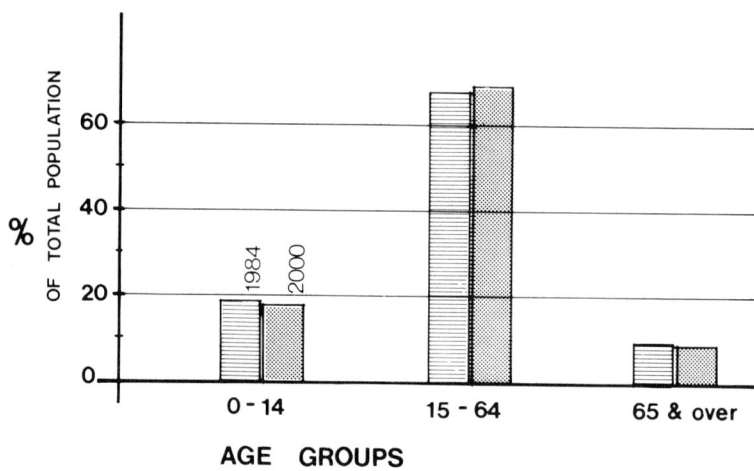

Danish population structure.

of income. Old-age pensions can be divided into two groups: those associated with social security and those provided through special employment contribution plans. The social security pension schemes consist of the national old-age pension, the supplemental pension (labor market), and early retirement pay.

National Old-age Pension

The old-age pension is not based on paid contributions or accumulation of employment quarters. It is paid to all Danish citizens at age 67 and includes additional benefit schemes:

1. Wife's supplement
2. Invalidity pension
3. Interim old-age pension
4. Additional supplements: housing supplement, personal subsidy

The national old-age pension is planned to provide elderly citizens with a modest, but comfortable, life without the need for income supplements. In 1984 single pensioners received DKR 40,068 (US$4,007) (based on US$1 = DKR 10.00) and married couples each received DKR 37,728 (US$3,773) annually. Additional benefits include:

- Wife's supplement: supplemental payment to a married couple when the husband is a pensioner and the wife is between 62 and 67 (supplement increases the single pensioner payment to that of a married couple when both are pensioners).
- Invalidity pension: social security pension for those who are invalids.
- Interim old-age pension: pension is granted prematurely (usually after age 60) in cases of failing health or other special circumstances.
- Housing supplement: municipal grant to subsidize rent or mortgage. Pensioners with an income of less than DKR 96,800 should not spend more than 15 percent of their income on housing. Maximum supplement = DKR 1,569 per month.
- Personal subsidy: municipal grant to the individual on an emergency basis (heating, medical, travel, and so on).

Supplemental Pension (Labor Market)

Labor market supplemental pensions are based solely on the number of years of contribution. A full pension attained after 40 years of service is equal to DKR 4,000 per year (pensions are prorated for fewer years of service). These pensions are financed by a contribution scheme of DKR 36 per month of which the employer pays two-thirds and the employee pays one-third.

Early Retirement Pay

Early retirement pay is available to persons over age 60 who have been a member of an unemployment insurance fund for at least 10 of the past 15 years. Payments, as of 1984, are equal to 90 percent of the person's past income, to a maximum of DKR 2,010 per week. Early retirement pay is restrictive, requiring full retirement from the labor market.

Housing

Purpose-built housing for the elderly includes a variety of concepts aimed at different portions of the aged population. Goals of increased independence and privacy have led to housing reforms and new housing standards. Danish policy has always supported the right to live in one's own home for as long as practicable. Support services, such as home help and home nursing, have made it possible for the elderly to live in their own homes for longer periods of time; two-thirds of those over age 85 still live at home.

For those unable to maintain themselves in the community (14 percent of the elderly population), a variety of housing schemes is available. It is difficult to categorize housing schemes; labels imply a static system of care rather than an evolving, adaptable environment. Danish housing facilities vary greatly by municipality and by urban or rural context. New concepts in residential care have led to the combination of different services and levels of care in a campus setting.

Ordinary Dwellings

Since 1979, pensioners are eligible for rent subsidies, which maintain housing expenditures at a maximum of 15 percent of their taxable income. To obtain full assistance, the dwelling must meet certain basic requirements, such as having running water, a toilet, a kitchen, and adequate weather protection. In addition, it can be no larger than one room per occupant, exclusive of the living room and kitchen. Homeowners are also eligible for municipal grants, which are part loan and part subsidy.

A 1977 study of elderly Danish households revealed an interesting picture of those living at home. The National Institute of Social Research (Pedersen, 1982) found that 35 percent of the elderly (over age 67) had been living at the same address for more than 30 years. The study also found that 68 percent of those over age 67 live in housing constructed before World War II—housing that

SUMMARY

Ministries:	*Ministry of the Interior*	*Ministry of Social Affairs*	*Ministry of Labour*
Boards:	National Health Service Board Medico-Legal Council	National Social Welfare Board Social Security Board Appeals Board	Directorate of Labour Labour Inspection Service Labour Market Development
State Appointed:		Special Care	14 Labour Inspection Districts Labour Exchanges* Labour Market Boards
	Medical Officers		
Regional Level:	Hospital Committees Hospitals Midwives	Social Welfare Committees Social Welfare Centres Rehabilitation & Pensions Board County Appeals Board Institutions	
Local Level:	Doctors Specialists Dentists	*Social Welfare Committees:* Payment and computation of daily sickness benefit, pensions, family allowances, rent support etc., sickness grants-in-aid and estimated cash assistance. Counselling etc., home help, aids for the handicapped, welfare facilities for the aged and infirm, day nurseries, nursery schools and other benefits in kind.	* Labour Exchange Branch Offices Unemployment benefit societies under trade unions

Citizens

Summary of services provided by levels of government. (FROM *SOCIAL WELFARE IN DENMARK*, ERNST MARCUSSEN, DET DANSKE SELSKAB, 1980; REPRINTED WITH PERMISSION FROM DET DANSKE SELSKAB)

is often substandard and without basic amenities. Other studies of the elderly population in Copenhagen have found that approximately 43 percent of the elderly live in housing that has no private toilet or bath or central heating.

Municipalities provide technical and financial assistance to make specific alterations for the disabled in a dwelling, making it more feasible for the pensioner to remain at home. Municipalities also provide technical aids and specially designed household equipment to normalize daily living activities.

Pensioners' Dwellings

Since the 1930s municipalities have been providing a small supply of specially designated pensioners' apartments in large multifamily apartment blocks. Essentially they are normal apartments for those elderly who can care for themselves with only minimal home-help service. These apartments typically have a lower than market-rate

Type of Housing	Percent of Elderly Population	Comments
Ordinary Dwellings	83%	43% in flats; 56% in single-family houses
Pensioners' Dwellings	4%	
Collective Dwellings		
Sheltered Dwellings	6%	64% are over age 80
Service flats		
Nursing Homes	7%	1/3 of those over age 85 live in nursing homes
Long-term Care Centers, Hospitals	0%	

Where the Danish elderly live. (STATISTICS COMPILED FROM: MARCUSSEN, 1980; FRIIS, 1980; AMMUNDSEN, 1982; MATTHIESSEN, 1982; RAMIAN, 1982; PEDERSEN, 1982)

rent. An evolution of this idea has led to "collective dwellings," which provide a greater measure of central services, such as restaurants and laundry facilities.

Sheltered Dwellings

Sheltered dwellings share strong similarities with the English model of sheltered housing (see page 119). Danish sheltered dwellings are for pensioners who can manage on their own with the assistance of on-call staff and domestic help, but do not require placement in a nursing home. The apartments are complete with kitchens, although meals usually can be purchased at a common restaurant. Sheltered dwellings may be established as a small enclave or as part of a larger family housing development. Formerly this type of dwelling was referred to as a "service apartment," which was commonly combined into a facility with a nursing-home unit. This housing model still popularly exists as a care center, which combines sheltered dwellings, nursing-home units, and an activity center (day center).

A variation of the sheltered-dwelling scheme is a rural solution that combines six to twelve light service flats with a common lounge, kitchenette, laundry, and 24-hour emergency call system. The facility is staffed only by local home helpers and home nurses.

Nursing Homes

The overwhelming reform in housing care was the establishment of municipal control over the private nursing-home industry in 1964. Government reimbursement is made only to nursing homes established and run by the communities, to nonprofit organizations approved by the local authority, or to county councils (though county councils rarely get involved). A high degree of privacy and gracious space requirements, accompanied by competition among municipalities during the 1960s and 70s, have produced extremely high quality residential settings. Former old-age homes have disappeared in favor of sheltered dwellings and nursing homes. Also, geriatric hospitals do not exist in the Danish housing system because they are inconsistent with residential care, which respects privacy.

Nursing home standards are extremely high, requiring private rooms with a private toilet and bath. Rooms are a minimum of 162 square feet (15 sq m), and are commonly equipped with small refrigerators and hot plates. Residents are permitted to decorate their rooms and bring their own furniture (except for the bed). Nursing units commonly consist of 20 to 30 resident rooms with shared lounges and dining rooms.

Day nursing homes are becoming a new form of residential care. They provide either a temporary, intensive form of care for a few weeks or day care to those who can return home at night to a spouse or family.

Supportive Special-care Services

Municipalities are required to provide trained home helpers to pensioners requiring assistance with domestic work or personal care. In 1983, 26 percent of the elderly over 67 years of age received regular home help (75 percent of the elderly population receives one to six hours per week). Home helpers can do the laundry, shopping, mending, cooking, and cleaning, as well as provide assistance in bathing or hair washing. Home help is free to those with only the national old-age pension; those with more money pay on a sliding scale. Other home-help services include meal delivery, friendly visits, telephone checks, and special transportation.

Additional services and recreational activities are available at day centers. Day centers are established to "preserve and strengthen the capabilities of the aged," as well as to "put more life" into the retirement years. Physical health maintenance is stressed through exercise classes, physical therapy, and chiropody. Mental well-being is encouraged through a variety of educational and recreational settings such as hobby areas, game rooms, and restaurants. These facilities and programs vary greatly by community and are not always sponsored by the municipality. Social organizations, pensioners' groups, and voluntary organizations such as Ensomme Gamles Vaern (The Society for the Care of Lonely Old People) sponsor adult-education classes, organize trips to museums, and establish minimarkets in the form of kiosks in various housing facilities.

Supportive Medical Care

Home nursing has become a growing form of health care both for the elderly who live at home and for those living in independent settings such as pensioners' dwellings and sheltered dwellings. Home nurses are provided by the municipality to carry out specific medical treatment at home.

Home nursing has two positive effects. Consumption of medical services provided by hospitals and local practitioners is reduced; and an elderly individual can be maintained in a more independent setting.

Summary

Denmark's system of housing for the elderly is based on maximized independence in a normalized setting with respect for individual privacy. The unique concept of residential care in the Danish system is the reshaping of traditional long-term care into a model for housing rather than one for health care. The governmental structure allows for a comprehensive approach to care of the elderly through a system that integrates the many facets of living to an old age. Financial security, housing, housing assistance, home help, nursing care, and recreational services are all administered and coordinated by the local government.

The major difficulty with Denmark's system has been the impact of welfare issues on other required services. Denmark's thrust of maintaining the elderly at home has not kept pace with the creation of quality housing. Obviously policies that support living at home must make the home livable. Social services, such as home help and home nursing, must be linked with housing subsidies that improve older dwellings—particularly those in the urban areas of Copenhagen.

D-1
ORDRUP VAENGE

GENTOFTE, COPENHAGEN, DENMARK

TYPE OF HOUSING:	Collective dwellings
NUMBER OF UNITS:	48 efficiency apartments
ARCHITECT:	Ejlers and Graversen
BUILT:	1968
OWNER:	Municipality of Gentofte

Physical Description

The site is on the edge of the Gentofte business district in the northeast region of Copenhagen. The 48 "collective" living units are located across the street from two nursing-home buildings (see D-2) and a day care center (see D-3). The units are grouped into 4 clusters with 10 to 15 apartments in each. These single-story buildings have large sloping corrugated roofs with wood siding and small fenced garden court entrances. All four housing clusters enclose a small landscaped park. The site is extensively paved to provide fire-truck and automobile access. Much of the paving is made of paver blocks, which allows the grass to grow through while meeting the extensive, but unnecessary, parking requirements.

Residential Care

These apartments are part of a campus approach to care for the elderly. The built-up infrastructure provides access to meals and contact for staff without overobtrusive protection. Within the complex, a common dining room provides meals for those who choose to take them. The day care center (see D-3) is also available to the residents for various arts and crafts activities. The residents' independence is enhanced by the close proximity of the downtown shopping district. Services and goods are available for purchase from the community at large.

Apartments

The apartments are one-room efficiencies with an area for the bed and a small kitchen and bathroom. The major focus of each unit is the garden court. Its value can be measured by the tremendous amount of personalization and variety of plants provided by the residents. All apartments have large windows looking onto the private gardens, which face southwest or southeast—important criteria in this northern climate.

Commentary

These apartments represent an era in Danish care when efficiency apartments were considered adequate. The current thinking provides one-bedroom apartments for single elderly residents and two-bedroom apartments for couples. Although the apartments themselves are small, they are attractive and handsomely scaled. The apartment blocks step back between units to break the long, somewhat repetitive facades and the roof line.

The siting of these units across a narrow secondary street from the main nursing home allows the independent elderly residents to live their own lives away from the institutional setting but within the protective enclave of the amenities, services, and security that the institution offers.

Strengths

Residential scale, materials, and detailing.
Garden courts coupled with large windows extend the living area in these otherwise small apartments.
Location of these units on the edge of the Gentofte business district.

Each apartment has a private garden entry court. (PHOTO COURTESY OF EJLERS AND GRAVERSEN)

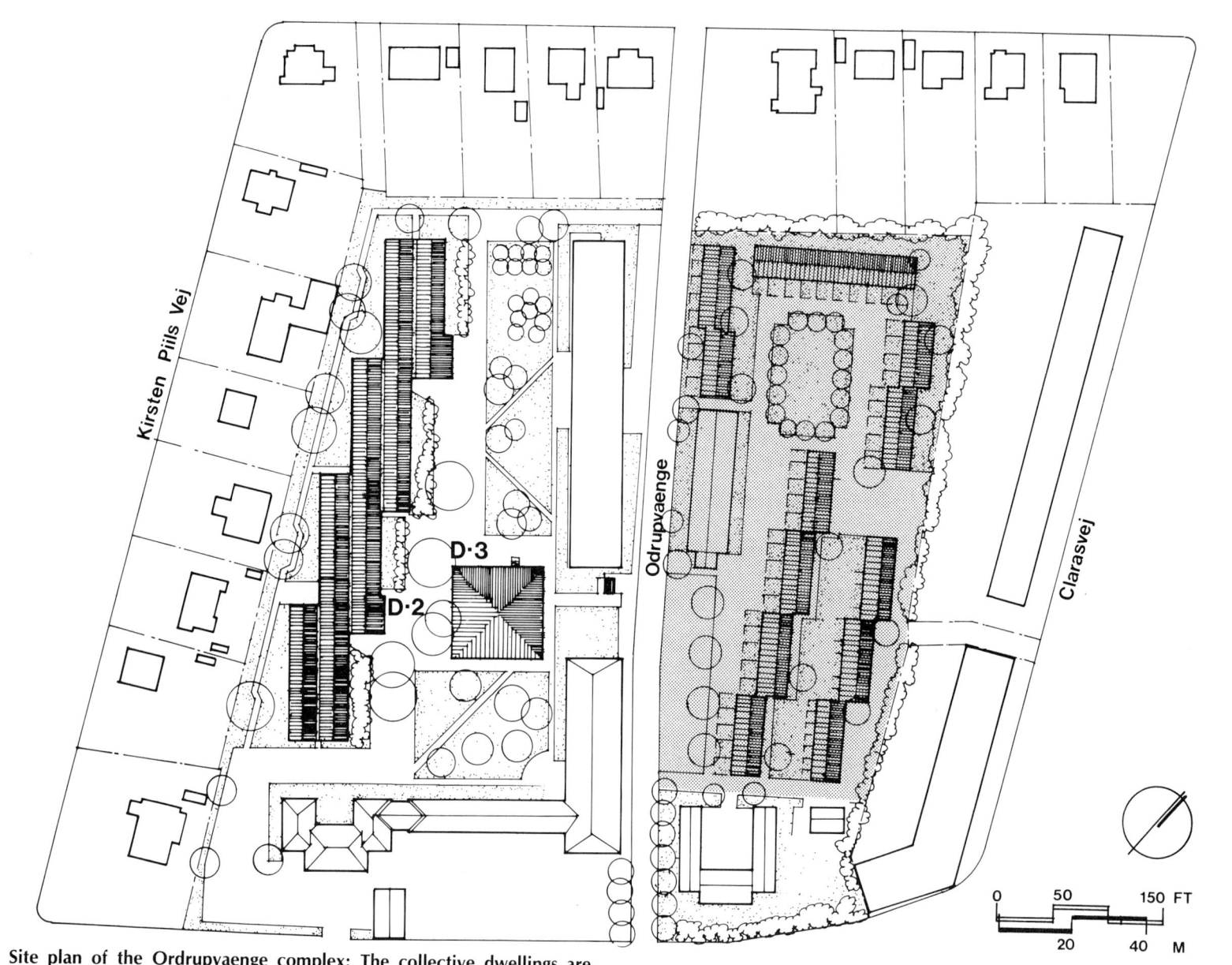

Site plan of the Ordrupvaenge complex: The collective dwellings are indicated by the shaded area.

84

The private garden areas are well utilized, and at times overgrown with large flowering bushes.

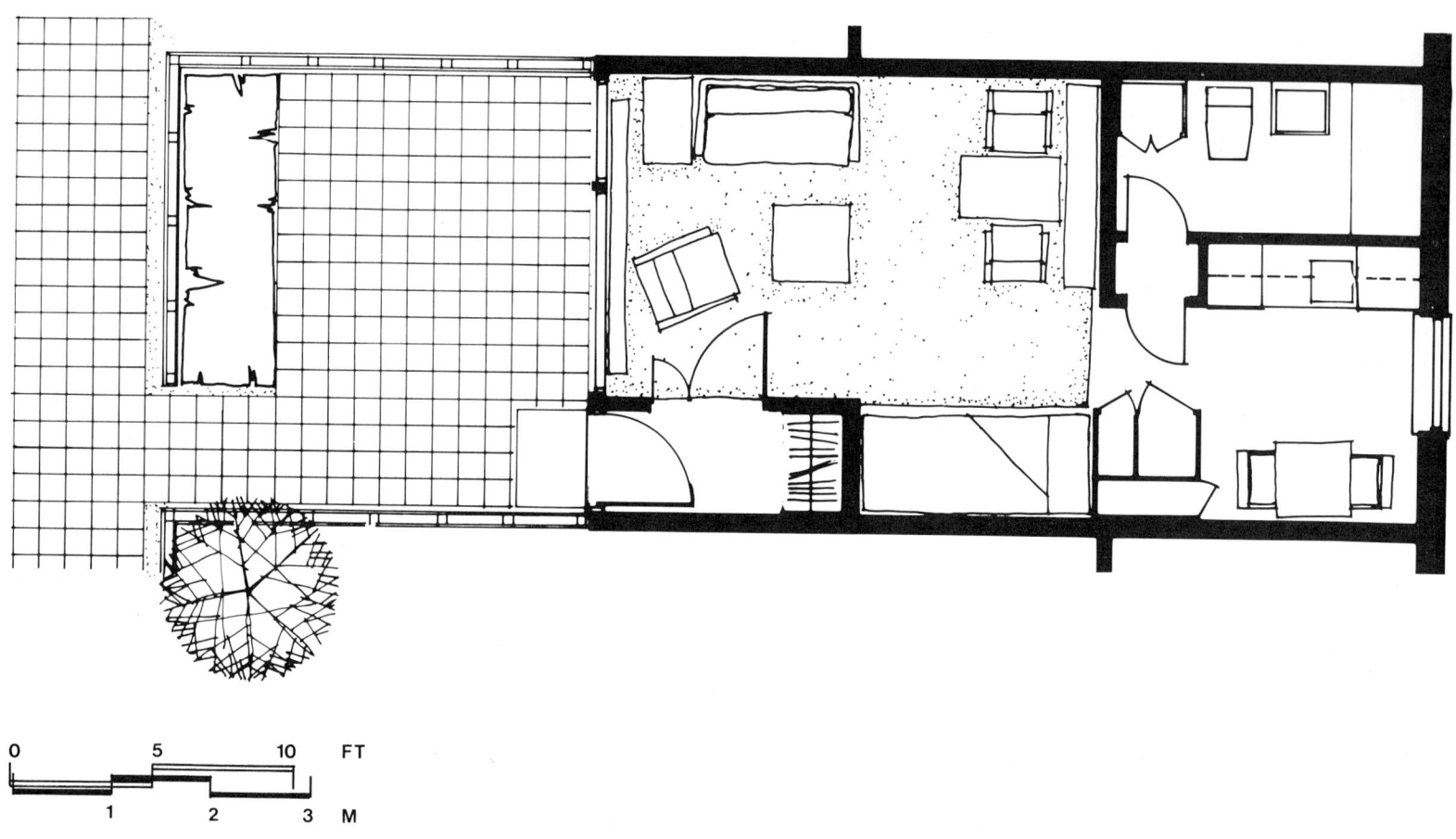

Typical apartment plan: The private garden entry court expands the private territory of the individual into the public zone.

The buildings enclose a private courtyard. The extensive paving provides vehicular access and parking. (PHOTO COURTESY OF EJLERS AND GRAVERSEN)

Clarity and hierarchy of public and private areas typically found in the private, detached home (for example, the private entrance, which serves as a buffer between public circulation and the semi-private living area of the house).

The layout of the typical unit allows the resident to shield the bathroom, kitchen, and sleeping areas from the view of guests at the entrance.

Weaknesses

The size of the apartments.

All apartment units are the same.

The residents are stranded in their apartments in inclement weather; no easy access exists to other apartments or to central facilities.

D-2

KØBENHAVN OG OMEGNS SYGEHJEM
(*Copenhagen and Omegns Nursing Home*)

ORDRUP VEJ, GENTOFTE, COPENHAGEN, DENMARK

TYPE OF HOUSING:	Nursing home
NUMBER OF UNITS:	48 single rooms
ARCHITECT:	Ejlers and Graversen
BUILT:	1976
OWNER:	København og Omegns Sygehjem

Physical Description

This one-story, 48-unit skilled-care nursing home shares an architectural vocabulary with Ordrup Vaenge (see D-1) located across the street. The site also has a day center (see D-3), administrative offices, and an additional nursing home built in the 1950s. The "campus" is linked by an underground system, which provides resident access and service delivery (food comes from a central kitchen). The rooms are grouped into two clusters of 24, with a shared dining room, living room, kitchen, laundry facility, and bathing room. The building is essentially one continuous double-loaded corridor, which steps back with common facilities at each break. The stepping enhances the scale and breaks the facade into smaller-scaled elements. The large sloping roof, gardens outside each room, and wood siding contribute to the residential image of the complex.

Residential Care

The design of this building is steeped in the Danish approach to normalization. The theory of normalization (adopted by the Danish government) stresses deinstitutionalization of health care. For the elderly, this means living in small groups, in a residential setting with a range of opportunities and activities similar to life's ordinary patterns (shopping, socialization, and so on).

The 48-room nursing home is broken down into two clusters of 24 each. This group of 24 is further broken down into two neighborhood wings of 12 with common facilities at the juncture between wings. Each resident has a private room with his or her own toilet, and a private patio and garden outside his or her room. Similar to recreational opportunities in the community at large, activities and therapy are provided in buildings that are not part of the residential environment. Residents have the opportunity to go downtown (two blocks away) with the assistance of staff or family.

Rooms

The private rooms are somewhat typical of Danish nursing-home rooms. The toilet is entered off a vestibule to the room, where there are built-in storage units. The room is spacious enough to permit personal furnishings for a small sitting area. A large window and a door onto the private garden and patio enhance the rooms.

Commentary

This project is a significant step in Denmark's approach to residential care for its frail elderly population. The approach to small nursing-home facilities (40 to 50 residents) dispersed in the community guarantees that residents can maintain neighborhood and family ties.

This project also represents a commitment to residential care rather than to a health care–oriented model. The scale, use of traditional residential building forms, and careful attention to detail reinforce the residential aspect. Incorporating small private gardens, a multitude of ways to enter and leave the buildings, and an unobtrusive nursing station minimize the feeling of being controlled and observed, promoting self-sufficiency, individuality, and privacy.

The building setbacks create a villagelike appearance, rather than a large institutional block. (PHOTO COURTESY OF EJLERS AND GRAVERSEN)

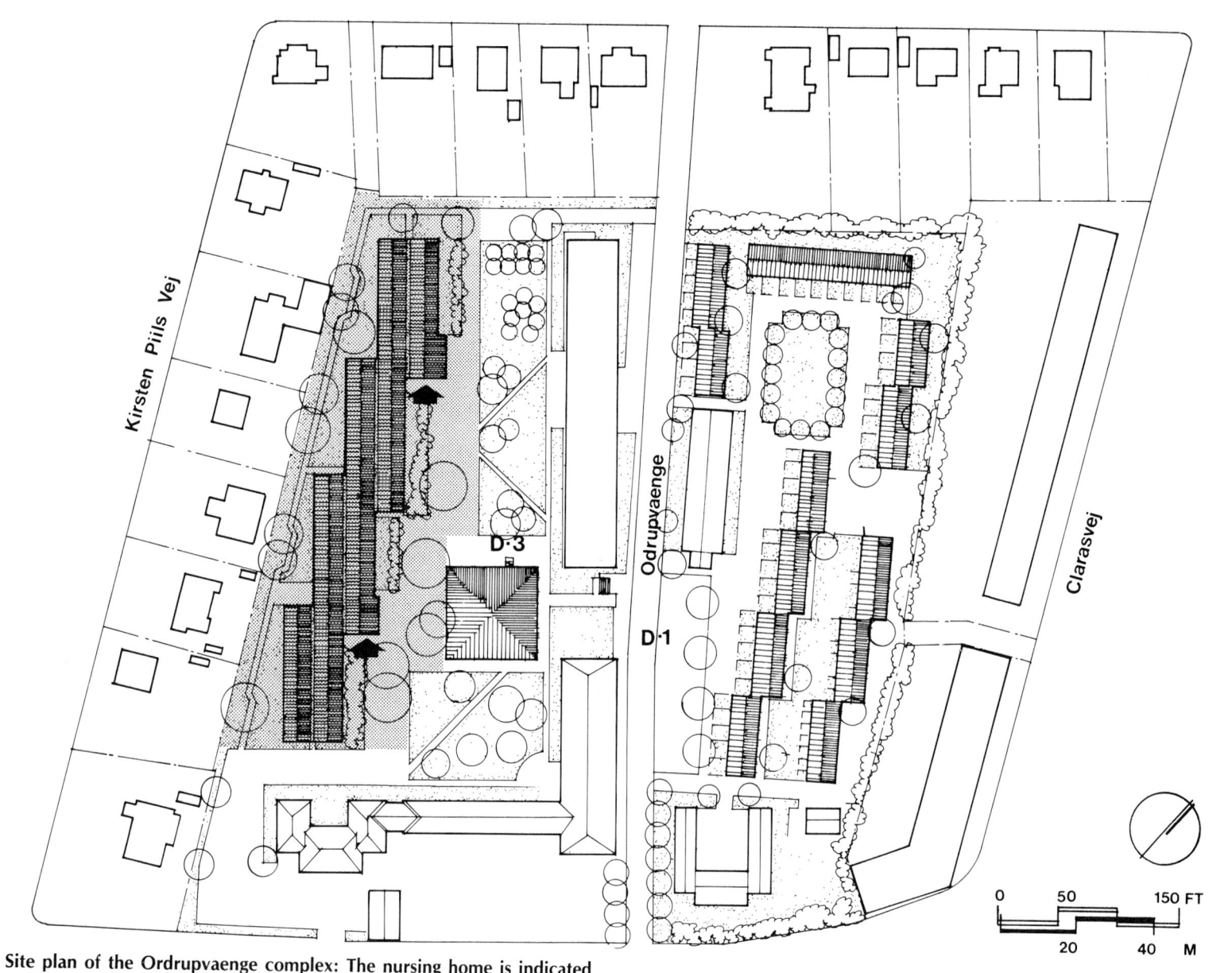

Site plan of the Ordrupvaenge complex: The nursing home is indicated by the shaded area.

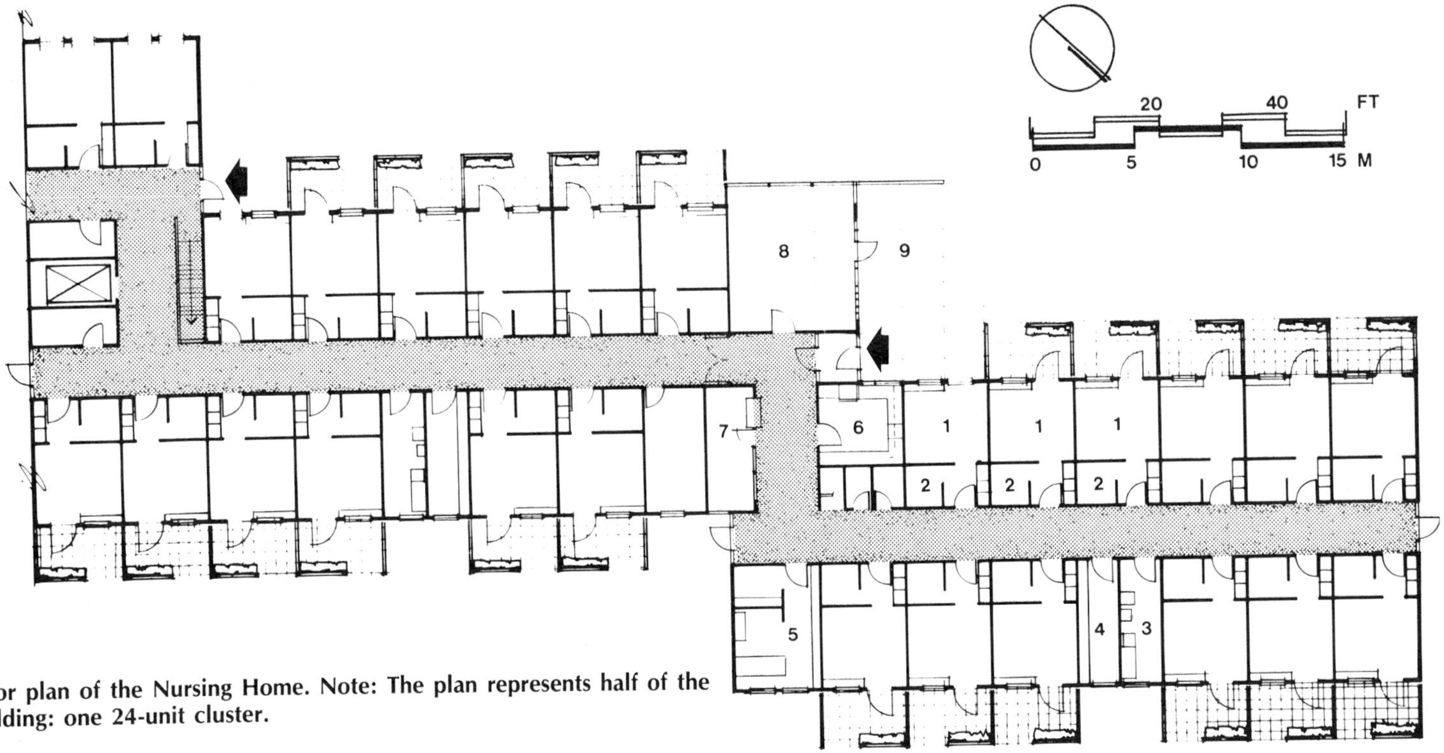

Floor plan of the Nursing Home. Note: The plan represents half of the building: one 24-unit cluster.

1. Private room
2. Private bathroom
3. Laundry room
4. Storage
5. Central bathing
6. Kitchenette
7. Nurse's station
8. Dining room
9. Terrace

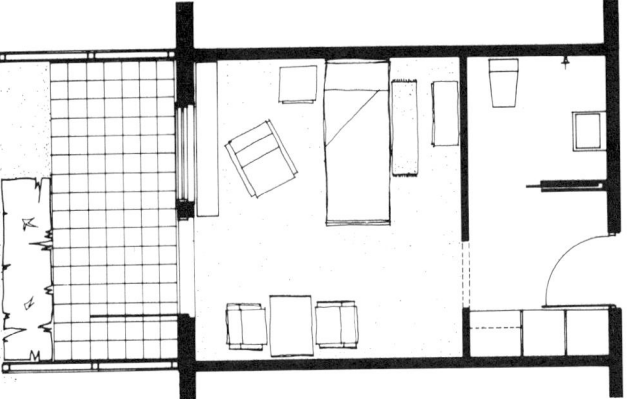

Typical resident room: Each resident has a private room, a private bath, a private terrace, and a door that can remain closed.

Each nursing-home resident has a private garden court. (PHOTO COURTESY OF EJLERS AND GRAVERSEN)

Strengths

Residential scale, materials, and detailing.
Private gardens for each resident.
The use of clustering to create smaller groups of residents. (Some facilities are shared by groups of 12 residents, others by groups of 24.)
The dispersal of nonresidential facilities gives residents a reason to leave their "home" and attend therapy or workshop activities elsewhere.

Weaknesses

The corridors are disappointingly similar and evenly modulated to create a repetitious pattern of doors.
The entrances and windows at the end of the corridors create glare, which is difficult for the elderly residents' eyes.
The smallest group (12 rooms) shares services but has no lounge or sitting room, which would formulate the basis of a smaller social grouping.

D-3
KØBENHAVN OG OMEGNS DAGCENTER
(*Copenhagen and Omegns Day Center*)

ORDRUP VEJ, GENTOFTE, COPENHAGEN, DENMARK

TYPE OF SERVICE:	Day care and therapy
ARCHITECT:	Ejlers and Graversen
BUILT:	1976
OWNER:	København og Omegns Sygehjem

Physical Description

This 3,600-square foot (335 sq m) day center is linked by an underground circulation system to the 1976 nursing home (see D-2) and an older nursing home on the same site. The building is a large open-plan square box wrapped in glass, with an exterior covered walkway on all four sides. The exterior appearance is in direct contrast to the residentially scaled housing buildings on the same site (see D-1 and D-2). Its appearance is one of a functional machine representative of other manufacturing and factory buildings around Denmark—a fitting prototype for a building that conducts workshop-type activities in metalwork, weaving, ceramics, and woodworking. It follows the theory of normalization by providing a place to live and a place to work.

Commentary

It is important to point out that, although adult day care in Scandinavia shares some similarities with American occupational therapy, the differences can be very striking. The Scandinavians have taken the concept of occupational therapy to a higher plane, committing resources and trained personnel. Danish adult day care is respectful of an individual's dignity—participants are not forced to paste paper doilies or make yarn puppy dogs to cover spare rolls of toilet paper. It is common to find wood- and metalworking shops fully equipped with power saws, drills, lathes, and sanders. The Copenhagen and Omegns Day Center also has traditional weaving looms (weaving is currently the most popular activity throughout Scandinavia) and sewing machines. Common products sold in the center's kiosk include baby clothes, bolts of weaving, and traditional Scandinavian wood toys.

Strengths

The open-plan flexibility allows the staff to accommodate new interests or activities of the residents.

The building form and appearance are consistent with its workshop activities inside.

The use of flexible task-lighting allows the user to maneuver the light as she or he needs it. Luxo-type lamps are used, as well as hanging counterbalanced lamps, which slide along a wooden rod attached to the ceiling.

Physical therapy is viewed as an activity rather than as a medical treatment.

The commitment of facilities, equipment, and staff to create a program that capitalizes on the users' abilities and talents while maintaining their dignity as adults.

Weaknesses

The built-in flexibility of the open plan does not spatially zone "clean" activities (sewing) from dirty ones (sanding wood), or quiet activities (weaving) from noisy ones (power drilling). This severely limits the number of activities that can be accommodated in what is essentially one space.

The building would have benefited from an exposure to the community edge as an interface on the business district. It is now rather insular and protected.

The day center responds to life's rhythms and patterns by providing a place to "work" that is different from the place one lives. (PHOTO COURTESY OF EJLERS AND GRAVERSEN)

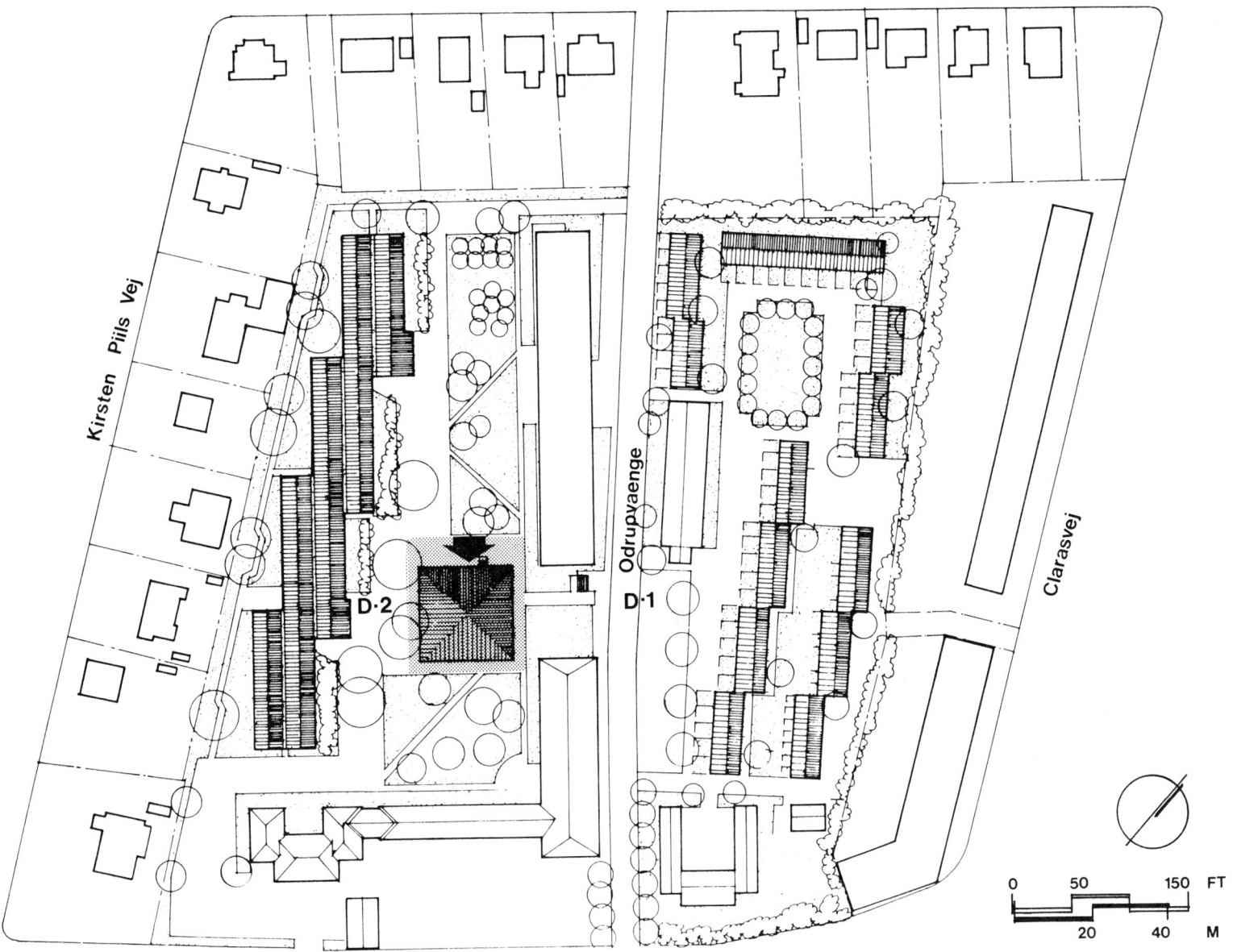

Site plan of the Ordrupvaenge complex: The day center is indicated by the shaded area.

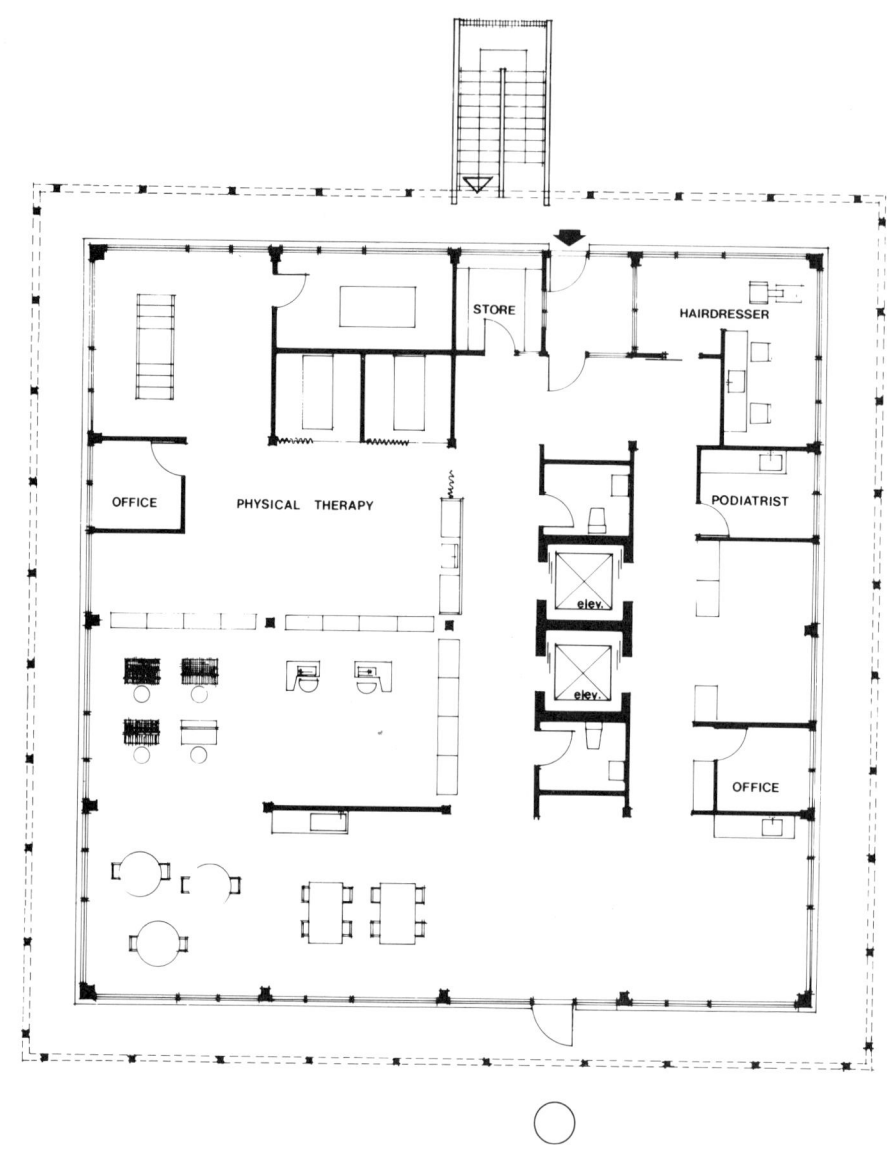
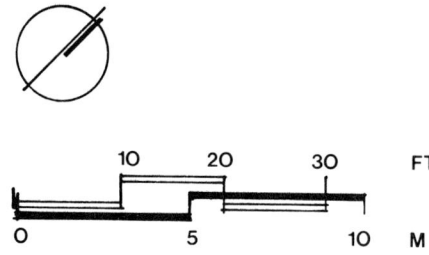

Floor plan of the day center.

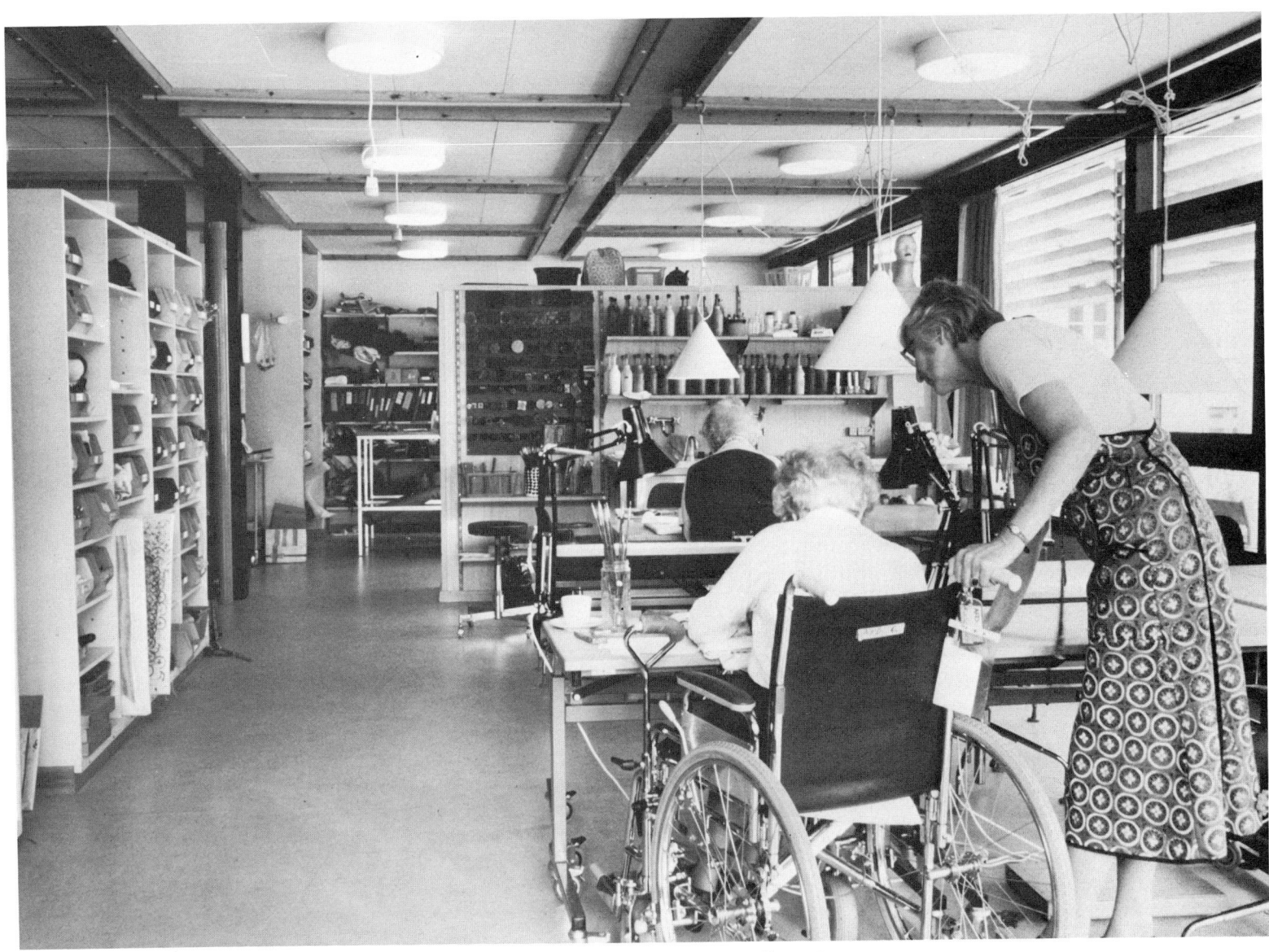

The day center is designed to be flexible for a variety of activities. Lighting is generally task specific and storage units provide spatial definition. (PHOTO COURTESY OF EJLERS AND GRAVERSEN)

D-4

OMSORGSCENTRET MØLLEGÅRDEN
(*Møllegården Care Center*)

GLADSAXE, COPENHAGEN, DENMARK

TYPE OF HOUSING:	Nursing home
	Sheltered dwellings
OTHER ELEMENTS:	Day center
NUMBER OF UNITS:	56 single rooms (nursing care)
	50 sheltered dwellings
ARCHITECT:	Ejlers and Graversen
BUILT:	1976–77
OWNER:	Municipality of Gladsaxe

Physical Description

Similar to the Gentofte campus (see D-1, D-2, and D-3), the Møllegården Care Center offers two levels of residential care through the nursing home and protected dwellings. The center also has a community day center. It is similar to any new planned community. Dispersed one- and two-story wood-clad buildings are arranged along a narrow winding road dotted with trees and bus shelters. This community for the elderly is nestled in an existing single-family area, adjacent to a major road.

The pedestrian street (originally a vehicular street until speeding traffic became a problem) links a series of green courtyards and parking areas to the existing fabric of the neighborhood. The road is used as a shortcut by children going to school and pedestrians going shopping.

The nursing home and the day center are separate two-story barnlike buildings, which are linked by a bridge and entrance. The sheltered dwellings are a series of one-story attached houses arranged around large green courtyards. All of the dwellings are linked by an enclosed circulation spine and underground tunnel to the day center.

The nursing-care portion of the center has 56 private rooms, which are arranged into a 28-room nursing unit on each floor. The group of 28 residents share a central lounge for programmed activities, and each residential cluster of 14 rooms shares a lounge/dining room.

The day center has a restaurant-style dining room with stage, central kitchen, and small meeting rooms on its ground floor. The upper floor has physical therapy and occupational therapy suites.

The 50 sheltered dwellings are one-bedroom apartments arranged around six courtyards. The apartments are wood-sided with large sloping corrugated roofs. The units can be entered through private terraces off the major courtyards or through the corridor at the back of the unit, which links it to all other units and the day center.

The buildings are constructed of a prefabricated concrete post-and-beam system with light infill panels clad with vertical wood siding. The roof and sunscreens are constructed of black corrugated transite.

Residential Care

The Møllegården Center addresses the continuum-of-care issue by offering three levels of service to its community. Those elderly individuals who can still remain at home but require occasional services are able to use the day center for therapies, meals, and socialization. Residents living in the sheltered dwellings require a variety of support services to maintain a challenging level of independence. Those residents too frail to maintain themselves in the independent setting are cared for in the nursing-home portion of the center. Placement in the nursing home is usually the sign of a weakening medical condition, since meals, house cleaning, shopping, and laundry services are all available to those living in the sheltered dwellings. The apartments are also linked to the nursing home by a call system for emergencies.

Apartments

All of the apartments are identical one-bedroom arrangements with a small living room, dining area, open kitchen, and bathroom. Each apartment has a private patio entrance off the major courtyard.

The pedestrian street winds through Møllegården and connects the "community" for the elderly with the community at large. (PHOTO COURTESY OF EJLERS AND GRAVERSEN)

Sheltered dwellings, each with a private garden court. (PHOTO COURTESY OF EJLERS AND GRAVERSEN)

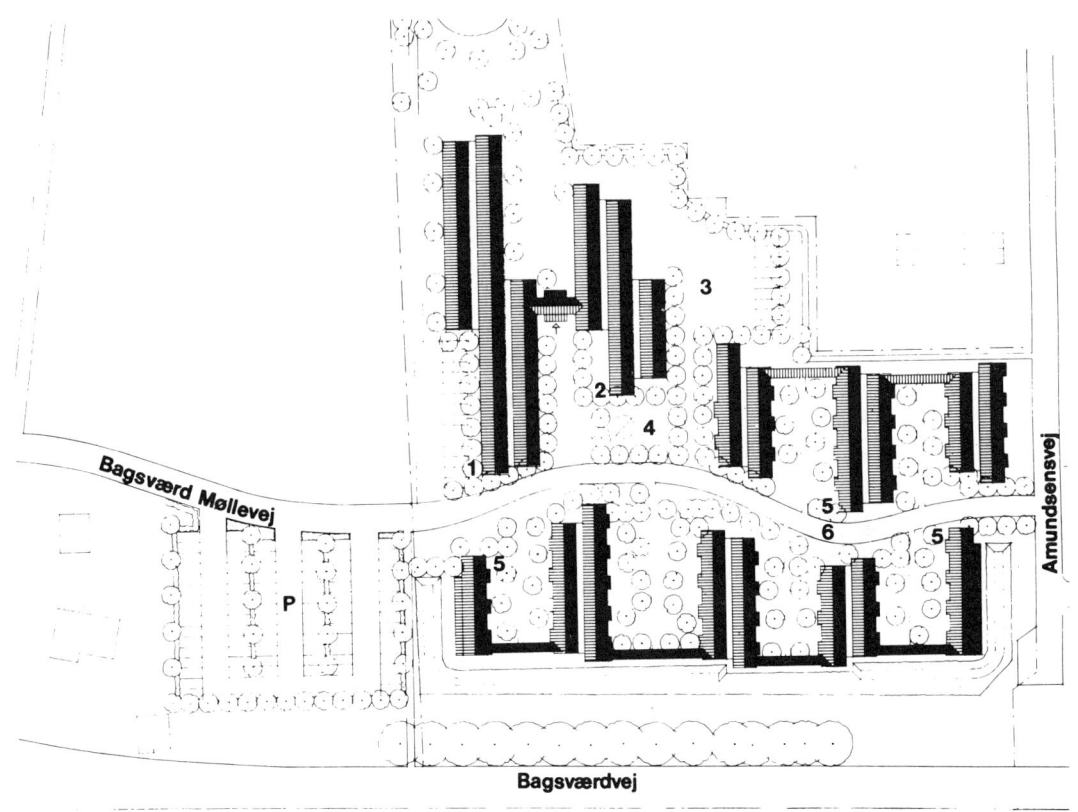

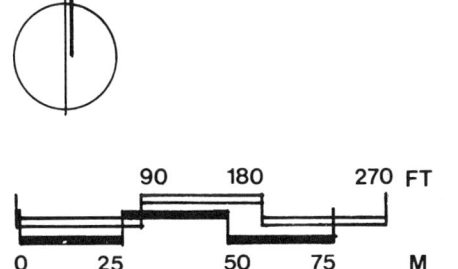

Site plan of Møllegården Center

1. Nursing home
2. Day center
3. Courtyard
4. Plaza
5. Sheltered dwellings
6. Pedestrian street

(COURTESY OF EJLERS AND GRAVERSEN)

Main entrance to the nursing home (left) and the day center (right).
(PHOTO COURTESY OF EJLERS AND GRAVERSEN)

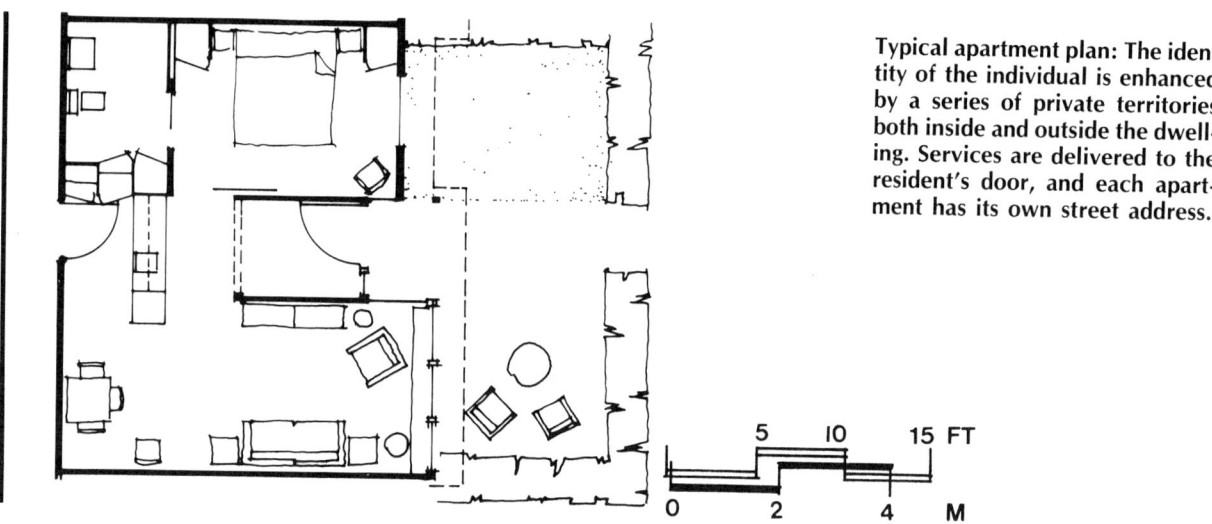

Typical apartment plan: The identity of the individual is enhanced by a series of private territories both inside and outside the dwelling. Services are delivered to the resident's door, and each apartment has its own street address.

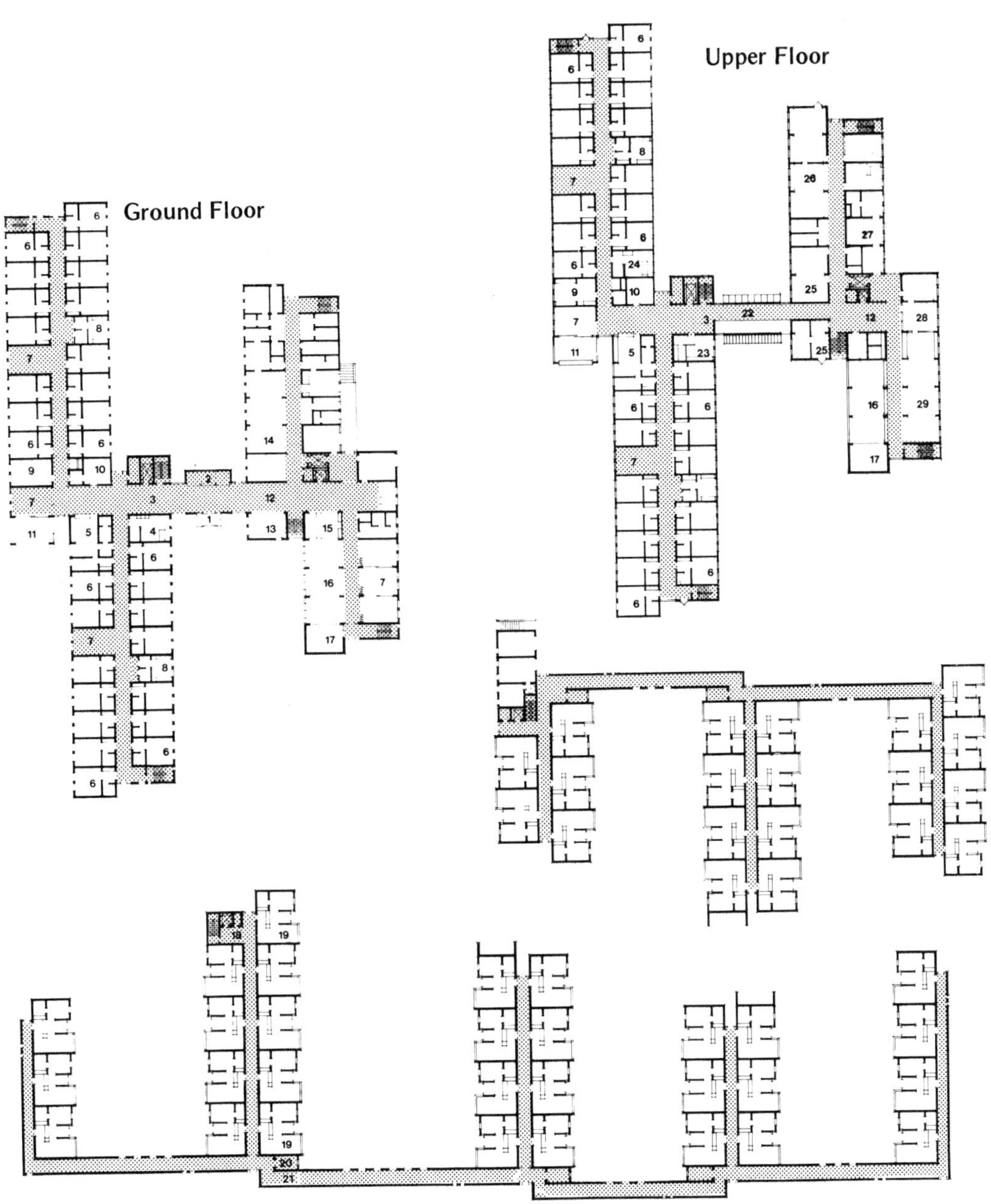

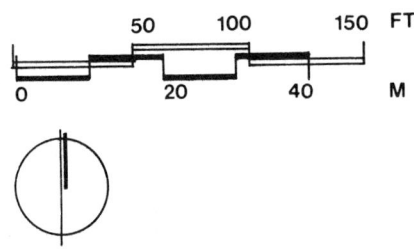

Floor plans of Møllegården Center.

1. Main entrance
2. Shop
3. Foyer of nursing home
4. Consultation room
5. Nurse's station
6. Private room
7. Living room
8. Staff workroom
9. Kitchen
10. Storage
11. Terrace
12. Foyer of day center
13. Sitting area
14. Central kitchen
15. Canteen kitchen
16. Dining room and activity space
17. Stage
18. Foyer
19. Sheltered dwelling
20. Office
21. Connecting corridor
22. The bridge
23. Hairdresser
24. Bathing
25. Administration
26. Physical therapy
27. Hand wash
28. Occupational therapy
29. Balcony/occupational therapy

(COURTESY OF EJLERS AND GRAVERSEN)

Soft lighting, beamed ceilings, and plants add to the residential character of the corridor linking the day center to the nursing home. (PHOTO COURTESY OF EJLERS AND GRAVERSEN)

The large living room window connects it with the garden and helps expand the sense of private territory. The entry vestibule is responsive to the extreme northern climate and provides a traditional Scandinavian energy-lock, or vestibule, entrance. The secondary entrance off the corridor opens into the kitchen area and is mainly a service entrance.

Nursing-care Rooms

The rooms are essentially the same as those in the Gentofte Nursing Home (see D-2). All rooms are singles, with private toilets and showers. The vestibule to each room has a wardrobe and a small tea kitchen so that residents can prepare their own snacks and tea or coffee. The ground-floor rooms all have small private terraces.

Adult Day Care

The program of this day care center is remarkably different from that of the Gentofte facility (see D-3). In the Møllegården Center the emphasis is not on producing craft items but rather on the restoration of independent living skills. The physical therapy suite assists nursing-home and independent dwellers in retaining or rehabilitating physical mobility and functioning. The ergotherapy suite conducts classes to develop independent living skills such as meal preparation, doing laundry, and other domestic activities. Classes may involve retraining stroke victims or teaching widowers to prepare their own meals. The goal is to encourage elderly residents to live as independently as possible.

Commentary

The complex achieves a villagelike appearance and has avoided institutional characterizations. The center has a masterfully designed series of public and private zones that mimic the "garden city" idea of small residential neighborhoods clustered around the town center. The street, while dividing the village, is also a unifying element that connects the center to the larger neighborhood. The public zone actually exists as a public zone for the community rather than as an internal street only for the elderly residents. The street becomes an area for mothers pushing babies in carriages or for children bicycling to school. The age-segregated community of Møllegården Center retains its protected enclave aspects while acknowledging that the residents are part of a larger social community.

Strengths

Residential scale and villagelike quality.

The public street connects the elderly, age-segregated community to the larger social community and residential fabric.

The juxtaposition of the most frail (nursing-home) elderly to the most active area of the center.

The gardens for the nursing-home rooms and apartments create small private outdoor territories.

Each apartment has its private main entrance to which mail is delivered.

Weaknesses

The apartment layouts have problems:

The bathroom is accessible only through the bedroom.

The kitchen is small, open to the living area, and difficult to screen from the view of guests.

An inordinate amount of living space is given up by having two doors at the entrance to each apartment.

The corridor that connects the apartments is a sterile, uninteresting pathway, which has become a storage area for wheelchairs and walkers. Also, the corridor is extremely long and circuitous.

D-5
RYGÅRDCENTRET (Rygård Center)

NIELS ANDERSENSVEJ 22, HELLERUP, DENMARK

TYPE OF HOUSING:	Nursing home
	Sheltered dwellings
	Day nursing home
OTHER ELEMENTS:	Day center
NUMBER OF UNITS:	32 single rooms (nursing home)
	54 sheltered dwellings
	8 beds (day nursing home)
ARCHITECT:	Ejlers and Graversen
BUILT:	1978–80
OWNER:	Municipality of Gentofte

Physical Description

The heart of this complex is two atrium buildings. The southern atrium is surrounded by the physical therapy and occupational therapy areas, as well as by a day nursing home for eight residents. This building is flanked by a series of two-story L-shaped components, which contain sheltered apartments. The northern atrium is surrounded by the community activity spaces—a large assembly hall, a dining room, and a central kitchen. This building is flanked by more sheltered dwellings and a 32-bed nursing home on the second floor. Linking these two atrium buildings and their "appendages" is a central lobby containing a library, fireplace, hairdresser, and reception area.

The 54 sheltered apartments—36 one-room (efficiencies) and 18 two-room (one-bedroom) apartments—are arranged in six two-story L-shaped buildings. Each cluster of nine apartments has an independent entrance and its own elevator. Two apartment clusters share a communal lounge, and are connected at the upper floor.

The apartments are arranged along a single-loaded corridor and look out toward the community. The L-shaped components create small courts typical of many multifamily apartment buildings. A system of paths circles the apartment wings and connects with the pedestrian circulation of the park and elementary school next door.

The 32-room nursing home consists of five wings, each with four to eight residents. The wings all open onto a common zone with a dining room, living room, and craft area overlooking the northern atrium. The nursing home has its own entrance (and address) with a large covered terrace above.

The buildings are planned and constructed on a ten-foot (3 m) module using cast-in-place concrete and load-bearing brick walls. The exterior is faced in yellow brick, with wood infill panels around the windows, wood balcony railings, and a yellow tile roof.

Residential Care

In an arrangement similar to the Møllegården center (see D-4), Rygård Center offers a continuum-of-care through three typical levels of service to its elderly community—sheltered dwellings, nursing home, and day-center activities (therapies, meals, and socialization). Rygård Center also offers a new level of residential care, the day nursing home, which attempts to delay institutionalization in a hospital or nursing home. Day nursing-home residents may be in need of a place to spend the day and receive extra care unavailable at home. Some day nursing-home residents are terminally ill and require a comfortable homelike environment rather than hospitalization.

Rygård Center is on the cutting edge of addressing the issue of integrating different levels of residential care. It integrates the frail and well elderly in the same building, but segregates them into separate zones, with their own facilities. One goal of the project was to economize on services by centralization under the same roof. A variety of inpatient and outpatient services can be provided by the same staff. The approach offers interesting opportunities for integration, but unfortunately the nursing home is isolated on the upper floor and shares no common circulation for spontaneous interaction between nursing-home residents and community visitors.

PHOTO COURTESY OF EJLERS AND GRAVERSEN.

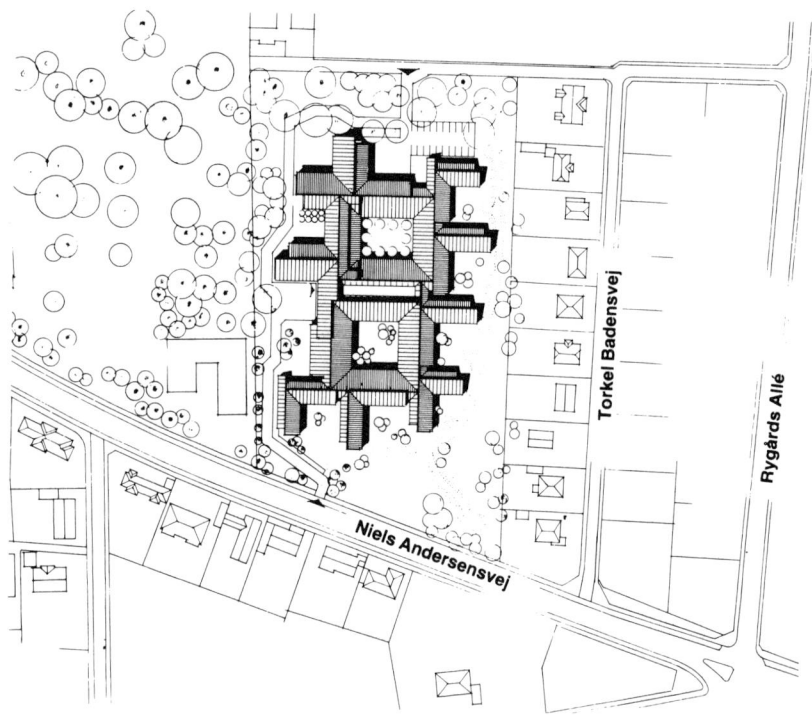

Site plan of Rygård center. (COURTESY OF EJLERS AND GRAVERSEN)

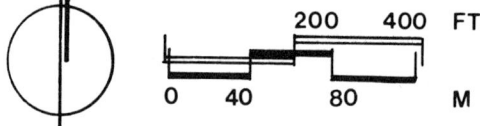

Apartments

The 54 sheltered dwellings consist of 36 one-room apartments for single persons and 18 two-room apartments for married couples or family members living together, which in all house 72 residents. This population is somewhat lower because of a reluctance to move residents. Spouses die, but the staff feels that this is not reason enough to relocate the resident; the dwelling is considered the resident's home as long as she or he wishes to live there.

The living portions of the two dwelling types are essentially the same. Each apartment has a grade-level terrace or balcony, which extends the living area. The kitchen consists of a wall-unit along one end of the living space with no definable eating area. The layout makes it very difficult to screen this area from the view of guests and visitors. The bathroom is located off the entry vestibule, placing it in a neutral zone accessible from either the private zone (bedroom) or public zone (living room). The entry vestibule is an important room in most Scandinavian homes; traditionally it becomes an area for display of personal items significant to the individual. Commonly a bureau or antique piece of furniture covered with photographs and knickknacks becomes a focal point on entering.

Nursing-home Rooms

The rooms, also referred to as one-room apartments, are similar to those reviewed in other Danish projects (see D-2, D-4). These rooms, however, lack the private outdoor space provided in the København og Omegns Sygehjem (see D-2). The rooms do have large windows looking out toward the community rather than into an interior court. Consistent with Danish policy, residents are free to furnish their own rooms (except for the bed) and decorate them as they wish.

Adult Day Care

The day care program places a strong emphasis on non–health care oriented activities. Day care is intended to provide opportunities for activity, socialization, and development of new or lost skills. No medical services are offered to community residents or on-site residents in the sheltered dwellings; they must maintain the use of their private doctors. For this reason the physical therapy suite (typically considered health care) is located at the center of the activity zone adjacent to the weaving rooms and off the main foyer. The space is a light-filled room with large windows opening onto the south courtyard.

The activity spaces, large meeting room, dining room, "fireplace

The corridor is softly lit and baffled from above with horizontal louvers. Interior spaces express the brick and concrete structure and have fine wood cabinetry and handrails. Floors are carpeted throughout.

room," library, hairdresser, chiropodist, and craft room are located along a main street, which is complete with sitting areas, plants, and directional signage.

Day Nursing Home

The day nursing home program has been in operation for only a few years, and is coming into its own. The original concept was to provide a noninstitutional setting for terminally ill patients who no longer need hospital care. The program, however, is under intense pressure to provide care for a growing segment of the elderly population in need of temporary extra care during the day. Young families find that they can no longer leave their parent or grandparent alone during the day while they are at work, or they may wish to take a vacation that their elderly family member cannot join in. The day nursing-home program fills this gap in services by providing a place for the resident to live for a few days, a week, or continuously, up to a month. This service prevents premature institutionalization and keeps family members at home in the community.

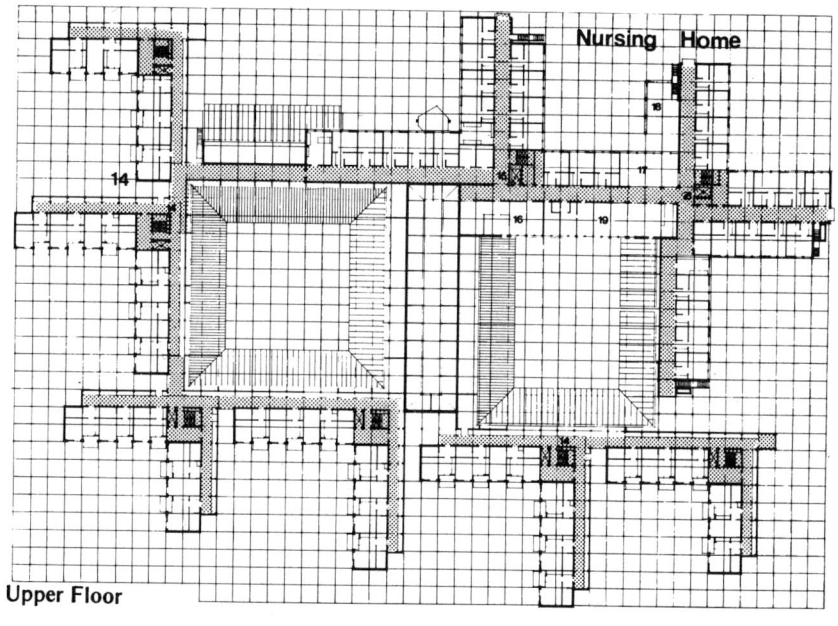
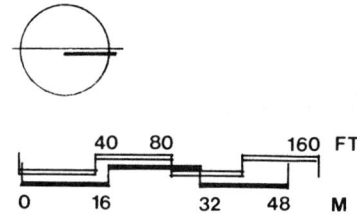
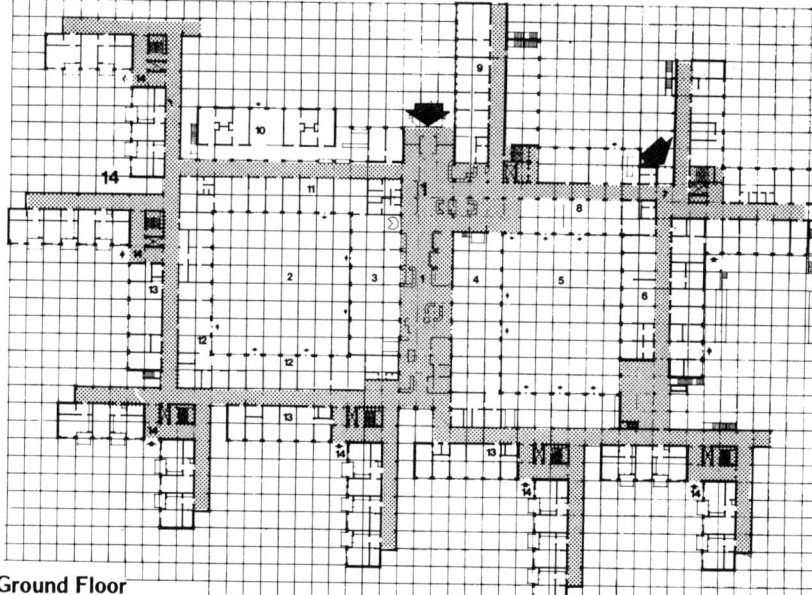

Floor plans of Rygård Center.

1. Foyer
2. South atrium
3. Occupational therapy
4. Large assembly space
5. North atrium
6. Kitchen
7. Foyer, nursing home
8. Dining room
9. Administration
10. Day and night nursing
11. Day home
12. Physical therapy
13. Communal area for 24 sheltered dwellings
14. Sheltered dwelling
15. Nursing home
16. Occupational therapy, sewing room, and TV room
17. Common lounge
18. Covered balcony
19. Dining room

(COURTESY OF EJLERS AND GRAVERSEN)

Detail plan of apartment buildings. (COURTESY OF EJLERS AND GRAVERSEN)

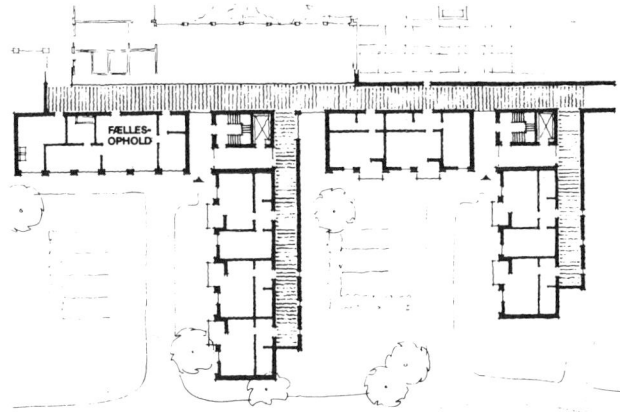

Typical apartment plans. (COURTESY OF EJLERS AND GRAVERSEN)

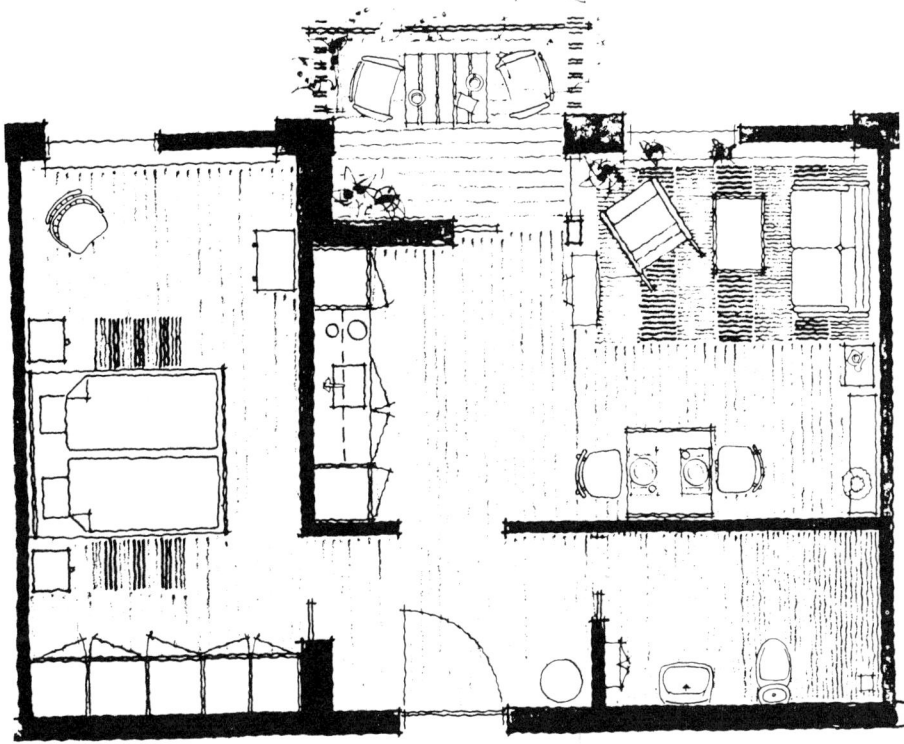

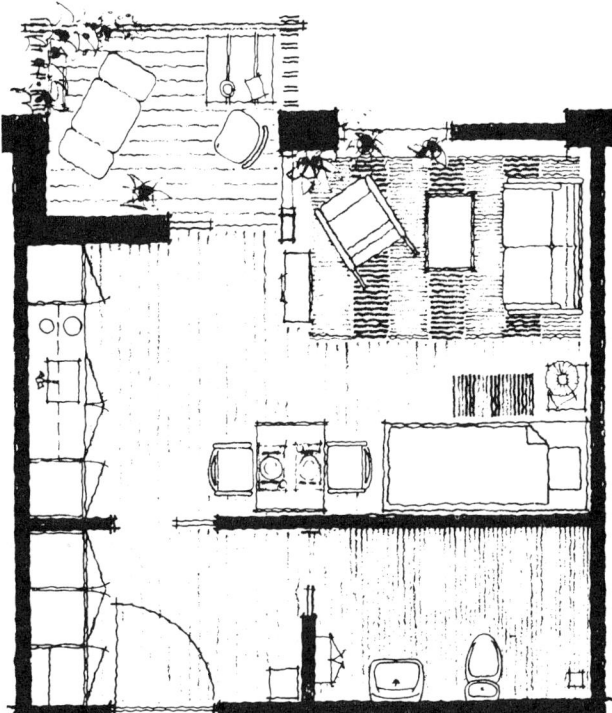

TWO-ROOM SCHEME

ONE-ROOM SCHEME

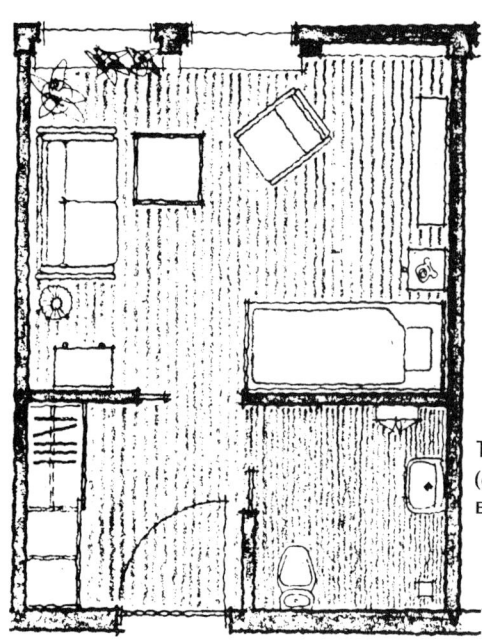

Typical nursing-home room. (COURTESY OF EJLERS AND GRAV-ERSEN)

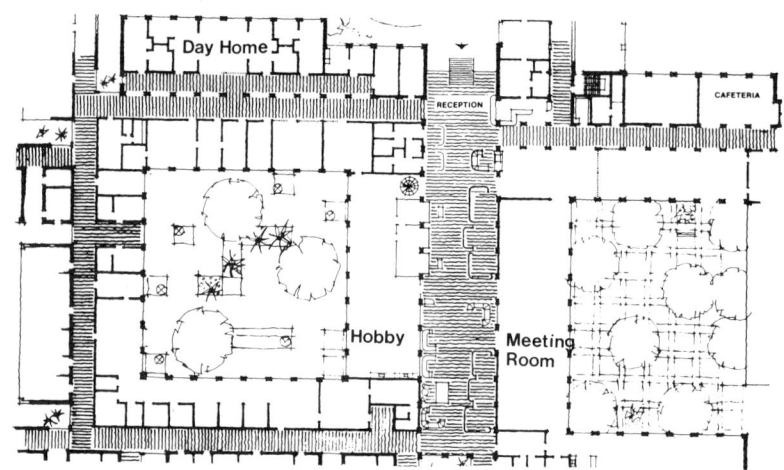

Detail plan of day center and day home. (COURTESY OF EJLERS AND GRAVERSEN)

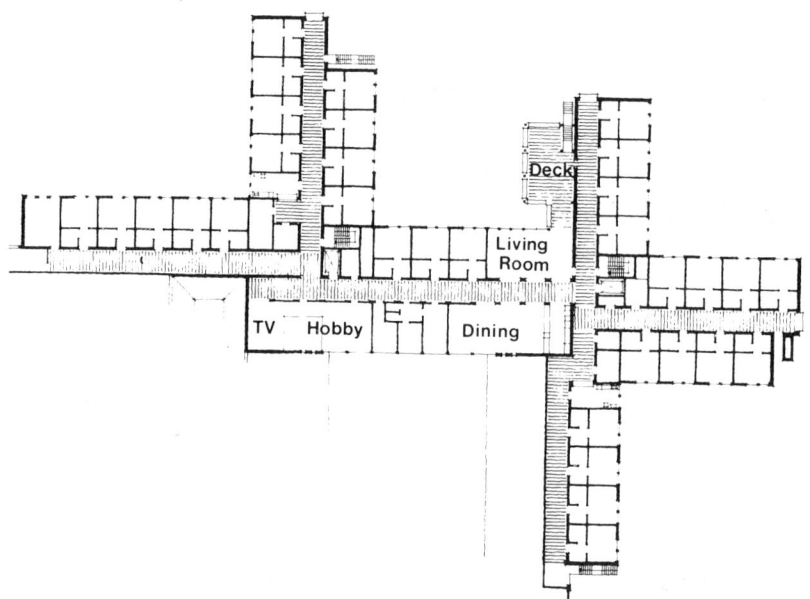

Detail plan of nursing home. (COURTESY OF EJLERS AND GRAVERSEN)

Commentary

Rygårdcentret takes the Møllegården center (see D-4) concept one step further by increasing the range of services and living arrangements. The diversity of residents—frail or well, short-term or long-term, community or in-house—under one roof implies a level of integration not often found in typical campus approaches or life-care communities. In actual operation, however, there may actually be more segregation than originally intended. There is a very careful hierarchy of private and public territories for the protected dwelling clusters, nursing home and day nursing home program. There may be too many zones for residents to withdraw and set up peer groups that exclude sick, disabled, confused, or terminally ill residents from their own peer groups. In fact, one could live within the complex and use its services without ever encountering any of the other user groups. It is an extremely interesting approach to the integration versus segregation issue. There is the clear choice of involvement or withdrawal; nothing is forced and no one is ma-

112 HOUSING FOR THE ELDERLY

Occupational therapy room. (PHOTO COURTESY OF EJLERS AND GRAVERSEN)

nipulated by the environment. It will be interesting to monitor this project to see whether the facility enhances a quiet acceptance of individual differences among its residents or creates a group of polarized individuals living independent lives.

Strengths

Residentially scaled complex created with small building components and traditional residential materials.

Innovative approach to integration of frail and well elderly.

The day nursing home program provides extra care for community residents when short-term support delays institutionalization.

The facility's location in a residential area next to an elementary school and a town park—and its linkage to these by a system of paths.

The use of natural light.

The variety of textures and colors, which act as cues in the environment.

The diversity and quality of spaces that were derived from a modular grid, which could have led to banal, repetitive elements.

The site development and landscaping are handled well. (Paver blocks let the grass grow through to conceal parking areas.)

Weaknesses

The kitchen is too prominent, located along one wall.

The nursing-care unit is isolated on the second floor away from the major activity zones.

The entry is hidden and rather difficult to find for the pedestrian visitor.

Detail of housing units. (PHOTO COURTESY OF EJLERS AND GRAVERSEN)

6 GREAT BRITAIN

Great Britain has a population of 55.7 million, 14 percent of whom are over the age of 65. The life expectancy (men: 70 years; women: 76 years) of British citizens is lower than that of Scandinavians, but higher than that of Americans. A portion of the newly retired population has settled in the warmer, often seaside climates along the English Channel.

British support for the elderly has never been as far-reaching as have Danish and Swedish policies. However, recent changes in pension benefits, expanded social services, and sheltered housing schemes signal new dimensions in care of the aged in Britain. New Town developments in Great Britain have also offered innovative sheltered-housing schemes integrated into the neighborhoods. Unlike the Scandinavian countries, volunteer activity and social philanthropy have played an important role in service provision for the elderly. Private enterprises have also had a strong role in supplying housing.

THE GOVERNMENT

Great Britain is governed by a parliamentary system with a sovereign head. The executive officers, who form the government, are chosen from legislators in the parliament. This cabinet of ministers, which is headed by the prime minister, is responsible for the administration of the country. Great Britain has no written constitution that defines the relationships between different political institutions and levels of government; custom and precedent have produced the existing relationships.

There are 25 governmental departments, each headed by a cabinet minister. Two of these departments, The Department of the Environment (DOE) and the Department of Health and Social Security (DHSS), are directly responsible for setting policy and directives for care of the elderly. DOE's primary responsibility is housing and the appropriation of funds. DHSS directs the social service and health authorities that provide home help, home health care, technical aids, and institutional accommodations.

The central government provides economic security through various pension arrangements. Local government is responsible for shouldering the provision of basic public services such as housing, health care, education, and care of the aged. Local government is a broad term for a complicated system of local authorities that have varying responsibilities based on their size. The Greater London

form, although now they are often supported by industry and trade unions. Private support for the elderly has bridged the gap between government support and the actual demand for housing services. Volunteer organizations, such as the Abbeyfield Society, have offered distinctive housing opportunities for the elderly.

Social assistance has always been an important part of British care. Social insurance, which is primarily a twentieth-century creation, started with the State Retirement Pension (1908) and the contributory pension schemes in 1925. A comprehensive system of social care was formalized in 1948 in conjunction with the National Health Service. This legislation, as well as the 1966 Social Security Act, formalized the provision of insurance as a responsibility of central government and assistance as the role of local authorities.

Central government has had the responsibility of directing policy through the various health and social service departments. Philosophical approaches to care of the elderly have been disseminated through DOE Housing Circulars and DHSS White Papers. A recent Department of Health and Social Security (DHSS) publication outlined three important goals of care for the elderly:

1. To ensure that retirement does not mean poverty.
2. To keep old people active and independent in their own homes.
3. To let the elderly make their own decisions about their own lives.

DHSS, 1978

Council, The London borough councils, the county borough councils, the administrative county metropolitan councils, and the district councils, are all local governmental units that provide different services for the aged.

As with Sweden and Denmark, financial security, good housing, supportive social services, and health care play important roles in care of the elderly in Great Britain.

Financial Security

The state retirement pension scheme was started in 1908, but was not formalized into an insurance program until 1948. Various pension and social security programs were consolidated in 1966, and in 1974–75 pensions became index linked and payment levels were raised 30 percent. Other earnings-related changes were made to

CARE OF THE ELDERLY

Care of the elderly in Great Britain grew out of a tradition of seventeenth-century almshouses established by monasteries for the elderly, the infirm, and the poor. Almshouses still exist in an altered

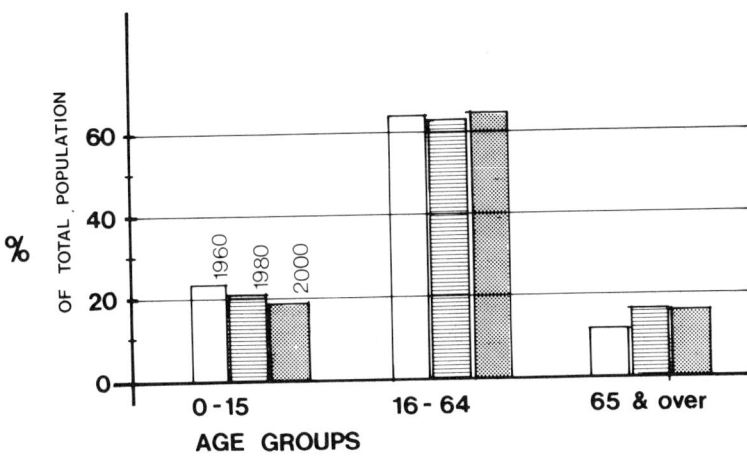

British population structure.

the pension system in 1978, but it will be twenty years before the new pension system is fully operational.

The pension system in Great Britain relies on a financial partnership between the state retirement pension plan and private occupational pension schemes. A 1978 study (DHSS, 1981) of elderly households found that only 47 percent of the weekly income came from social security benefits (23 percent private pensions, annuities, investments; 23 percent wages, salaries, and self-employment; 7 percent other sources).

The State Pension

The state pension system provides a basic weekly retirement pension at age 65 for men and age 60 for women. Other supplemental pensions, grant allowances, and benefits are available:

1. State retirement pension
2. Supplementary pension
3. Additional benefits: attendance allowance, mobility allowance, invalidity care allowance, Christmas bonus

The state pension plan is an entitlement program that requires contributions into the system. The weekly payment in 1984 was £35.80 (US$47.25) (based on £1 = US$1.32) for single persons and married women who earned their own contributions; married couple rates were £57.30 (US$75.64). The supplementary pension scheme is paid to those with insufficient resources from the state retirement pension and other schemes to cover their basic needs. The British pension system is not supportive of partial retirement; major reductions in benefits preclude many retirees from part-time work during the first five years of retirement (earning limits of £70 per week).

Additional payments are made for special housing, heating, and emergencies. House payments are proportional to the actual housing costs, and allowances are made to those unable to pay fuel bills. Special benefits for the disabled provide for attendants to assist with daily living, as well as funds to adapt existing housing.

Private Occupational Pensions

Approximately half the work force receives occupational pensions in addition to the state retirement plan. Most of the occupational pensions are related to the individual's most recent salary. Problems arise because schemes vary widely in their benefits (only some are protected from inflation), and occupational pensions can be lost when individuals change jobs before retirement.

Housing

Great Britain operates primarily from custom and tradition. Evolutionary changes are slow; new approaches in housing for the elderly are adopted sporadically and unevenly across the country. The housing categories reflect a mixture of current housing schemes and early twentieth-century models. The quality and quantity of housing for the elderly vary greatly by location and are dependent on the strength of the local housing authority. Britain is proud that 90 percent of the elderly population live outside a "sheltered" setting.

Housing associations and private and volunteer organizations play a role in providing housing. These groups provide approximately

Type of Housing	Percent of Elderly Population	Comments
Ordinary Dwellings: Houses, Bungalows	76%	59% own their own residence or rent privately. 38% "rent" from public
Purpose-built Flats	12%	
Converted Flats		
Old People's Accommodation without Warden	3%	
Sheltered Housing (Old People's Accommodation with Warden)	5%	
Almshouses	½%	
Residential Homes	2½%	35% are over age 85 on admission
Geriatric Hospitals Nursing Homes	1%	

Where the British elderly live (STATISTICS COMPILED FROM: DHSS, 1978; DHSS, 1981; FOX, 1981)

15 percent of the required places in residential homes. Many of these groups provide places for former employees of a particular firm, while others provide places for elderly individuals supported by local authorities. Organizations such as the Abbeyfield Society purchase old homes and convert them into familylike units for six to eight elderly residents and a housekeeper.

Local housing authorities are currently providing the majority of the purpose-built housing for elderly and physically disabled residents. Sheltered housing schemes have become the most recognized form of British housing for the elderly. Sheltered housing, which began in the early 1960s, has become a main thrust of most housing authorities.

Ordinary Dwellings

Ordinary dwellings include a variety of housing settings not controlled by housing authorities (although 12 percent of the pensioners receive rent assistance). Single-family homes, flats in multifamily buildings, and bungalows are common forms. Bungalows were a popular "old people's accommodation" built on large housing estates at the beginning of the twentieth century. Some New Towns have developed one-bedroom flats that can be allocated to pensioners or young couples.

Housing studies in Great Britain have found that the elderly who rent private dwellings have the worst housing conditions. The 1981 Department of Environment study on housing found that 20 percent of private renters had an outdoor toilet. This study also found that 27 percent of all households in Great Britain are headed by people over age 65. Of these households, 39 percent of the homes required rehabilitation and 54 percent lacked major amenities. In addition to rent assistance, energy costs are subsidized by grants that are available to pensioners.

Flats (Converted and Purpose-Built) and Old People's Accommodations without "Wardens"

Organizations such as the Abbeyfield Society and Age Concern supplement the independent housing stock provided by the local housing authorities. Housing associations and volunteer organizations operate a variety of independent settings such as small hostels, and purpose-built flats. Other schemes include the "granny flat," "mobility housing," and "wheelchair housing."

Typical characteristics include small-scale developments, adaptation of existing housing stock, and conversion of large houses into hostels and dormitorylike settings. Residents are expected to care for themselves and lead independent lives. Abbeyfield homes, for instance, usually consist of six to eight bed/sitting rooms with a shared dining room, kitchen, parlor, and bathrooms. Abbeyfield homes have a housekeeper who prepares two meals a day during the week and provides a measure of companionship.

Mobility housing and wheelchair housing include flats that maintain the elderly in noninstitutional settings in the community.

The goal of mobility housing is to convert the houses and flats of the disabled elderly, so that they remain in their own homes among their friends and family. The granny flat (or annex) is a private-sector solution that provides independent flats attached to single-family houses. The original concept was for families to provide care for their aged relatives.

Sheltered Housing

Sheltered housing, in its most basic form, is a grouping of 28 to 35 dwellings for the elderly, with a supervising "warden." Sheltered housing schemes provide a varied range of amenities but are usually not considered to be a resource-rich type of accommodation for the elderly. DOE publications in the early 1960s led to the formulation of the concept, and in 1969 DOE circular 82/69 detailed specific design criteria as part of a comprehensive housing policy for the aged. This circular also outlined two types of sheltered housing: Category I, which was "to accommodate one or two people of the more active kind," and Category II, which was "to meet the needs of less active elderly people" (Fox, 1981). Category II was originally envisioned as having bed/sitting rooms with shared bathrooms, communal lounges, and laundry facilities. Common practice, however, has been to provide all residents of both types with a one-bedroom apartment of approximately 360 to 525 square feet (34 to 48 sq m). Category I housing would typically not include a common lounge and might not include elevator service for a two-story facility. Category II schemes require central laundry facilities and a shared activity room, as well as an enclosed corridor and elevator service to connect all flats.

Category I and II have become artificial distinctions. Category I schemes have common activity rooms and elevators. The residents of both types are very similar in their ages, degree of physical mobility, and level of activity. The concept was for residents of Category I to move to Category II when they became less mobile, then on to residential homes when they required more care, and eventually into a nursing home or geriatric hospital. This has not proven to be the pattern. Residents are very comfortable in their homes and are unwilling to move into schemes that limit their independence. This continuum-of-care hierarchy also requires residents to make major moves when they may be least able to cope with them. Increasing pressure requires wardens, who are primarily service/management oriented, to become caretakers for residents with debilitating physical conditions.

The result has been that some housing authorities are examining linked schemes with residential homes (Category III). Category II½, "very sheltered housing," is a new concept, which provides a higher ratio of management to residents. Concern exists that there is really no difference between very sheltered housing and residential homes. Also, the development of another level of care does not remove the need for residents to relocate to different facilities.

Sheltered housing is an important type of housing for the aged because it stresses independence and self-sufficiency. Derek Fox, a former Advisor on Housing Management to the Secretary of State for the Environment, notes the following successes of sheltered housing.

1. providing old persons with housing specifically designed to take account of their needs, capabilities, and limitations, free of the frustrations many experience in normal housing in a nonsheltered environment;
2. freeing elderly people from worries like "what's going to happen to me if I'm ill, or fall?" and giving them greater opportunities to live independently longer in life—often until the end of life itself;
3. encouraging easy social intercourse with elderly people of similar interests, and generally improving the quality of their lives.

DEREK FOX, 1981

Almshouses and Residential Homes

Residential homes provide care for the elderly who are unable to care completely for themselves in the community. Residents may be disabled or "confused," but they do not require hospital-type care. Some residential homes are very similar to American nursing homes without the emphasis on medical care.

Residential homes are commonly resource-rich, with many common facilities for personal care and meals. Residents have small private rooms (although they may share bathrooms) with a recommended minimum of 110 square feet (10 sq m). Residential homes are limited to a maximum of 50 rooms to avoid large institutional settings.

Almost half the residential homes are provided by private and voluntary organizations. Some trade unions provide these homes for former employees. Homes operated by private groups must be registered with the local housing authority, which reviews their facilities, staff, and general operation.

Nursing Homes and Geriatric Hospitals

Approximately 50,000 hospital and nursing-home beds are occupied by pensioners—25 percent of all hospital beds are used daily by those over 65. Commonly a coupling of physical difficulties or illness with mental confusion makes residential placement in traditional British settings difficult. The result is that residential care has been divided from more intensive long-term care. This is particularly true of mental infirmity that includes abusive and wandering behavior, which cannot be handled in sheltered housing or residential homes. Private and voluntary hospitals and nursing homes provide half of the long-term care beds.

Supportive Special-care Services

The range of British social services is as extensive as that found in other countries; however, the coverage of the elderly population does not compare to the Scandinavian countries. About 9 percent of the elderly receive home-help assistance each year. Programs include Meals-on-Wheels, laundry service, cleaning, and technical aids for daily living. Social centers in the community offer meal programs, advice, and socialization opportunities. The development of social centers is inconsistent from community to community, but about 10 percent of the pensioners attend day centers at least once per week.

Supportive Medical Care

Medical health care is provided through the National Health Service. Family doctors and general practitioners provide primary health care through office visits or home visits (two-thirds of all home visits are for those over age 75). District nurses provide follow-up health care, information, and referrals, as well as advice for families caring for an elderly relative at home. Visiting dental and chiropody services can also be arranged. Approximately 12 percent of the pensioners are visited by a district nurse during the year.

"Short-stay" residences (day hospitals) have become increasingly important for pensioners who need a place to recuperate following a hospital stay. Residential homes have begun to set places aside for use by local residents. Residential homes have also begun to share communal facilities with pensioners who require a day care program. Short-stay and day care accommodations are an important part of maintaining the elderly in the community by providing support for families caring for older relatives.

Summary

British care of the aged follows the Scandinavian pattern of decentralized government, with responsibility belonging to the local authority. The difficulty, however, is the lack of a cohesive national policy to direct local government in providing services, such as housing. The quantity and quality of housing vary among communities, and it is often supplemented by private housing associations that follow different policies.

British sheltered housing has been internationally recognized for the high-quality housing that it affords independent pensioners. In practice, sheltered housing is really a term for a variety of accommodations that have evolved differently from the way in which they were conceptualized. Concepts such as Category I and Category II sheltered housing conflict with the natural aging process and deny residents the opportunity to live the rest of their years in one home. As the facility ages, so does the average age of the residents. With increasing age, additional measures of care, prostheses in the environment, and supportive services are required. Plans that do not provide housing for the elderly with elevators lack forethought. Initially, residents may need elevators only from time to time, but with advancing age they may become a constant necessity.

E-1

SPRINGFIELD COURT

MILTON KEYNES, ENGLAND

TYPE OF HOUSING:	Sheltered housing (Category II)
NUMBER OF UNITS:	26 sheltered apartments
ARCHITECT:	Milton Keynes Development Corporation Central Area (CSMK Division)
BUILT:	1977–78
OWNER:	County Council

Physical Description

Springfield Court is one of several sheltered housing schemes in the New Town of Milton Keynes (see also E-2).

Springfield Court is located in a neighborhood of attached dwellings at the center of a "grid square," which adjoins an activity center and small convenience store. The L-shaped building contains 26 apartments on one floor, with a warden's apartment at the apex of the two wings. The common lounge and library form the internal angle of the L and look out across a terraced garden court. The simple, almost drab, brick exterior with corrugated tile roof belies the excitement of the interior.

The highlight of this project is the circulation space, which uses an internal street concept. Large planters are situated in front of each apartment with large skylights to daylight the "street" and plants. White stucco walls and dark tile floors enhance the street concept. Each apartment has a front stoop complete with porch light, mailbox, and milk-bottle shelf.

Residential Care

Sheltered housing in Great Britain has long been regarded as an innovative housing concept for the independent elderly. A current refinement of British housing policy has led to the development of Category I and Category II housing. Programmatically they are very similar. Category I housing typically has no communal space, elevators, or common hallways. Category II housing provides more supervision, although both housing schemes have on-site residences for the warden. The original concept was that Category II residents would be more frail and in need of more supervision. In actuality, it has become a difficult policy issue. As residents age they become more frail—Category I residents become Category II with no desire to move, and debilitating physical conditions confine active Category I residents to their second-floor apartments with no elevator service to the ground floor.

Springfield Court is considered to be a Category II sheltered housing scheme. It provides a shared community room, and all apartments are connected by an enclosed, heated corridor. The warden is responsible for providing supervision, companionship, and emergency medical assistance. All residents prepare their own meals and are responsible for their own laundry and housekeeping (unless they arrange for special home-help service). Each apartment is linked to the warden's apartment by an emergency call system.

Apartments

The apartments are somewhat conventional in layout; all are typical one-bedroom arrangements. The innovative features result from the architect's exploration of the concept of privacy and of the internal street.

Each apartment has a private stoop at the front door recessed off the internal public street. The garden planter at each apartment entrance enhances and reinforces the semipublic zone of the street. The apartments also have a private garden/sitting area off the living room, which is defined by low brick walls. The forced open plan of a small apartment usually leads to an overly exposed kitchen, but in Springfield Court the architect created a low wall screening the kitchen from the view of people seated in the living room. The kitchen also has a skylight and a window over the sink, which looks onto the street.

Each apartment has a landscaped terrace.

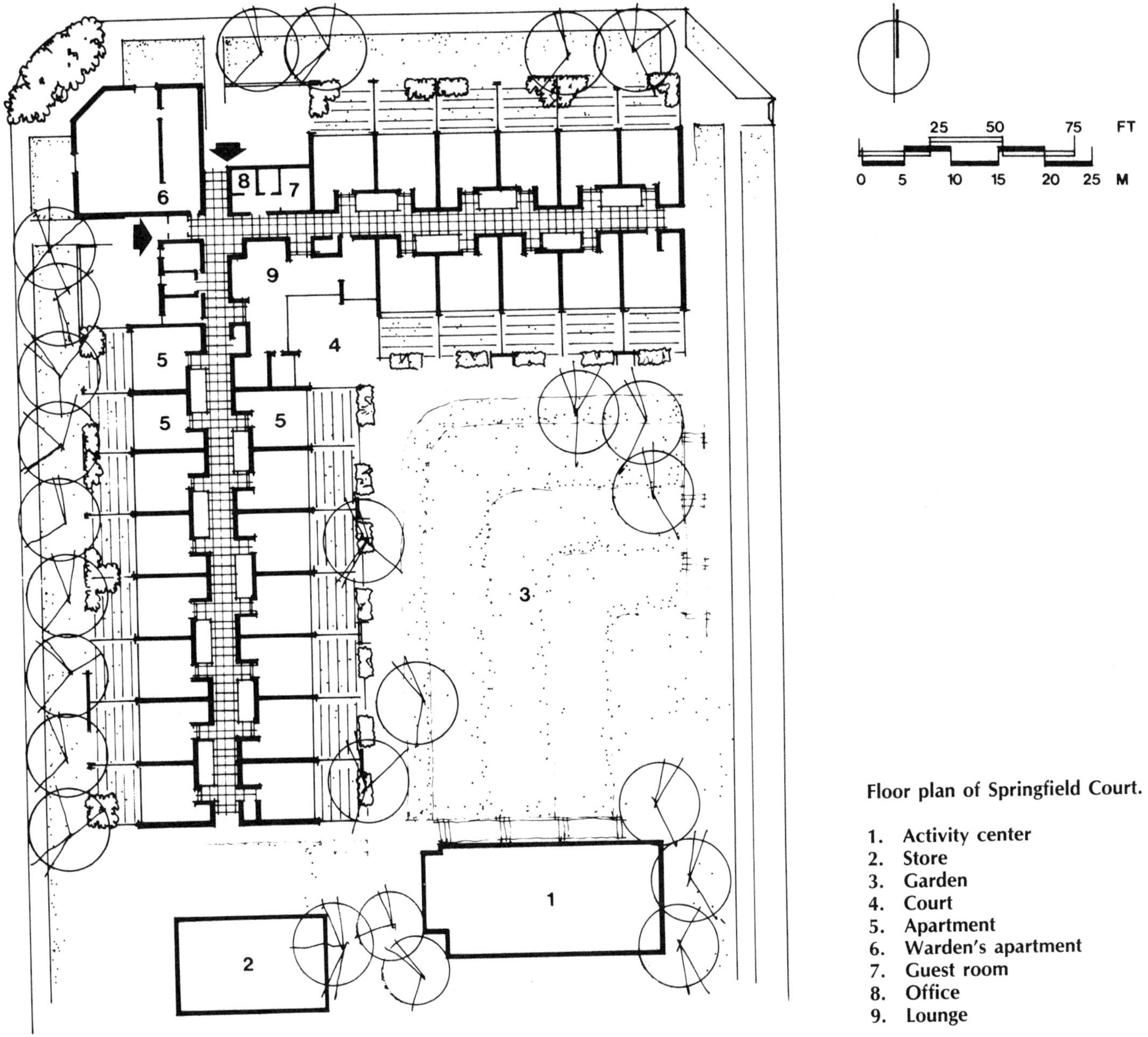

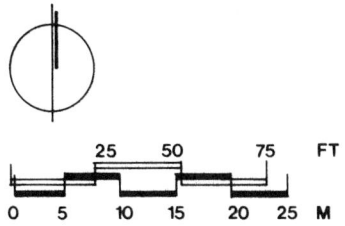

Floor plan of Springfield Court.

1. Activity center
2. Store
3. Garden
4. Court
5. Apartment
6. Warden's apartment
7. Guest room
8. Office
9. Lounge

Springfield Court is built into a hillside at the center of a residential neighborhood. The convenience store is at the forefront in the photo.

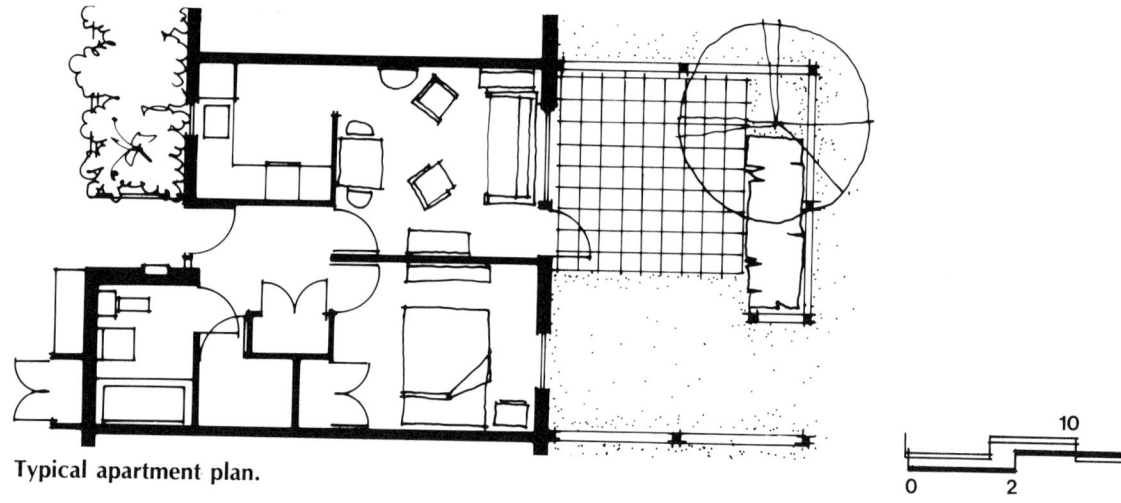

Typical apartment plan.

Commentary

The corridor as a street concept in apartment buildings is not new. It has been successful in some cases and sadly inappropriate in others (for example, Pruitt Igoe, in St. Louis). Springfield Court includes features characteristic of a residentially scaled neighborhood street—front stoops, gardens, porch lights, natural (overhead) light, kitchen windows, doorbells, milk boxes, and doors with sidelights—in an entirely appropriate setting: a single-level housing scheme for elderly residents in a cold northern climate. Whether the street concept encourages socialization among residents remains to be seen, but it provides the opportunity for such activity in a delightfully pleasant space.

Strengths

The street concept strengthens the corridor as a "place" and enhances the building's residential qualities for independent living.

Careful attention to residential detail, which breaks down the institutional quality of congregate housing.

Location in the midst of a residential area that is adjacent to local shopping.

Quality and richness of landscaping both externally and internally.

Weaknesses

Site perimeter has a steep incline, which decreases accessibility.

The warden's apartment has a Big Brother appearance, controlling the major building entrances at the apex of the two wings (the apartment entrance is also elevated—creating a sense of domination and limiting access).

The kitchen window that looks onto the street is very small and too high for most residents to see out of.

The front stoop along the interior street—complete with welcome mat, milk box, porch light, house number, doorbell, and planter.

E-2
CARPENTER HALL

MILTON KEYNES, ENGLAND

TYPE OF HOUSING:	Sheltered housing (Category II)
NUMBER OF UNITS:	29 sheltered apartments
ARCHITECT:	Milton Keynes Development Corporation
BUILT:	1978–79
OWNER:	County Council

Physical Description

Carpenter Hall is located along a footpath between a small neighborhood park and the village green, which contains several shops and a pub. This two-story, L-shaped building encloses a residential court that abuts the city footpath. Activity spaces and the warden's apartment are located at one end of the L near the main building entrance. The paved parking court provides a common entrance zone for other multifamily housing. The exterior is a rather stark, unadorned brick box with square window openings and underdeveloped landscaping.

The interiors have a warm, playful quality that comes from the use of a variety of materials, textures, and lighting. The architects have explored the concept of the corridor as a street and interpreted it in a different way from Springfield Court (see E-1). The corridor wall consists of traditional exterior materials (brick and wood-paneled doors), with narrow recesses to delineate front stoops at the entrance to each apartment. A combination of central storage closets (for refuse, milk bottles, and newspapers) and wood benches creates a variegated and interesting corridor. The residents seem to like the stoops and benches, personalizing them with plants, flowers, and name plates.

Residential Care

Carpenter Hall is considered a sheltered-housing Category II scheme (see E-1, Residential Care, for an explanation of Categories I and II). The building, however, deviates from a typical Category II in that it does not provide elevator service to the second floor. Although the residents are independent enough to live unassisted in their own apartments, their physical condition is such that elevator service may be required constantly or intermittently. Segregating disabled people on the first floor may be an immediate solution to economize construction costs but may prove an expensive operational issue.

Commentary

Sheltered housing schemes offer elderly residents the opportunity to live in age-integrated neighborhoods but to live privately in the company of their peers. Carpenter Hall is a good example of a building located among multifamily housing without identifying itself as special. Residents are guaranteed their privacy without the stigma of an institutional setting.

Strengths

Location in a residential setting near the village center.
The corridor is used to define semipublic zones at apartment entrances.
Site development provides a variety of spaces for individuals and small groups.
The meeting room is planned as a special (somewhat remote) place for common activities rather than as a central lounge in the middle of the building (which tends to be more institutional).

Weaknesses

The lack of access to the second floor for people unable to climb stairs.
The warden's apartment appears to dominate the main entrance in an authoritarian manner.

The landscaped court abuts the city footpath. A trellis-covered walkway provides a shaded path.

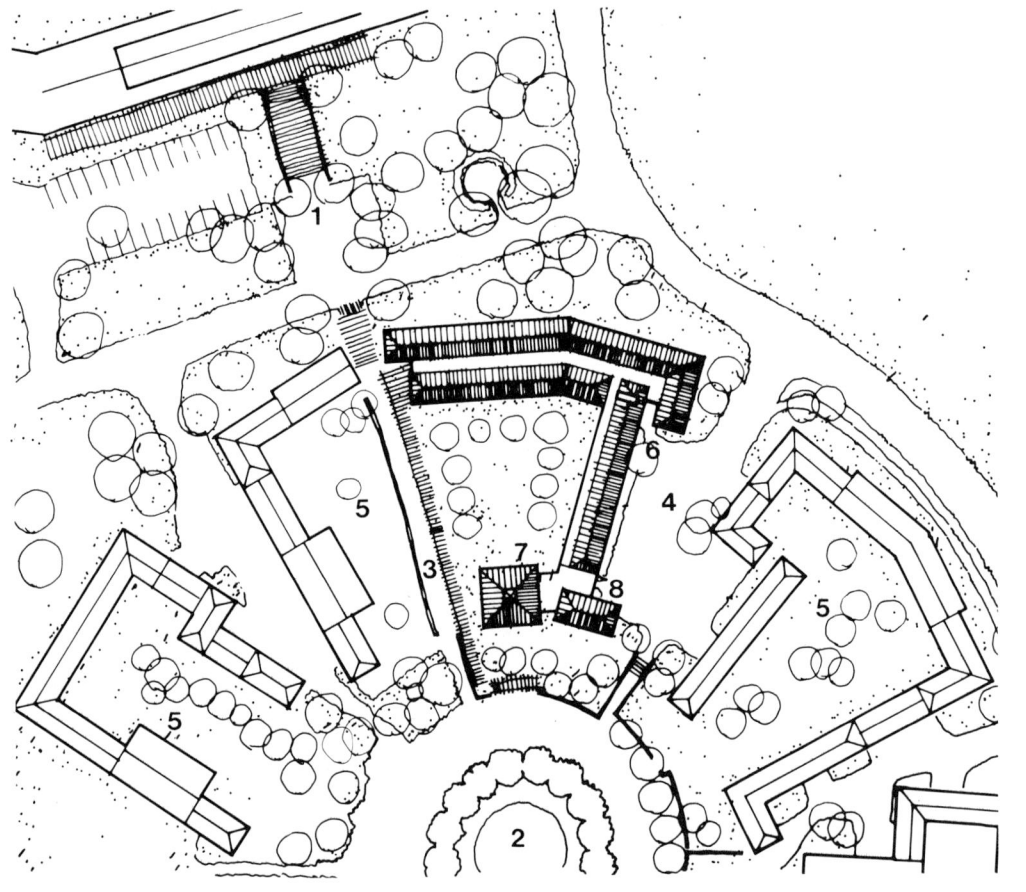
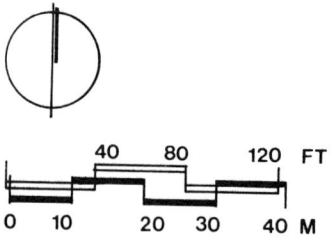

Site plan of Carpenter Hall.

1. The Village Green
2. Neighborhood park
3. Footpath
4. Parking court
5. Multi-family housing
6. Sheltered dwellings
7. Lounge
8. Warden's apartment

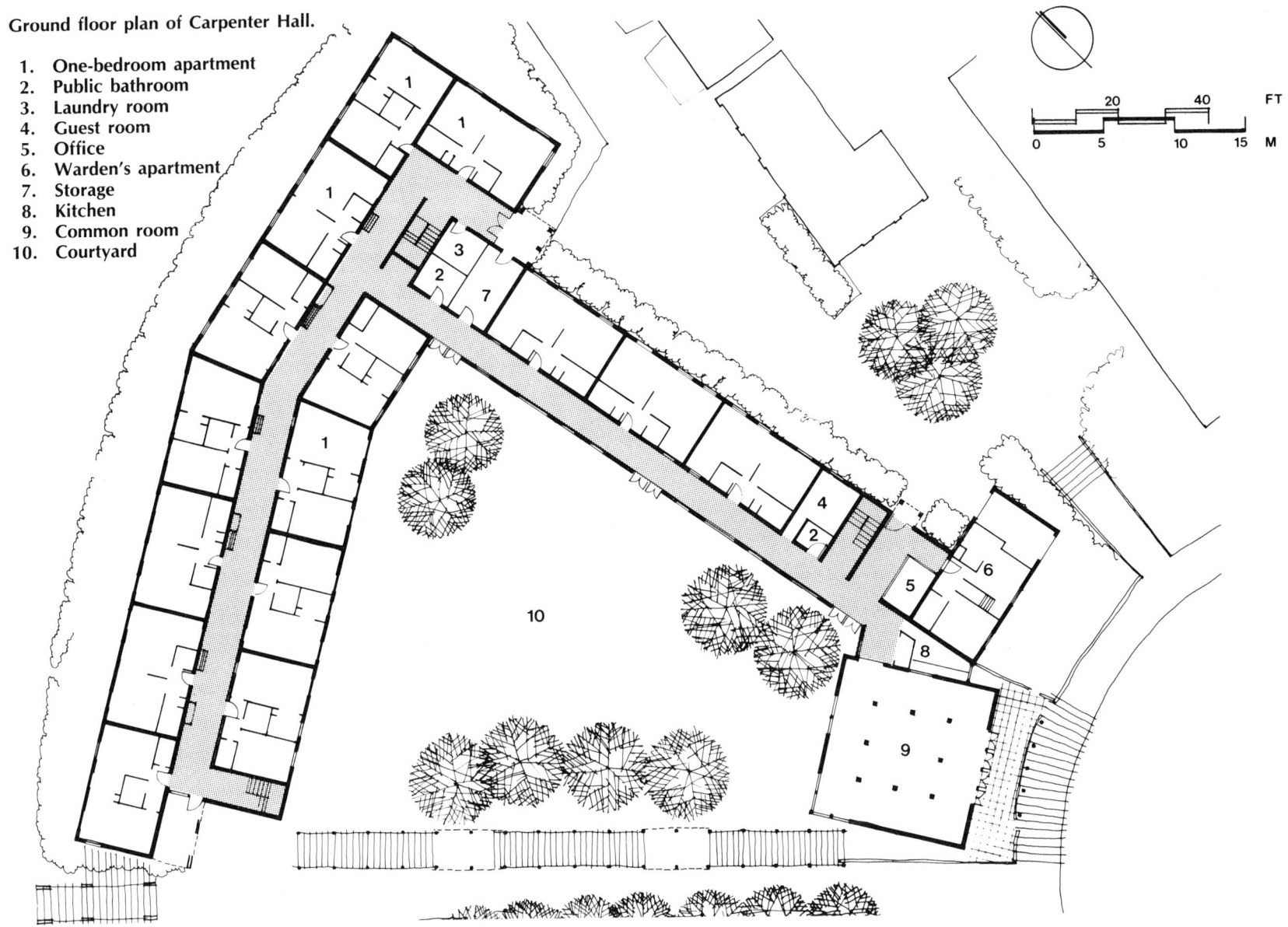

Ground floor plan of Carpenter Hall.

1. One-bedroom apartment
2. Public bathroom
3. Laundry room
4. Guest room
5. Office
6. Warden's apartment
7. Storage
8. Kitchen
9. Common room
10. Courtyard

Detail of Carpenter Hall.

Changes in material, ceiling, and lighting reinforce the public and semipublic zones of the Carpenter Hall corridor.

E-3
18-24 BANIM STREET

BOROUGH OF HAMMERSMITH, LONDON, ENGLAND

TYPE OF HOUSING:	Sheltered housing (Category I)
NUMBER OF UNITS:	34 sheltered apartments
NUMBER OF RESIDENTS:	40
ARCHITECT:	Borough Architects Department
BUILT:	1977–78
OWNER:	London Borough of Hammersmith

Physical Description

Hammersmith is a nineteenth-century working-class borough of London. The existing infrastructure consists of simple, two-story brick row houses and Victorian warehouses. Banim Street is a narrow, typically nineteenth-century street that straddles a residential area and the commercial heart of Hammersmith, which the residents call "Broadway."

18-24 Banim Street consists of nine typical two-story housing blocks grouped in three clusters. The blocks are set back from the street to open it to daylight and allow for planting along the street edge. Although 18-24 Banim Street does not follow the conventional nineteenth-century attached form, it is sympathetically scaled with the row houses on the opposite side of Banim Street. The building clusters are surrounded by landscaped paths, raised gardens for the residents, a fish pond, and an aviary.

Each block contains four typical one-bedroom apartments, two per floor. The center cluster on the site uses the space of two apartments for a common meeting room, laundry, and warden's office. The warden's apartment is located at the extreme end of the site on the ground floor of one building.

Architect's account:
While designing the Banim Street project we were very conscious of the fact that housing is only one of the many uses which compete for land in inner urban areas; infill sites are often in areas of housing shortage and open space deprivation. Therefore it is necessary to avoid producing a development which is viewed as an intrusion and threat within the neighborhood. Even if good quality housing can be achieved economically it doesn't follow that a redevelopment will contribute to the local amenities and preclude vandalism. Inhuman and inefficient council housing has become "type-cast" with all the related problems for the residents of the neighborhood. Much of the overall layout and detailing of this project stems from a desire to positively counteract any ill-feeling that might be engendered by a new council development occurring on the site.

MICHAEL PADDON, 1979

Residential Care

The aim of sheltered housing is to allow elderly people to maintain an independent life and level of activity in the community. The Banim Street project represents this concern by maintaining the residential fabric of the urban environment. The facility is not stigmatized by institutional elements or nonresidential qualities. The project has no building name; each apartment is identified only by its address on Banim Street—mail is delivered by the postal service to each resident.

Category I sheltered housing avoids institutional qualities such as elevators and enclosed corridors that remind residents that they live in something other than a private home (see E-1, Residential Care, Springfield Court, for a description of Categories I and II). The meeting room and laundry facilities are the only communal facilities not typical of private housing developments. The warden is linked to each apartment through a call system that is used only for emergencies. The warden at Banim Street also acts as an area warden for other elderly people living in their own private homes in the immediate neighborhood.

Apartments

In the Borough Architect's words: "it is our opinion that what people manifestly want is a house, a garden, a little community life and a lot of privacy."

MICHAEL PADDON, 1979

This new housing for the elderly was conceptualized to fit as unobtrusively as possible into the existing urban fabric.

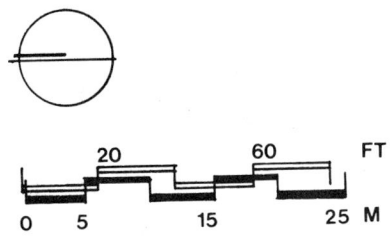

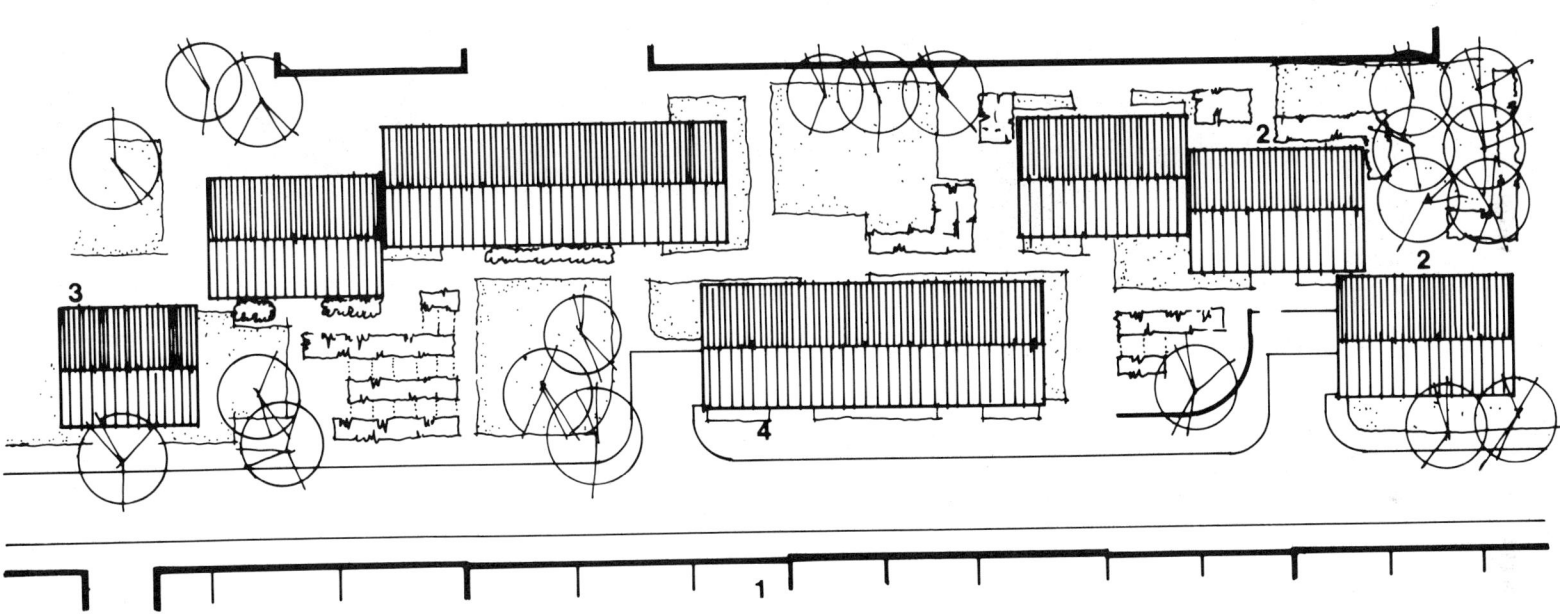

Site plan of Banim Street.

1. Existing row houses
2. Building block of four apartments
3. Warden's apartment
4. Community room, laundry, and warden's office are on the ground floor

Raised planters and green courts provide open spaces throughout this development.

The living rooms and bedrooms all face west toward the activity of Banim Street. The kitchen and bathroom face the small private courts and paths between the apartment and adjacent office building. Ground-floor apartments have access to grade-level terraces from the kitchens.

Commentary

The project is largely consistent with its goals established both for the elderly residents of the complex and for the community as a whole. At the same time, however, the solution offers contradictory approaches that defeat some of the major guiding design principles.

The large open spaces do indeed bring light into narrow Banim Street and open up vistas. The gardens and terraces, however, are not accessible to community residents, which segregates housing for the elderly from the community at large. The vast majority of apartments are removed from the street edge, and visual participation in the urban street life is difficult. In fact, much of the street edge is taken up with private parking for the warden, service vehicles, and buses.

The buildings are sympathetic to the row house scale, but the attached form is unusual, so the project is immediately obvious to a passerby traveling down Banim Street.

Category I housing raises planning concerns for elderly residents who can become trapped on upper-floor apartments. This has already occurred at Banim Street—an active woman in an upper

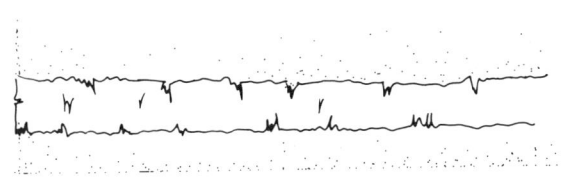

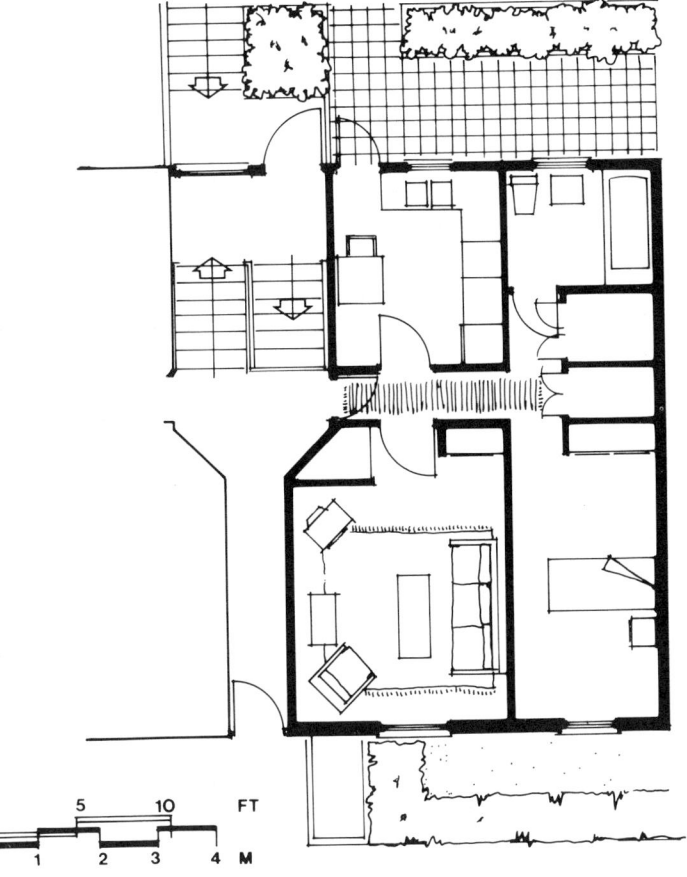

Typical apartment plan.

floor apartment was confined due to a broken hip. If she needed to get out she had to be carried down the stairs. The planning documents outlining the concept of Category I housing indicate that she should have been moved into a ground-floor apartment. In reality she was kept on the upper floor because there were no ground-floor apartments available. This woman's independence was not promoted by Category I sheltered housing; instead, she became dependent and frightened.

This project is exciting because it dares to address the issue of housing for the elderly as infill housing in an urban context. The facility has promoted a dialogue because the architects confronted these issues directly and thoughtfully. On the whole, the project is quite positive—it creates an urban residential environment that is subtly supportive for its elderly residents.

Strengths

Location in an urban setting.
Residential scale and lack of institutional qualities and forms.
The exterior development responds to elderly users by careful attention to paving materials, raised garden planters, and places to sit.

Weaknesses

The attached housing form and massing is at variance with the row house development. This tends to make the complex stand out as different from the local context.
The apartment arrangements maintain the functional privacy of each element, but as a result they feel extremely small.
The organization of rooms around a hallway makes it very difficult for wheelchair-bound residents to move about.
The upper floor apartments are not accessible to people unable to climb stairs.

E-4

40-70 MUNDEN STREET

BOROUGH OF HAMMERSMITH, LONDON, ENGLAND

TYPE OF HOUSING:	Sheltered housing (Category II)
NUMBER OF UNITS:	32 sheltered apartments
NUMBER OF RESIDENTS:	33
ARCHITECT:	Borough Architects Department
BUILT:	1979–80
OWNER:	London Borough of Hammersmith

Physical Description

Located a short 15-minute walk from Banim Street (see E-3) is the Munden Street sheltered housing scheme. Munden Street is an old, narrow street that makes a sharp left turn at its intersection with another street. Both streets are lined with nineteenth-century worker's housing. The buildings are characteristically two and three stories and are made of brick with cast-stone windowsills, frames, or copings. Buildings march rhythmically along the street in large identifiable blocks, reflecting different builders, architects, and styles.

The Munden Street sheltered housing facility is an L-shaped building located at the apex of the two streets. The building is primarily two stories with a third floor that steps back from the street edge. The brown brick harmonizes with the brick buildings in the vicinity, and the cast-stone window frames mimic other similar details. Unlike Banim Street, the Munden Street project is consistent with the neighborhood pattern. The building is built to the street edge and pulls back only at the entrance. Behind the building there is an intimate courtyard-style garden complete with raised planters, large mature trees, and a goldfish pond.

The building has two elevators, which connect all three levels of apartments. The ground floor has a large two-story, skylight-covered community room. Other activity spaces include a billiards room, kitchenette, laundry, and greenhouse. The first two floors of apartments are essentially double-loaded corridors. The upper floor corridor has windows that look down into the community room, as well as two outdoor terraces. The top floor has five apartments with corridor windows that open onto Munden Street. The warden's apartment is a completely independent structure separated by a driveway from the rest of the facility.

Residential Care

As with other sheltered housing schemes, this facility allows residents to live as part of the community, rather than as observers. The residents all came to Munden Street from the local community. They have maintained connections with their community roots, continuing shopping and social patterns. As an age-segregated facility in an age-integrated area, Munden Street offers subtle support and security from live-in staff. Residents (aged 67–90) can continue leading independent lives with the assurance that when they need assistance it is available. The warden and her family become different people to different residents. Mrs. McGee, the warden, commented that the "clients" see her as an advisor, nurse, or daughter. For some residents, the warden is only a convenient service provided by the borough; for others, she is the friend, companion, confidante, or daughter who is missing in their lives.

Apartments

All the apartments are similar one-bedroom arrangements. Two apartments are specifically detailed for use by disabled residents. The door from the corridor opens into an entry/hallway with a storage closet. From here there are entrances into the bedroom, bathroom, and living room. The kitchen is located off to one side of the living room. The apartments are comfortable, although they would not be considered overly large. Residents can completely redecorate their apartments, and they are permitted to keep pets.

The Munden Street buildings imitate the existing nineteenth-century housing.

Munden Street housing for the elderly.

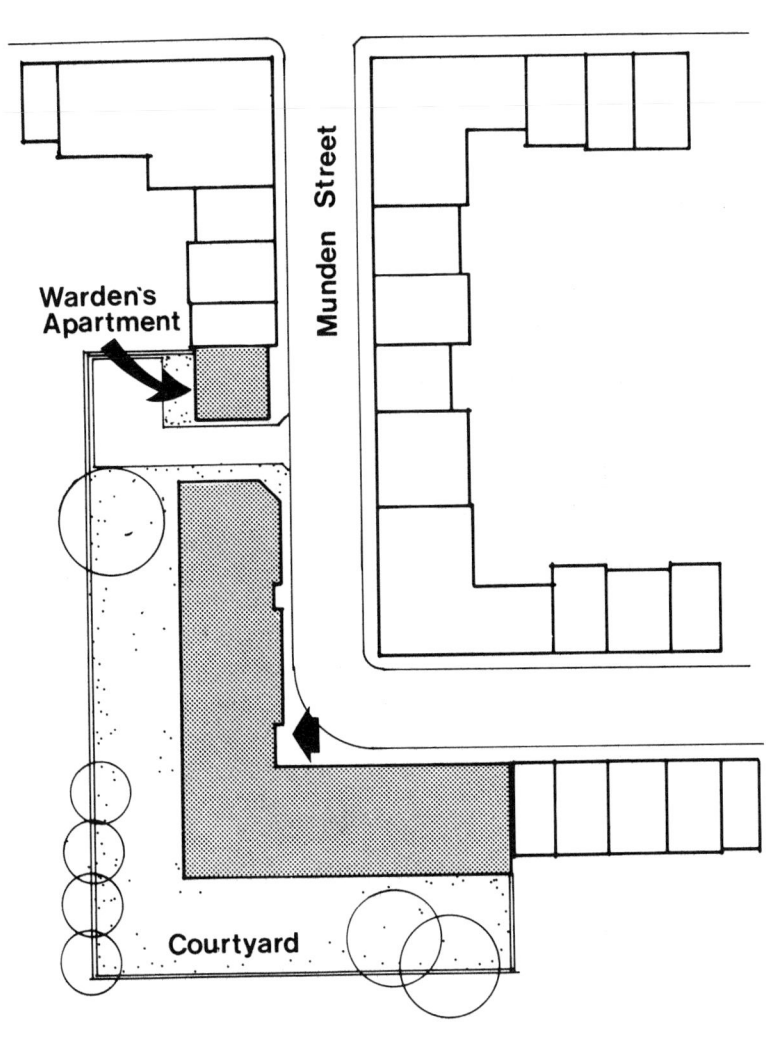

Conceptual plan.

The private courtyard along the back of the building provides the elderly residents a secure green space in the urban environment.

Commentary

Both the Banim Street (see E-3) and Munden Street sheltered housing schemes address the issue of community-integrated urban housing for the elderly. It is intriguing to see how different the results have been. Both facilities were designed by the Borough Architects Department of Hammersmith and have obvious similarities and peculiar differences. The Munden Street facility becomes a more cohesive part of the community by reflecting the massing, scale, and detail of its neighbors. It is conspicuous only by its newness and its lack of front doors and stoops.

The facility has lost the confusing, boring, and repetitive qualities of a typical apartment building with double-loaded corridors. The variety of interior spaces, the interesting views from the corridor, and the quantity of extra spaces such as sitting areas and terraces provide easy orientation and excitement. The patterned, repetitive exterior masks the variety and diversity of the interior spaces.

Strengths

The physical form, scale, and detailing, which blend with the neighborhood.

The degree of independence afforded the residents.

The use of natural light and views to break up the monotony of the conventional double-loaded corridor.

The courtyard is intimately scaled with a variety of sitting spaces, as well as gardens, rabbit hutches, and a goldfish pond.

The kitchens in the apartments are on the exterior wall, receiving light and providing a view.

Weaknesses

All apartments are alike.

The apartment planning could have been cleaner and better zoned:

The bathroom is not adjacent to the bedroom and can be reached only by going through the entry/hallway.

The kitchen can be reached only by going through the living room.

The living room is primarily a circulation zone, especially where ground-floor apartments have French doors onto the courtyard.

7 FUTURE DIRECTIONS

THE RELEVANCE OF PURPOSE-BUILT HOUSING FOR THE ELDERLY

Population projections remind us of the increasing number of elderly, particularly the most frail, who will place increasing demands on social services and housing care. Demographic studies indicate changes in the upcoming elderly generations; the elderly of the year 2000 will be better educated, wealthier, and living in suburban, not urban, settings. Young couples who settled the postwar suburbs will reach retirement age in the next 10 years. Within the next 20 years this same group will find itself in need of special supportive care—care that must be delivered to those who may no longer be able to drive and obtain services for themselves. Existing housing forms will not respond to the future generations of the elderly.

The need for special housing settings will not cease to exist. Although purpose-built housing provides care for only a small segment of the aged population at any one time, a large number of elderly people spend some period of time in "special" supportive housing. Studies done by Kastenbaum and Candy (Lawton, 1980) show that there is a 25 percent chance that a person over age 65 will spend some time in a nursing home. These statistics do not address the increased chance that an individual will spend time in another form of institutional housing. Institutions for the aged have a profound effect on the vast number of people who live in them, as well as on the family and friends who visit residents.

If purpose-built housing is to respond to future generations of elderly people, there must be a greater awareness of what standards will be used to measure their housing. Privacy and independence will undoubtedly have greater meaning than they have had in the past. Cubicle curtains will not provide privacy in a nursing home, and sidewalk curb cuts will not provide independence for an elderly individual unable to make his or her wheelchair move. Minimum standards in nursing homes and congregate housing have created a frozen image of housing quality. Accessibility standards of the late 1970s and 80s have not been meshed with space standards established in the 1960s and early 70s. Standards of privacy respond to institutional requirements of the 1940s and 50s. Life safety codes compound the issue by creating laws that conflict with accessibility for frail, wheelchair-bound elderly.

Housing for the elderly, by and large, has not been conceptualized as a home. Large apartment buildings for the elderly provide cell-like containers for people to live life as observers, rather than as participants. Long-term care centers dispense care and medication to elderly residents who may live only a very short time. Housing for the elderly is viewed as a transient form of housing that simply fills a need for shelter. Policy standards alone will not change the way in which housing for the elderly has been conceptualized. Standard, "boiler plate," forms of housing originate from the drawing boards and files of architects. As a profession, we architects and designers have been too willing to blame standards for our lack of imagination and ability to present clients and housing administrators with alternative solutions.

BEYOND CUBICLE CURTAINS; PRIVACY AS A RELEVANT PURSUIT

Privacy is a quality of life that we generally agree should exist for everyone. Institutional settings have ignored privacy because the mentally infirm and physically debilitated were viewed as incapable of appreciating the subtle qualities of human life. Viewpoints have changed somewhat, but standards have not. Privacy is often viewed as a quality that is expensive to provide, difficult to maintain, and unattainable with current reimbursement rates. It may be said that privacy costs, but how is this expense measured, and is it truly more expensive?

Expense in purpose-built housing is often viewed from two related perspectives—the cost to construct the housing unit and the cost to operate it (that is, primarily staff). The production cost of the unit is usually measured by the amount of money spent per unit or the amount of money per square foot of area. Minimum area standards become maximum because of the cost of increasing the number of square feet per person (or per unit). Operational costs are based on staff efficiency and the maximized use of space. Travel distances and the number of beds per nurse in nursing homes become the measure of operational efficiency.

Does Privacy Have to Cost?

Privacy has not been viewed as an economically feasible goal. If changes are to occur, the issue of privacy must be addressed from the standpoint of cost and spatial requirements. Nowhere is this issue of cost more apparent than in nursing-home standards for semiprivate rooms. Semiprivate rooms provide no standard of privacy for the individuals forced to share the same space. The common, rubber-stamped semiprivate room of the 1970s (which meets accessibility standards) is 17 feet (5.2 m) by 12 feet (3.7 m) with a shared toilet and vestibule. There is one large window, which becomes the domain of the bed nearest to it. Cubicle curtains provide the only spatial separation. The television, telephone, lights, access to the bathroom, clothes storage, and room temperature become common elements over which neither person has full control.

Approximately the same space standards can be used in a room that maximizes individual privacy and spatial control. However, at best it is still only *semi*private. The reconfigured room provides a private space for each resident with his or her own window, storage space, television, and telephone. The vestibule and bathroom are still shared, but they provide equal access and control. Auditory privacy is increased, although not to the degree of that of a private room. The additional cost appears to be only 16 square feet (1.5 sq m) per room, or 8 square feet (.75 sq m) per bed (approximately the size of a coat closet). Over the lifetime of a building the cost is negligible when considering the quality of life it provides to the hundreds of people who will live in the room. The reconfigured room is not the ultimate goal, but rather a step toward maximizing privacy.

American standards of privacy are certainly not at the level of Sweden or Denmark, where residents are all provided with private rooms. The private interior and exterior spaces of the Copenhagen nursing home (see D-2) and the private rooms of Papegojelyckan (see S-1) indicate space standards that are changing worldwide. Apartment standards that provide a private bedroom (rather than a sleeping alcove), private terraces, and residentially scaled environments are likely to become common in the future. Facilities such as Møllegården

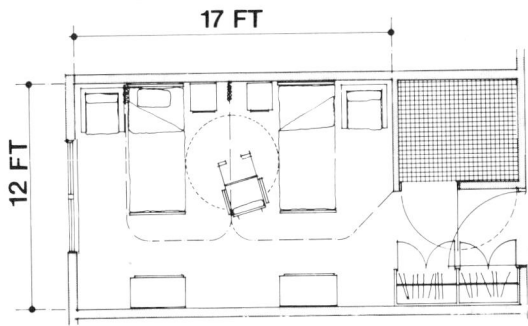

Conventional Semiprivate Room
Living area = 12 ft × 17 ft = 204 sq ft
No visual or auditory privacy.
Neither resident has control over television, telephone, temperature, or lights.
The bed nearest the window has control over it.
The resident nearest the door is distracted by roommate's use of the toilet.
Neither resident has an area that is entirely individually controlled.

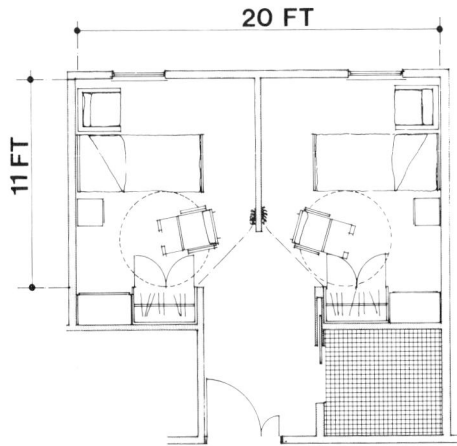

Reconfigured Semiprivate Room
Living area = 11 ft × 20 ft = 220 sq ft
Visual privacy is maximized.
Auditory privacy is better.
Each resident has a private territory complete with window, lights, and clothes storage.
The bathroom is in a zone of neutral access.
Accessibility to the wardrobes is improved.

Center (see D-4), Gränna (see S-4), Springfield Court (see E-1), and Ordrup Vaenge (see D-1) signal new dimensions and alternative approaches to housing that maximize privacy and a self-determined life-style.

Operational Efficiency

Staff efficiency is hardly a worthwhile trade-off when it removes an individual's rights to privacy and control over his or her environment and body. Shortened travel distances, ease of surveillance by staff members, and idealized economic standards have not touched the heart of what makes a facility economical to operate. Architects conceptualize purpose-built housing as freestanding facilities autonomous from the environment. Idealized standards that require 100 apartments for the elderly per building ignore the existing infrastructure that can provide support services. Special internal services such as meals, general stores, libraries, and laundries must give way to generic services available in the community.

European facilities such as Kv. Dalen (see S-7), Örnen (see S-6), and Teckomatorp (see S-2) have responded to their urban or rural context by sharing services with the community at large. Services that may not have been economically feasible for a small elderly population become possible when they are shared with other groups in need of similar services. Schools and dwellings for the elderly can share central kitchen facilities and staff. Passive and active alarm systems can provide a sense of security and help for elderly residents, without the need for increased staff for surveillance. Future housing developments must offer creative solutions to increased operating costs by utilizing generic rather than special services.

BEYOND CURB CUTS; INDEPENDENCE IN THE ENVIRONMENT

The issue of independence for the elderly does not lie with cost and economics, but rather with the way in which we have conceptualized housing care. Housing for the elderly will achieve a level of independence when we have fulfilled all of an elderly individual's physical and emotional needs for shelter, medical care, social opportunities, and financial security. We have become blinded by accessibility standards that have little to do with the true concept and meaning of an independent life. Housing for the elderly must provide greater adaptability, flexibility, and variety.

The balancing of dependence and independence may require an individual to make environmental changes. These changes may be as simple as the movement of furniture or as difficult as the relocation to a totally new environment. Housing policy in the United States has focused on the latter; increased need for housing support has meant a change in physical setting for the individual. This step system of housing care requires individuals to move to settings that provide greater levels of care. The level of environmental support within a particular setting can be altered only marginally.

Facilities that provide a continuum-of-care or campus approach to housing for the elderly vary greatly in quality. Many become so large and insular that they become isolated communities and take on institutional qualities. Others provide quality care by utilizing a combination of outreach programs for the community and in-house support for residents. Facilities such as Papegojelyckan (see S-1) and Gränna (see S-4) allow residents to increase services as they need them without changing the physical setting. The Knivsta Center (see S-5), Kv. Dalen (see S-7), Rygård Center (see D-5), and Mollegården Center (see D-4) allow residents to stay within the same neighborhood but to change the level of environmental support. Västra Fäladen (see S-3), Banim Street (see E-3), and Munden Street (see E-4) provide one environmental setting, but maximize the chance that residents will remain independent and involved in the community from which they came. The change in physical setting from the private home is less difficult when other social patterns can be maintained. Housing that is conceptualized as providing "dependent" care or "independent" care does not recognize the constant balance that the individual elderly person strives to maintain.

FOCUSING ON THE INTANGIBLE QUALITIES OF HOUSING

Privacy and independence have gained importance within our society. In the rush to provide housing units for the elderly, we have lost track of the individual and his or her needs—needs that extend beyond a mere place to sleep. The bricks and mortar meet our temporal need for shelter, but it is the intangible qualities of housing that give life meaning, purpose, and joy. Variety and imagination have been lost to standard-practice housing. We must learn to create environments that restore an individual's dignity and encourage frivolity, spontaneity, and creative pursuits. Our energies must focus on the rhythms and patterns of life, restoring old age to a period of fulfillment, advantage, enchantment, and unparalleled freedom.

BIBLIOGRAPHY

Abrams, Mark. "Demographic Trends." In *The Impact of Ageing: Strategies for Care*, edited by David Hobman. London, England: Croom Helm, Ltd., 1981.

Age Concern England. *Profiles of the Elderly: Volume 5*. London, England, 1980.

Age Concern England. *Profiles of the Elderly: Volume 1*. London, England, 1977.

American Institute of Architects. *Architectural Graphic Standards*. Edited by Robert T. Packard. New York: John Wiley and Sons, Inc., 1981.

Ammundsen, Esther. "Care of the Elderly in Denmark: General Aspects." *Danish Medical Bulletin*, vol. 29, no. 3, March 1982.

Ammundsen, Esther. "The Transition from Private to Public Provision of Nursing Homes in Denmark." *Danish Medical Bulletin*, vol. 29, no. 3, March 1982.

Atchley, R. C. *The Social Forces in Later Life: An Introduction to Social Gerontology*. Belmont, California: Wadsworth, Inc., 1972.

"Banim Street," *Architects' Journal*, February 20, 1979, p. 365.

Bank-Mikkelsen, N. E. "Legislative and Administrative Services for Handicapped Persons in Denmark." Copenhagen, Denmark: National Board of Social Welfare, 1980.

Bednar, M. J. *Architecture for the Handicapped in Denmark, Sweden, and Holland: A Guidebook to Normalization*. Ann Arbor, Michigan: University of Michigan, 1974.

Bednar, M. J. *Barrier-Free Environments*. Stroudsburg, Pennsylvania: Dowden, Hutchinson, and Ross, Inc., 1977.

Bensman, Joseph and Robert Lilienfeld. *Between Public and Private: The Lost Boundaries of the Self*. New York: The Free Press, 1979.

"Boligbebyggelsen Västra Fäladen, Landskrona." *Arkitektur DK*, Nr. 6, 1979.

Bowe, F. *Rehabilitating America: Toward Independence for Disabled and Elderly People*. New York: Harper and Row, 1980.

Byerts, Thomas O. "Toward a Better Range of Housing and Environmental Choices for the Elderly." In *Back to Basics: Food and Shelter for the Elderly*, edited by Patricia Wagner and John McRae. Gainesville, Florida: University of Florida Press, 1978.

Department of Health and Social Security (Welsh Office). "A Happier Old-Age: A Discussion Document on Elderly People in Our Society." London, England: Her Majesty's Royal Stationery Office, 1978.

Department of Health and Social Security. "Growing Older." London, England, 1981.

Dickson, Niall. "Age Concern at Work." London, England: Age Concern England, 1980.

Erdal, Inger. "Social Services for the Elderly." *Danish Medical Bulletin*, vol. 29, no. 3, March 1982.

Fox, Derek. "Housing and the Elderly." In *The Impact of Ageing: Strategies for Care*, edited by David Hobman. London, England: Croom Helm, Ltd., 1981.

Friis, Henning. "Social Programmes for the Aged in Denmark." Graz, Austria: European Federation for the Welfare of the Elderly, June 1980.

Goffman, Erving. "Stigma and Social Identity." In *The Handicapped Person in the Community*, edited by David Boswell and Janet Wingrove. London, England: Tavistock Publications, 1974.

Goldenberg, Leon. *Housing for the Elderly: New Trends in Europe*. New York: Garland STPM Press, 1981.

Goldsmith, Selwyn. *Designing for the Disabled*. London, England: RIBA Publications, 1976.

Goldsmith, Selwyn. "Mobility Housing." *Architects' Journal*, July 3, 1974.

Gustafsson, A. *Local Government in Sweden*. The Swedish Institute, Ministry of Local Government, 1978.

Heal, L. W. "Ideological Responses of Society to its Handicapped Citizens." In *Integration of Developmentally Disabled Individuals into the Community*, edited by A. R. Novak and L. W. Heal. Baltimore, Maryland: Paul H. Brookes, 1980.

Helander, Jan. "Gerontology of the Future: What Measures Should Be Taken in a World in Which There Will be So Many Senior Citizens?" Lund, Sweden: Gerontologiskt Centrum, 1982. Presented at the United Nations World Assembly on Aging.

Helander, Jan. "Rhythms." Presented at the EURAG International Congress, June 3-7, 1979.

Hoglund, J. D. "The Application of Normalization Principles to Housing for the Elderly." Champaign, Illinois: The University of Illinois, April 1981.

Howell, Sandra C. *Designing for Aging: Patterns of Use*. Cambridge, Massachusetts: MIT Press, 1980.

Jones, Michael A. and John H. Catlin. "Design for Access." *Progressive Architecture*, April 1978.

Jung, Carl Gustav. *Memories, Dreams, Reflections*. New York: Vintage Books, 1961.

Kira, Alexander. *The Bathroom*. New York: Viking Press, Inc., 1976.

Koncelik, Joseph A. *Aging and the Product Environment*. Stroudsburg, Pennsylvania: Hutchinson Ross Publishing Company, 1982.

Koncelik, Joseph. *Designing the Open Nursing Home*. Stroudsburg, Pennsylvania: Dowden, Hutchinson and Ross, Inc., 1976.

Lawton, M. Powell. *Environment and Aging*. Monterey, California: Brooks/Cole, 1980.

Lifchez, Raymond and Barbara Winslow. *Design for Independent Living: The Environment and Physically Disabled People*. New York: Whitney Library of Design, 1979.

Lindsley, Ogden R. "Geriatric Behavioural Prosthetics." *The Handicapped Person in the Community*, edited by David Boswell and Janet Wingrove. London, England: Tavistock Publications, 1974.

Marcussen, Ernst. *Social Welfare in Denmark*. Copenhagen, Denmark: Det Danske Selskab (The Danish Institute), 1980.

Matthiessen, P. C. "The Demography of the Elderly in Denmark." *Danish Medical Bulletin*, vol. 29, no. 3, March 1982.

McRae, John. *Elderly in the Environment: Northern Europe*. Gainesville, Florida: University of Florida, 1975.

Ministry of Housing and Local Government. "Housing Standards and Costs Accommodation Specially Designed for Old People." London, England: Circular 82/69.

Ministry of Local Government. "Local Government in Sweden." Stockholm, Sweden, 1978.

Moore, Charles, Gerald Allen and Donlyn Lyndon. *The Place of Houses*. New York: Holt, Rinehart, and Winston, 1974.

Newman, Oscar. *Defensible Space: Crime Prevention through Urban Design*. New York: Collier Books, 1973.

Nirje, B. "The Normalization Principle." In *Normalization, Social Integration, and Community Services*, edited by R. J. Flynn and K. E. Nitsch. Baltimore, Maryland: University Park Press, 1980.

Nusberg, Charlotte. "Programmes and Services for the Elderly in Industrialised Countries," In *The Impact of Ageing: Strategies for Care*, edited by David Hobman. London, England: Croom Helm, Ltd., 1981.

"Omsorgscentret Møllegården Undearealer." *Arkitektur DK*, Nr. 6, 1978.

Paddon, Michael, and Gregory Butcher. "The Banim Street Case." *Architects' Journal*, April 25, 1979.

Pedersen, Dan Ove. "Housing Problems of the Elderly." *Danish Medical Bulletin*, vol. 29, no. 3, March 1982.

Penton, John. "Excellence For the Elderly." *Architects' Journal*, October 24, 1979.

Ramian, Knud. "The Needs for Housing of the Elderly." *Danish Medical Bulletin*, vol. 29, no. 3, March 1982.

Rosenblad-Wallin, Elsa. *Kläder for Äldre*. Göteborg, Sweden: STUs Konsumenttekniska Forskningsgrupp, 1977.

Rudfeldt, Kirsten. *Care of the Aged in Denmark.* Copenhagen, Denmark: Det Danske Selskab (The Danish Institute), 1973.

Rush, Richard. "The Age of the Aging." *Progressive Architecture,* August 1981.

"Rygårdcentret, Plejehem og Beskyttede Boliger i Gentofte." *Arkitektur DK,* Nr. 7, 1981.

Schaie, K. Warner. "Age Changes in Adult Intelligence." In *Aging: Scientific Perspectives and Social Issues,* edited by Diana S. Woodruff and James E. Birren. New York: Van Nostrand Company, 1975.

Seligman, M. E. P. *Helplessness: On Depression, Development, and Death.* San Francisco, California: W. H. Freeman and Company, 1975.

Socialstyrelsen. "After 65: Activities, Services, and Medical Care for Seniors in Sweden." Stockholm, Sweden, 1979.

Sommer, Robert. *Personal Space: The Behavioral Basis of Design.* Englewood Cliffs, New Jersey: Prentice-Hall, Inc., 1969.

Sommer, Robert. *Tight Spaces: Hard Architecture and How to Humanize It.* Englewood Cliffs, New Jersey: Prentice-Hall, 1974.

Swedish Planning and Rationalization Institute of Health and Social Services (SPRI). "Primary Care and Care of the Elderly." Stockholm, Sweden, 1980a.

SPRI. "Redovisning av Tävlingsresultat." Stockholm, Sweden, 1980b.

SPRI. "SPRI Rapport 35: Lokala Sjukhem." Stockholm, Sweden, 1980c.

Stephens, Suzanne. "Hidden Barriers." *Progressive Architecture,* April 1978.

"Sweden 81." Stockholm, Sweden: National Central Bureau of Statistics, 1981.

Swedish Institute. "Old Age Care in Sweden." Stockholm, Sweden, 1981.

Tortora, Gerald J., Ronald Evans, and Nicholas P. Anagnostakos. *Principles of Human Physiology.* New York: Harper and Row, Publishers, 1982.

Trier, Adam. "Old-Age Pensions, Social Security, and Other Schemes." *Danish Medical Bulletin,* vol. 29, no. 3, March 1982.

Walsh, David A. "Age Differences in Learning and Memory." In *Aging: Scientific Perspectives and Social Issues,* edited by Diana S. Woodruff and James E. Birren. New York: Van Nostrand Company, 1975.

Weg, Ruth B. "Changing Physiology of Aging: Normal and Pathological." In *Aging: Scientific Perspectives and Social Issues,* edited by Diana S. Woodruff and James E. Birren. New York: Van Nostrand Company, 1975.

Wolfensberger, Wolf. *The Principle of Normalization in Human Services.* Toronto, Canada: National Institute on Mental Retardation, 1972.

Woodruff, Diana S. "A Physiological Perspective of the Psychology of Aging." In *Aging: Scientific Perspectives and Social Issues,* edited by Diana S. Woodruff and James E. Birren. New York: Van Nostrand Company, 1975.

Zeisel, John, Gayle Epp, and Stephan Demos. *Low Rise Housing for Older People: Behavioral Criteria for Design.* U.S. Department of Housing and Urban Development, 1977.

INDEX

activity theory, social passage and, 13
aging process, 5–14
    biological aging, 6–11
    communicating systems and, 6–8
    control systems and, 9–10
    detection senses and, 10–11
    mechanical systems and, 8–9
    social passage, 11–14
Alexander, Christopher, 2
almshouses, in Great Britain, 119–20
aloneness, privacy and, 20
apartments
    in Denmark, 82, 98, 105, 108
    in Great Britain, 121, 131, 134, 136
    in Sweden, 42, 45, 50, 56, 59, 63, 65, 69, 73
Atchley, Robert, 13

Banim Street (Borough of Hammersmith, London, England), 131–35
    apartments, 131, 134
    care, residential, 131
    commentary, 134–35
    description, physical, 131
    strengths, 135
    weaknesses, 135
Bank-Mikkelsen, N. E., 77
barriers, independence and, 23–25
biological aging, 6–11
    communicating systems, 6–8
    control systems, 9–10
    detection senses, 10–11
    digestive system, 9
    mechanical systems, 7–9

campus care. *See* Continuum-of-care facilities
Candy, S., 141

cardiovascular system, aging and, 9–10
care. *See* Medical care; residential care
Carpenter Hall (Milton Keynes, England), 126
    care, residential, 126
    commentary, 126
    description, physical, 126
    strengths, 126
    weaknesses, 126
Clevestam, Arne, 59
communicating systems. *See* Aging process
competence, social passage and, 14
continuity theory. *See* Social passage
continuum-of-care facilities
    in Denmark, 82–93, 98, 106
    in Sweden, 42, 54, 59
control systems. *See* Aging process
Copenhagen and Omegns Day Center (Ordrup Vej, Gentofte, Copenhagen, Denmark), 93
    commentary, 93
    description, physical, 93
    strengths, 93
    weaknesses, 93
Copenhagen and Omegns Nursing Home (Ordrup Vej, Genofte, Copenhagen, Denmark), 88–92
    care, residential, 88
    commentary, 88
    description, physical, 88
    rooms, 88
    strengths, 92
    weaknesses, 92

Dalen District of Enskede, Residential Hotel (Stockholm, Sweden), 69–74

apartments, 69, 73
care, residential, 69
commentary, 73, 74
description, 69
strengths, 74
weaknesses, 74
day care, adult
    in Denmark, 93, 105, 108–9
    in Sweden, 36
    See also Medical care; residential care
Denmark, v, 76–114
    care of elderly in, 77
    financial security in, 77–79
    government in, 76–77
    housing in, 79–80
    medical care in, supportive, 81
    special-care services in, supportive, 80–81
    See also Copenhagen and Omegns Day Center; Copenhagen and Omegns Nursing Home; Møllegården Care Center; Ordrup Vaenge; Rygård Center
dependence. *See* Independence
design, responsive
    independence and, 27–28
    privacy and, 20–22
detection senses. *See* Aging process
digestive system. *See* Aging process
dignity, as housing setting concern, v
disengagement theory, social passage and, 12–13
dwellings, ordinary
    in Denmark, 79–80
    in Great Britain, 118
    in Sweden, 54
    See also Apartments; housing; rooms

economics of housing settings, v, vi, 142–43
    privacy and, 18
Ejlers and Graversen (architects), 82, 88, 93, 98, 106
elderly, housing settings for; facts, concerns, and approaches to, v–vi
    as social group, 4–5
    See also Aging process; *names of countries; aspects of elderly (e.g., independence; privacy)*
endocrine system, aging and, 6
environmental press and competence, 14
environment, implications of aging process on
    communicating systems and, 7–8
    control systems and, 10
    detection senses and, 11
    mechanical systems and, 8–9
    social passage and, 14
equilibrium, aging and, 10
event, privacy of, 17

financial security
    in Denmark, 77–79
    in Great Britain, 116–17
    in Sweden, 31–33
flats (converted and purpose-built), in Great Britain, 118–19
    See also Apartments; housing; rooms
Flensborns, Helmer, 54

geriatric hospitals, in Great Britain, 120
geriatric vs. gerontology, 5
goals
    independence and, 25
    social and behavioral, housing and, 2

Goldsmith, Selwyn, 26
Gränna Service House for the Elderly (Gränna, Sweden), 54–58
    apartments, 56
    care, residential, 54, 56
    commentary, 56
    description, physical, 54
    strengths, 56, 58
    weaknesses, 58
Great Britain, v, 115–40
    care of elderly in, 116
    financial security in, 116–17
    government in, 115–16
    housing in, 117–20
    medical care in, 120
    special care services in, 120
    See also Carpenter Hall; Banim Street; Munden Street; Springfield Court

Hall, Edward, 2
Hansson, Olle, 42
Heal, L. W., 24
hearing, aging and loss of, 10
homes, residential, in Great Britain, 119–20
    See also Apartments; dwellings; flats; rooms
hospitals, geriatric, in Great Britain, 120
housing, 15–16
    in Denmark, 79–80
    focus for, 144
    future of, 141–46
    in Great Britain, 117–20
    privacy and independence, and, 16
    social and behavioral goals in, 2
    in Sweden, 33–35
    See also Apartments; dwellings; flats; rooms; *aspects of housing; names of housing settings*
Howell, Sandra, 2
Hultquist, Arvid, 41

identity, individual
    independence and, 25
    privacy and, 18
independence, v, vi, 22–28
    concepts of, 25–26
    and dependence, 26
    and the elderly, 26–27
    in Europe, 28
    forms of, 23–25
    as freedom from barriers, 24–25
    future environments and, 146
    and goals, 25
    as housing quality, 1–2
    and individual identity, 25
    physical barriers and, 23
    psychological barriers and, 24
    and responsive design, 27–28
    rhythms and patterns and, 26–27
    and risk, 25–26
    social barriers and, 23–24
individual focus on, 3
institutions, privacy and, 18–19

Jung, Carl Gustav, 11

Kastenbaum, R., 141
Kira, Alexander, 21
Knivsta Service House and Nursing Home (Knivsta, Sweden), 59–62
    apartments, 59
    care, residential, 59
    commentary, 62
    description, physical, 59
    strengths, 62
    weaknesses, 62

Lawton, M. Powell, 14, 141
life-style, privacy of, 17
loneliness, privacy and, 20

mechanical systems. *See* Aging process
medical care, supportive
    in Denmark, 81
    in Great Britain, 120
    in Sweden, 35
Møllegården Care Center (Gladsaxe, Copenhagen, Denmark), 98–105
    apartments, 98, 105
    care, residential, 98
    commentary, 105
    day care for adults, 105
    description, physical, 98
    rooms, nursing-care, 105
    strengths, 105
    weaknesses, 105
Moore, Charles, 3
Munden Street (no. 40–70) (Borough of Hammersmith, London, England), 136–40
    apartments, 136
    care, residential, 136
    commentary, 140
    description, physical, 136
    strengths, 140
    weaknesses, 140
muscular system, aging and, 8

Nahemow, L., 14
nervous system, aging and, 67
Newman, Oscar, 2
nursing-care homes, rooms, or units
    in Denmark, 80, 88–92, 105, 108
    in Great Britain, 120
    in Sweden, 54, 56

Ordrup Vaenge (Gentofte, Copenhagen, Denmark), 82–87
    apartments, 82
    care, residential, 82
    commentary, 82
    description, physical, 82
    strengths, 82, 87
    weaknesses, 87
Örnen Service House (Uppsala, Sweden), 63–68
    apartments, 63, 65
    care, residential, 63
    commentary, 68
    description, physical, 63
    strengths, 68
    weaknesses, 68

Paddon, Michael, 131
Papegojelyckan Home for the Aged (Lund, Sweden), 36–41
    care, residential, 36
    commentary, 40
    day care center, 36
    description, physical, 36
    rooms, 36
    strengths, 41
    weaknesses, 41
pensions
    in Denmark, 78
    in Great Britain, 117
    in Sweden, 31, 33
personal care, privacy and, 20–21
press, environmental, social passage and, 14
privacy, v, vi, 16–22
    aloneness, loneliness and, 20
    concepts of, 18–19
    and costs, 142–43
    and design, 20–22
    and economics, 18
    and the elderly, 19–20
    in Europe, 28
    of event, 17
    forms of, 17–18
    future pursuits for, 142–45
    as housing quality, 1–2
    and individual identity, 18
    and institutions, 18–19
    of life-style, 17
    and operational efficiency, 145
    and personal care, 20–21
    and shrinking space, 19
    and sleeping, 22
    of thought, 17–18

research, environmental design, 2–3
residential care
    concepts of, 2
    in Denmark, 82, 88, 98
    in Great Britain, 121, 126, 131, 136
    in Sweden, 36, 42, 48, 54, 56, 59, 63, 69
Residential Hotel in Dalen District of Enskede (Stockholm, Sweden), 69–74
respiratory system, aging and, 9–10
retirement, early pay for, in Denmark, 78–79
rhythms and patterns, independence and, 26–27
risk, independence and, 25–26
rooms
    in Denmark, 88, 105, 108
    in Sweden, 36
    See also Apartments; dwellings; flats

Rygård Center (Niels Andersensvej 22, Hellerup, Denmark), 106–14
    apartments, 108
    commentary, 112, 114
    day care for adults, 108–9
    day nursing home, 109
    description, physical, 106
    rooms, nursing-home, 108
    strengths, 114
    weaknesses, 114

Samuelson, Sten, 36, 48
Schaie, K. Warner, 7
senescence, 5
sheltered housing
    in Denmark, 98, 106
    in Great Britain, 119, 121, 126, 131, 136
    in Sweden, 42, 48, 54, 59, 63, 69
sight, aging and, 10
skeletal system, aging and, 8
sleeping, privacy and, 22
smell, aging and sense of, 10–11
social passage, 11–14
    activity theory, 13
    continuity theory, 13–14
    disengagement theory, 12–13
    environmental press and competence, 14
Sommer, Robert, 2
space, shrinking, privacy and, 19
spatial manipulation, as design issue, v
special-care services, supportive
    in Denmark, 80–81
    in Great Britain, 120
    in Sweden, 35
Springfield Court (Milton Keynes, England), 121–25
    apartments, 121
    care, residential, 121
    commentary, 125
    description, physical, 121
    strengths, 125
    weaknesses, 125
Stoltz, Inge, 48
Sweden, v, 29–74
    care of elderly in, 31–35
    financial security in, 31–33
    government in, 29–31
    housing in, 33–35
    medical care in, 35
    special-care services in, 35
    See also Gränna Service House for the Elderly; Knivsta Service House and Nursing Home; Örnen Service House; Papegojelyckan Home for the Aged; Residential Hotel in Dalen District of Enskede; Teckomatorp Service Center; Västra Fäladen Service Center

taste, aging and, 10–11
Teckomatorp Service Center (Teckomatorp, Sweden), 42–47
    apartments, 42, 45
    care, residential, 42
    commentary, 45, 47
    description, physical, 42
    strengths, 47
    weaknesses, 47
therapeutic relationships of spaces as design issue, v
thought, privacy of, 17–18
touch, aging and, 10–11

United States, lag in housing settings in, *vs.* Europe, v

Västra Fäladen Service Center (Landskrona, Sweden), 48–53
    apartments, 50
    care, residential, 48
    commentary, 50
    description, physical, 48
    strengths, 53
    weaknesses, 53

wardens, accommodations without, in Great Britain, 118–19